The Anatomy of Secret Sins, Presumptuous Sins, Sin in Dominion, and Uprightness

wherein divers weighty cases are resolved, in
relation to all those particulars delivered in
divers sermons preached at Mildred's,
in Bread-Street, London,
on Psalm 19:12-13

together with

The remissibleness of all sin, and the
remissibleness of the sin against the Holy Ghost

Preached before an Honorable Audience

By that Reverend and Faithful Minister of the Gospel,

Mr. Obadiah Sedgwick, B.D.

Edited by Don Kistler, M.Div.

Soli Deo Gloria Publications
...for instruction in righteousness...

Soli Deo Gloria Publications
P.O. Box 451, Morgan, PA 15064
(412) 221-1901/FAX 221-1902

*

*

ISBN 1-877611-78-6

Contents

Contents

Appendix

Two sermons on Matthew 12:31

To The Christian Reader

The name of the reverend author of this work will commend it to the acceptance of all those who were either acquainted with his ministry or have attentively perused his treatises formerly published. He was a workman who needed not to be ashamed. As the matter of his discourses was solid and profitable, so his language was pregnant and delightful, both which took much upon his gracious and ingenious auditors. This is to be acknowledged a great abatement of the church's loss by his death, that though he is dead he yet speaks from the press by the useful treatises left written by his own hand which through God's mercy may prove rich blessings unto posterity by edifying Christians in grace and comfort. As the reasonable immortal soul is the more noble part of man, so supernatural grace truly ennobles it by introducing the likeness and life of God.

This grace, which is the good work, the good and perfect gift of God, may be promoted both in its habit and exercise, by such helps as this which divine providence puts into your hand. And therefore, since sanctifying grace (which is the strength, beauty, riches of the soul, and the best thing on this side of Christ Himself, from whose fulness we all receive grace for grace) is wrought, preserved, enlarged, and quickened by these means, they should

be gladly welcomed and diligently improved by all
serious, sincere Christians. And whereas humility
and sincerity are graces eminently excellent and
useful throughout the whole course of Christianity,
rendering every other grace and every duty the more
lovely and acceptable, helps in both these you may
expect from this ensuing treatise. The text here
handled holds forth, at the first view, both sinfulness and uprightness of God's servants; their sinfulness bitterly bewailed, and their uprightness seriously designed; whence we have the anatomy of secret sins, presumptuous sins, sins in dominion, and
uprightness.

Every self-considering Christian sees so much
sin in his heart and life that he is abased under the
burden of it. How heavy, then, is this thought upon
his heart, that there are many thousands of secret
unseen errors chargeable upon him by the all-know-
ing, heart-searching God! And yet this adds further
load unto the burdened spirit, that besides his former guiltiness of, and inclination to, presumptuous
sins (things heinous and horrid), the seeds also of
that unpardonable sin (the thoughts whereof are
amazing and dreadful to every gracious heart) lie
and live in his depraved nature. These particulars
are here largely and convincingly discoursed of by
means whereof the secure sinner may be well awakened and the proud heart deeply humbled. What examples of bitter mourning, self-loathing, and
lamentable outcries upon this account are recorded
in the Holy Scriptures. How needful and seasonable
this too-oft-neglected endeavor would be in these
loose, lukewarm times might easily be manifested.

The manifold precious benefits of this practice may
persuade it; besides, divine acceptance and familiar
communion, together with many rich promises
hereby possessed, by means hereof the soul will pa-
tiently submit to God's afflicting hand and seriously
set upon real reformation. Thus Christ will become
much more precious and sweet unto the soul, and as
we shall be made more meek in our deportment towards all, so more peculiarly compassionate towards
bleeding, repenting sinners, viewing the number
and heinousness of our own irregularities, considering how much we ourselves still lie under sin's dominion with the guilt of some presumptuous iniquities.

Good Reader, you shall not only be thus edified
in humility (this product of sin's discovery), but in
sincerity also, by that which follows in the Anatomy
of Uprightness. Inexpressible are the comforts
which come into the soul by clearing up its sincerity
from Scripture evidence. If there is a messenger, an
interpreter, one of a thousand to show unto man his
uprightness, then he is gracious unto him and says,
"Deliver him from the pit. I have found a ransom."
His flesh shall be fresher than a child; and for the
enjoyment of satisfaction out of God's all-sufficiency, it is assured in the covenant of grace unto
upright walking with His majesty. Herein consists
God's image in man, which is His fairest beauty and
His greatest glory. The imperfect performances of
the sincere do not only find acceptance, but delight
in the Lord. Unto them He will not deny either
grace or glory or anything which may be truly good;
and, notwithstanding the saddest dispensations

imaginable, God will be constantly and superlatively good unto them. How bad they may be in their own eyes, yet they are perfect in God's account; and they may always rejoice with thanksgiving before the Lord, and with gladsome boldness. Look pale death itself in the face when it approaches.

But we will not enlarge ourselves in these matters, contenting ourselves with these short hints suggested to give you a taste of that sweet fruit which you may expect to reap by the careful perusal of this very savory, useful book which we commend to your improvement, and yourself therein to the blessing of the Almighty, through Jesus Christ in whom, and for whom, we are

Your Faithful Friends and Servants,

Humphrey Chambers
Edmund Calamy
Simeon Ash
Adoniram Byfield

September 1, 1659

Introduction

"Who can understand his errors? Cleanse thou me
from secrets: or from secret sins or faults."
Psalm 19:12

Chrysostom conjectures that the main intention
of the greatest part of this Psalm consists in the discovery of divine providence, which manifests itself
in the motions and courses of the heavenly bodies,
concerning which the Psalmist speaks much from
verse 1 to verse 7. Austin (upon that place) is of quite
a different opinion and conjectures that Christ is
the whole subject of this Psalm, whose Person is
compared to the Sun for excellency and beauty, and
the course of whose doctrine was dispersed round
about the world by His apostles, to which Paul
alludes, Romans 10:18, "Have they not heard? Yes,
verily their sound went into all the earth," and the
efficacy of whose gospel is like the heat of the sun
which pierces into the very heart of the earth, so
that into the secrets of the soul.

I confess this allegorical exposition is not altogether impertinent, neither is that literal exposition
of Chrysostom to be blamed, for it has its weight.

But to omit all variety of conjectures, this Psalm
contains in it:

1. A double kind of the knowledge of God, of
which one is by the book of the creature; and this
divines call a natural knowledge. There is not any

1

one creature but it is a leaf written all over with the description of God, "His eternal power and Godhead may be understood by the things that are seen," said the Apostle, Romans 1:20. And as every creature, so especially the heavens lead us to the knowledge of a God, so verse 1 of this Psalm, "The heavens declare the glory of God, and the firmament showeth His handiwork." They are the theaters, as it were, of His wisdom, power, and glory.

Another is by the book of Scripture. And this knowledge is far more distinct and explicit. With the other, even the heathens grope after a deity, but with this, Christians behold God, as it were, with open face. The characters here are new, fresh, spiritual, complete, and lively. The Word of God is the singular means to know God aright. Look, as the light which comes from the Sun, so that Word of God, which is light, is the clearest way to know God, who is light itself. Hence it is that the Psalmist stands much upon this, from verse 7 to verse 12, where he sets open the Word in its several encomiums and operations, namely, in its perfection, its certainty, and firmness; its righteousness, purity, and truth, and then in its efficacy: that it is a converting Word, an enlightening Word, an instructing Word, a rejoicing Word, a desirable Word, a warning Word, and a rewarding Word.

2. A singular and experimental knowledge of Himself; so it seems that the Word, which David so commended, he commended from an experimental efficacy. He had found it to be a righteous, holy, pure, and discovering Word, laying open not only visible and gross transgressions, but also, like the

light of the sun, those otherwise unobserved and secret atoms of senses flying within the house (I mean in the secret chambers of the soul).

Now in this there are two things which the Psalmist sets down:

First, a sad complaint of his ignorance, "Who can understand his errors?" As Paul said in his defense, "The law is holy, and just, and good, and spiritual, but I am sold under sin," Romans 7:12-14, so David here says that the law of the Lord is pure, righteous, and perfect, but I am very sinful. Many sins I see in myself, and more there are which I cannot see. I cannot find them out. "No, I think," he said, "that every man's sins arise beyond his accounts. He cannot give a full and entire list of them." Who can understand his errors?

Second, an earnest request, and that for three things:

One is to be cleansed from secret sins, which words some expound that he desires to be pardoned; not only his known, but also his unknown sin. Yet others conjecture that his desire reaches to sanctification, which might prevail not only against open, but the private and closer methods of sinning.

Another is to be kept back from presumptuous sins, verse 13. Austin and others read it "keep back Thy servant from prides." I think their reason is because (1) pride is a bold and presuming sin; and (2) it is that which is the main ingredient of a presumptuous kind of sinning. Even good men have the root of high transgressions within them, into which they may fall if corruption might have its swing; and if they do not fall into them, it is not because they are able alone to keep themselves, but because God, by His Spirit of grace, keeps them back.

A third is the ordering of his words and thoughts, which he desires might be so composed that they might be always acceptable in the sight of God, verse 14. It is as if he had said, "O Lord, I do not only desire to be kept from the viler ways of sin, but from all whatsoever. I would not only not be wicked, but I pray that I may be good. As I would not do evil, so I would not speak evil. Nay, as I would not speak, so I would not think evil. I desire to be so as that I may be acceptable before Thee. I desire to do so that I may be acceptable to Thee. I desire to speak so that I may be accepted by Thee. Yes, and I desire to think so that I may be acceptable in Thy sight."

In my poor conjecture, you have in David a lively copy of an upright heart, which is truly plain all over, and pitches upon this: that it may be acceptable with God. And that it may be so, it would be rinsed of all sins, not only notorious and visible but invisible and secret. And it would have not only an outward decency of religion in pious actions, but also an inward conformity even of the very thoughts and meditations of the heart.

I shall not speak of David's complaint, verse 13, "who can understand his errors?" Only a word and then away.

By "errors" he means his unwitting and inconsiderate mistakes. There are sins, some of which are committed when the sun shines, with light and knowledge, and then, as it is with colors when the sun shines, you may see them, so these a man can see and know, and confess them particularly to be transgressions. There are other sins, which are committed either in the times of ignorance or else (if there is knowledge) yet with inobservance. Either of these may be so heaped up in the particular number of them that, as a man (when he committed them) took no notice of them, so now, after the commission, if he should take the brightest candle to search all the records of his soul, yet many of them would escape his notice. And indeed this is a great part of our misery, that we cannot understand all our debts. We can easily see to many, yet many more lie, as it were, hidden and out of sight. To sin is one great misery, and then to forget our sins is a misery, too. If in repentance we could set the battle in array, point to every individual sin in the true and particular times of acting and reacting, O how would our hearts be more broken with shame and sorrow, and how would we adore the richness of the treasure of mercy which must have a multitude in it to pardon the multitude of our infinite errors and sins!

But this is the comfort. Though we cannot understand every particular sin or time of sinning, yet if we are not idle to search and cast over the books, and if we are heartily grieved for those sins which we have found out, and can, by true repentance, turn from them unto God and by faith unto the blood of Jesus Christ. I say that God, who knows our sins better than we know them, and who understands the true intentions and dispositions of the heart (that if it saw the unknown sins it would be answerably carried against them), will, for His own mercy's sake, forgive them and will not remember them. Nevertheless, though, David says, "Who can understand his errors?" As the prophet Jeremiah said, "The heart of man is desperately wicked, who can know it?" Yet, we must stir ourselves to get more and more heavenly light to find out more and more of our sinnings so the Lord can search the heart. And though we shall never be able to find out all our sins which we have committed, yet it is possible and beneficial for us to find out yet more sins than yet we now know. And you shall find this in your own experience, that as soon as ever grace entered your hearts, you saw sin in another way than ever you saw it before. Yes, and the more grace has traversed and increased in the soul, the more full discoveries it has made of sin. It has shown new sins, as it were; new sins, not for their being, not as if they were not in the heart and life before, but for their evidence and our apprehension and feeling. We now see such ways and such inclinations to be sinful, which we did not think to be so before. As medicine brings those humours which had their residence before now more to the sense of the patient, or as the sun makes open the motes of dust which were in the room before, so does the light of the Word discover more corruption.

But I pass by that point of the impossibility of a full apprehension of all sins committed ignorantly and inconsiderately.

I now proceed from David's complaint to David's request, and here I shall speak of his first request. "Cleanse Thou me from secrets," or secret sins. Austin, writing on these words, expressed it thus: "From those concupiscences which lie so hid, and so close, and so private within me, O Lord, cleanse

Thou me." And in his second exposition of this
Psalm (for he expounded the Psalm twice) he wrote,
"O Lord, take out of my very heart even the sinful
thoughts."

I will name the proposition, and then, perhaps,
we may open things more fully.

1

It is the desire of a holy person to be cleansed, not only from public, but also from private and secret sins. Romans 7:24, "O wretched man! Who shall deliver me?" said Paul. Why, O blessed apostle! What is it that holds you, what is it that molests you? Your life, you say, was unblameable before your conversion and since your conversion, Philippians 3. "Thou hast exercised thyself to have a conscience void of offence toward God and men," Acts 24:16. And yet you cry out, "O wretched man!" And yet you complain, "Who shall deliver me?" Verily, brethren, it was not sin abroad, but at home; it was not sin without, but (at this time) sin within; it was not Paul's sinning with man, but Paul's sinning with Paul. It was that "law of his members" warring (secretly within him) against "the law of his mind." This made that holy man so to cry out, so to complain. As Rebeccah was weary of her life not, as we read, for any foreign disquietments, but because of domestic troubles (the daughters of Heth within the house made her weary of life), so the private and secret birth of corruption within Paul, the workings of that was the cause of his trouble; that was the ground of his exclamation and desires, "Who shall deliver me?"

I remember that the same Paul advised the Ephesians to put off the former conversation so that they could put on the renewed spirit of the mind,

Ephesians 4:22-23, intimating that there are sins which are lurking within as well as sins walking about; and that true Christians must not only sweep the door, but wash the chamber. My meaning is this: We are not only to come off from sins which lie open in the conduct, but also labor to be cleansed from sins and sinning which remain secret and hidden in the spirit and inner disposition.

Now for the beneficial discovery of this assertion, let us inquire four things, each in its own section:

1. In what respects are sins called secret?
2. What is it to be cleansed?
3. Why we are to desire a cleansing from them?
4. What of all this to us?

SECTION I

In what respects are sins called secret? For the resolution of this, know that sin has a double reference.

It may refer to God, and so really no sin, nor manner of sinning, is secret. "Can any hide himself in secret places that I shall not see him?" said the Lord. "Do I not fill heaven and earth?" said the Lord in Jeremiah 23:24. It is true that wicked men with an atheistical folly imagine to hide themselves and their sinful ways from God. "They seek deep to hide their counsel from the Lord, and their words are in the dark, and they say, Who seeth us? And who knoweth us?" Isaiah 29:15. But really it is not so, though the cloud may somewhat eclipse the light of the sun, and though the dark night may shut it

forth altogether; yet there stands no cloud, nor curtain, nor moment of darkness or secrecy between
the eyes of God and the ways of man. "The ways of a
man are before the eyes of the Lord, and He pon-
dereth all his goings," Proverbs 5:21. He speaks principally there of the ways of the adulterer, which usually are plotted with the most cunning secrecy, yet
God sees all those ways. Hebrews 4:13, "There is not
any creature that is not manifest in His sight, but all
things are naked and opened even to the eyes of
Him with whom we have to do." Not a creature, not a
thing, not anything of any creature but it is naked, it
is without all fig leaves. It is uncased of his colors
and pretenses. Yes, it is opened, as it were, embow-
elled, cut into distinct pieces, the very inside of it
turned out to the eyes of God.

Sin may also refer to man, and thus indeed
comes in the division of sin into, first, open, and
second, secret. Now in this respect, sin may be
termed secret diversely:

1. *In respect of the person sinning, when his very sinning
is (formally considered) hidden from himself.* He does a
thing which is really sinful, but to him it is not ap-
prehensively. So what outrages Paul breathed out
against the church in the times of his ignorance,
which he did not know to be acts of sin but thought
to be motions of a warranted zeal. In this sense, all
the obliquities which may be fastened, at least, upon
invincible ignorance, may be called secret sins.

2. *In respect of the manner of sinning, and thus sins may
be termed secret either:*

1.) When they are colored and disguised,
though they fly abroad, yet not under that name, but

apparelled with some semblances of virtues (Cyprian complained of such tricks in his second epistle, which is to Donatus); or

2.) When they are kept off from the stage of the world. They are like fire in the chimney. Though you do not see it, yet it burns. Many people, like those in Ezekiel, commit abominations in secret, as long as the public eye is not upon them. He is sinful, and acts it with the greatest vileness. All the difference between another sinner and him is this: he is a sinner, but the other one admits he is a sinner. It is the same with an open book and a shut book. The one which is shut has the same lines and words, but the lines in the one which is opened may be read and seen; or

3.) When they are kept not only from the public eye, but from any mortal eye. The carnal eye of him who commits the sins does not see them. He does see them with the eye of conscience, but not with an eye of natural sense. Even those persons with whom he converses, and who highly commend the frame of his ways, cannot yet see the secret discoursings and actings of sin in his mind and heart for, brethren, all the actings of sin are not external. They are not visible. But there are some, yes, the most dangerous acting within the soul, where corruption lies as a fountain and a root. The heart of man is a scheme of wickedness. A man says that in his heart which he dares not speak with his tongue, and his thought will do that which his hands dare not execute. Well, then, sin may be called secret when it is sin and acted as sin even there, where none but God and conscience can see.

I think sin is like a candle in a lantern, where the shining is first within and then bursting out at the windows; or like boils and ulcerous humours which are scabs and scurvy stuff. They are first within the skin, and afterwards they break out to the view on the outside. So it is with sin. It is a malignant humour and a fretting leprosy, diffusing itself into several secret acts and workings within the mind, and then it breaks abroad and dares adventure the practice of itself to the eye of the world. Though that sin may never see the light, it is still like a child who is alive, but buried in the womb. Yet as that child is a man, a true man there closeted in that hidden frame of nature, so sin is truly sin, though it never gets out beyond the womb which conceived and enlivened it.

Now, whether David speaks of secret sins in opposition to the eyes of men, or to his own sensible eye, such as corrupt nature committed within his own heart, or whether he intends both, may be much disputed. For my part, I think that it may be understood both of such sins as he committed in private (and so the words respect the actings of sin in secret) and also those sins which his own heart and thoughts might commit within themselves. And so the words respect the secret actings of sin, though principally they may be most fitly expounded in this latter sense.

But what were those secret sins from which David desired to be cleansed?

Nay, that is a secret. He does not instance in any one because his desire is to be freed from every one. He speaks indefinitely. He found many secret inclinations (without all doubt) in several kinds of sin, now in one, now in another; from all of which (not some only) he desires to be cleansed.

SECTION II

But what is that to be cleansed? There are two expositions of it.

One is that he desires to be justified, to be pardoned for those sins, and so the Hebrew word imports in the second conjugation.

Indeed, the blood of Christ which justifies is a cleansing thing. It wipes off the guilt.

Now, if this is it, then this much is evident, that secret thoughts and inclinations may be sinful, and are damnable, or else they were not pardonable.

Another is that he desires more to be sanctified, and that his nature might be more changed, not only that outward sinnings might be abandoned, but even inward actings or motions might be subdued.

And observe, he desires to be cleansed. He does not desire to be dipped only into the water or sprinkled. He does not only desire to be slightly rinsed; but he desires to be washed until he is cleansed, until his soul is made clean and pure, free from those secret sinfulnesses. Where observe, by the way, three things:

1. *He who has received true grace needs more grace.* Our lives need to be still reformed and our hearts still to be cleansed. The soul is such a vessel as is continually gathering in and sending out what is corrupt

and evil. It is like a fountain which you are always having to clean.

2. *Again, the progress and perfection of cleansing the soul appertains to God as well as the beginning.* The physician must go through with his cure, or else the patient will relapse, the disease will prevail. No, the created grace in the soul is not enough to keep down sin, much less to pit it out, unless a divine and new assistance comes to the soul. Therefore David, though a holy man, prays to God to cleanse him.

3. *Lastly, persons who are truly holy desire still further measures of holiness.* David was cleansed before, and yet he desires to be cleansed. Why? Because though he had a radical purity, he did not have a gradual purity. The whole man was cleansed, but it was not cleansed wholly. He had some grace, but he wanted more. He was pretty well rid of some sins, but others he felt stirring and working. Though no man saw them, yet he felt them. No combat serves the Christian, but that which looks to victory, and he thinks the day is not yet won if he does not yet have the conquest of every sin as well as any one particular sin.

SECTION III

But why should we desire to be cleansed from secret sins, either from secret acting or secret motions? I will give you several reasons for it.

1. *Because secret sins will become public sins if they are not cleansed.* It is with the soul as it is with the body wherein diseases are first bred and then manifested.

And, if you suppress them not in their root, you shall shortly see them break out in the fruit. It is like fire which catches the inside of the house first, and there, if you do not suppress it, will make a way to get to the outside. "Lust when it hath conceived, bringeth forth sin," James 1:15. Beloved, remember this, that though the first ground of sin is within the heart, yet the propensity of sin is to come forth into public. The child in the womb does not have stronger throes to get out of its private lodging than sin secretly wrought to fly into open and manifest action. Amnon is sick with the sinful conceptions of incestuous lust, and what ado was there till he had committed that villainy. Let a man set up any sin in delightful contemplation and meditation, that same inward acting of his sin, either actually casts him upon the outward adventures, or invites them. This is the least that it does. It strangely ripens his natural inclination; and, besides that, it prepares him for a temptation that suits that way. Satan shall not need to tempt him much who has already tempted himself: and he who will work sin in his heart, a weak occasion will draw it out into his life. Thirty pieces of silver will prevail with a covetous Judas, who already had gold as his master in his heart.

OBJECTION. But, will you say, suppose that secret sins uncleansed become public.

ANSWER. I say, therefore, should we the rather labor to cleanse them; for as much as the more public sin becomes, the worse it is. You know that if the word or letter of the mind is written in paper, it becomes something for others to copy, while secret sins are confined to the house, that is, to the soul

only, and do not break out into visible actions.
Though they are very damnable, yet they are but of
personal and proper danger, they only endanger
him who maintains them, as poison does the one
who takes the poison. But, when they come to public
and visible actions, then they are a copy. They are
exemplary sins and, like the plague infecting other
persons, others are capable of imitating them, and
so more souls are tainted and God now receives a
common dishonor.

2. *Secret sins are apt to deceive us most, and therefore
cleanse them.* There is a deceitfulness in all sinnings
whatsoever; the soul is deceived by sin whenever it
sins. But now secret sins deceive us most; they are
most apt to prevail with us:

First, because we do not have that strict and spiritual judgment of inward sins like we do of outward
sins. Many times we conceive of them as no sins at
all, or else as slight and venial. To draw a sword, and
run a man through the heart! O this is a fearful
murder, to draw a false word, and slanderously to
pierce through his good name, we likewise imagine
that this may be bad; but to kill a man with malicious thought, with revengeful plots and desires,
nay, this is scarcely thought as a matter culpable, or
at least very excusable. Beloved, it is the nature of sin
to come off easily in the soul without stir and debate, and no sins come off so easily as those which
we scarce imagine to be sins. Now we are apt to
think that secret sins are scarce sins.

Second, because most men decline sin upon outward respects, which do not reach the actings of secret sins, shame and fear, and observance are great,

and the only restraints to many. They do not live in, and visibly commit such sins, because they like not shame, and are afraid of punishment; but what are those to secret sinnings, where no law of man can reach, and no eye of man can search. It is true, that God has set some one or other to watch the sinner all over, as His law for inward and outward actings; conscience principally for the inward, and the eyes and mouths, and hands of men for the outward. But now for secret sinning, it being invisible, it therefore escapes all the outward restraints by the seeing, speaking, and judging of men. And it has mainly to attend to what conscience will say, which perhaps is ignorant or drowsy. And, if it does speak, yet it is not regarded. Now mark, of all sins, eye them most which most easily deceive you. These a man commits most, affects most, and continues in longest. Since, therefore, secret sins come under that form, is it not necessary to labor to be cleansed from them?

3. *The strength of sin is inward; therefore labor to be cleansed from secret sins.* If a man has a fever so that his tongue burns in his mouth and his flesh is even roasting with burning heat, yet the strength of that fever is not in his spirits and inward parts which are set on fire by some humorous distemper. So it is with sin. Though the outward actings are bad enough, yet the strongholds are within the soul.

Wherein Lies the Strength of a Sin

It lies in its nearness to the fountain, from whence it can take a quick, immediate, and continual supply; and so do our secret sins. They are as near to original sin as the first droppings are to the spring-head. They are indeed original sin immediately acting itself, which sin is a full sin, a feeding sin, a sinning sin, and never weary.

It lies in the acceptance of the affections. Love and liking set sin on its throne. They are the royal arms of sin. Now of the two, men are more apt to like and love secret sins than open sins.

It lies in the confidence of commission. Now a man takes more heart and boldness and courage to commit secret sins than open.

It lies in the iteration and frequency of acting, for sin often repeated and acted is like a cable doubled in strength by the manifold twistings, but secret sins are more frequently iterated; an unclean heart can keep a whore in his thoughts every day and moment who, perhaps, is afraid to be seen at the door of her house once a year. A proud person can disdain another in his heart all week who yet will not show it once a month; so for the malicious.

4. *The principal object of God's eye is the inward and secret frame of the soul; therefore, labor to be cleansed from secret sins.* Psalm 66:18, "If I regard iniquity in my heart, the Lord will not hear me." Psalm 51:6, "Behold, Thou desirest truth in the inward parts." Therefore is He often said in Scripture to "search the heart and reins," which intimates His special observation of the secret frame. It is true that God gives charge against open sins. Why? Because He would not have any to be profane; and so He gives singular charge against secret sins. Why? Because He cannot endure

any to be hypocritical. The man is to God what his inside is; if you work wickedness in your heart, God will destroy you. Plaster your visible part with all sorts of pious expressions, if yet you can set up a form of sinning within, you are notable hypocrites. The Lord sees you to be false and rotten, and He will discharge Himself of you. Treason is as bad as rebellion; rebellion is but open treason, and treason is but secret rebellion. The King will exact life justly for either; so will God for the secret sinnings, as well as for the open.

The Spirit of God is grieved by secret sins as well as dishonored by open sinnings.

SECTION IV

Now I come to the applications of this point. Is it the desire of a holy heart to be cleansed not only from public, but also from private sins; not only from gross and visible, but also from secret and invisible sins? Then these things will follow from hence as information.

1. *True holiness has a repugnancy and contrarity to all sins.* It is not contrary to sin because it is open and manifest, nor to sin because it is private and secret, but to sin as sin whether public or private, because both the one and the other is contrary to God's will and glory. As it is with true light, though it is but a beam, yet it is universally opposite to all darkness: or as it is with heat, though there is but one degree of it, yet it is opposite to all cold; so if the holiness is true and real, it cannot comply with any known sin.

You can never reconcile them in the affections. They may have an unwilling consistence in the person, but you can never make them to agree in the affections.

Beloved, there is a marvelous difference between things which are different by a respective and accidental repugnancy, and by a natural and pure contrarity. In the former there may be an accord, but in the latter, none. A hypocritical heart may fall out with its sin for the consequence of it, for the shame it brings, for the stinging guilt which it causes in the conscience; yet his heart has (in absolute terms) an inward cohesion and league with that sin. But now true holiness and sin are opposite with a natural contrarity, therefore you can never reconcile them in the heart; but the opposition is inward as well as outward to sin, wherever it is.

2. *Sanctification is not perfect in this life.* He who has the most grace still has some sin. Else, why does David, a holy person, desire to be cleansed? He who needs to pray that he may be cleansed cannot yet totally say, "My heart is clean."

There is a perfection of integrity which a holy heart has standing in opposition to hypocrisy and essential defectiveness, but there is not a perfection of eminency which consists in an opposition to all want. Grace, while in your hearts living on the earth, is as health rising in a sick body, like heat getting into the water, or like light spreading itself more and more to chase away darkness. There is yet more of sin to be conquered, and we have less grace than we should have, and where any part or degree of sin is yet as an enemy, being and rising, there grace,

though it may be sound and saving, is not yet absolute and perfect.

3. *Here you may understand the grounds and reasons of
the many troubles and heavy complaints of Christians.* It is
true that they may fail many times in their words
and speeches (and he is a very perfect man who does
not trespass therein), and they may be overtaken
with explicit sinnings. No holy person will profess
himself to be an angel, but he has many outward
sins to bewail, as he has many inward graces for
which to bless God. Yet the load of his soul is within
his soul. Commissions justly humble him, but the
secret inclinations of sin burst his heart asunder.

"Why do you look so sad," we oftentimes say to
good people, "and why are you cast down?" What is it
that troubles you? You have a good God, a good
Christ, and a good gospel. Yes, I have, but with all
that, I have a bad heart. In spite of all my conflict-
ings, strivings, and prayings, I am still molested with
sinful imaginations and sinful inclinations. If I do
not perform duty with any life, I am troubled for my
dullness. If I do it with any life, I am troubled with
pride. If I do not pray, I cannot bear the guilt of a
willing omission. If I do pray, I am even torn from
myself, and the crowd of other thoughts jostles out
the apprehension and affection of my praying.
Another Christian complains bitterly of secret blasphemies and atheistical risings. Another complains
of private murmurings, discontents, and unbeliev-
ings, though you hear no such word and see no
such carriage. "O wretched man that I am!" said
Paul. And verily so great is the insolence of secret
corruptions that the Christian is often times weary

of his life. Beloved, the main battle of a Christian is
not in the open field. His quarrels are mostly within
and his enemies are in his own breast. When he has
re-formed an ill life, yet it shall cost him infinitely
much more to reform an ill heart. He may receive so
much power from grace at the beginning, as in a
short time, to draw off from most of the former
gross acts of sinning, but it will be a work all of his
days to get a thorough conquest of secret corruptions.

4. *Then all the work of a Christian is not abroad if there
are secret sins to be cleansed.*

There are two sorts of duties. Some are direct,
which are working duties. They are the colors of
grace in the countenance and view of the conversation, setting it forth with all holy evenness, fruitful-
ness, and unblameableness.

Some are reflexive, which are searching duties.
They pertain to the inward rooms, to the beautifying
and reforming of them, for not only the life but the
heart is also the subject of our care and study. I am
not only to labor that I *do* no evil, but also that I *be*
not evil; not only that sin does not distain my paths,
but also that it does not defile my intentions; not
only that my clothes are handsome, but also that my
skin is white, that is, my inward parts are as acceptable to God as my outward frame is plausible with
man. Yes, let me tell you one thing. He who is a
hypocrite, who takes care to wash the outside only
(forasmuch as the greatest solicitude for the life may
be without any reformation of the heart; not that the
life must not be squared, but if that is varnished and
the heart is neglected), that person has not only the

same natural and lively frame of sinfulness, but he deceives himself, or at least another with a mere pretense and shadow. Therefore, brethren, let us have eyes to look inward as well as outward. God has given us a reflexive faculty. Besides that, know:

The first part of our work is to set upon the inward part. How vain it is to wash the distasteful streams which are yet fed by a sour fountain, and verily the conversation will be ever and anon unequal and unlike itself. If the heart remains unpurged and unchanged, corruption, which has often entertained your secret thoughts, will at length present these births to your very eyes.

The greater part of your work is within. It is true, an ill tongue, a lustful eye, and a stealing hand may challenge much prayer, care, observance, and watchfulness to reform them, but a beam of light is small to the vast body of light in the sun, and the dribbling rivers are more easily turned and dried up than the deep ocean. Sin within is sin in the fountain, and sin in the visible parts is sin in the streams. Yes, everything is strongest in its cause (and therefore sin is highest in the heart), for the strength and vigor of temptations is at the inward part of man.

Satan does not stir a naked eye, but a filthy heart to look through that sinful window. He does not come to the hand and say "Steal," but first to the heart, which will quickly command the hand. He does not say immediately to the tongue, "Swear and blaspheme," but the heart, which can easily command that hellish language into the tongue. If you should pluck out your eyes and never see any object

to excite your unclean heart, yet you may still be as
filthy a person as before. Your own corrupt heart
and Satan would incline you so. And though you
never had a foot to go, or a hand to stir, yet you
might be as much a thief as Judas. Your heart might
rob every passenger, and steal from every house you
come to.

Objects are but accidental things to man. They
have no necessary impressive influences. They only
deliver themselves in that nature with which God
has clothed them. But that which envenoms them,
and makes them to work so wickedly, is man's
wicked heart. You have many persons who complain
much against objects. Oh, they can see none or deal
with none but wickedness is stirring. Why, beloved,
the objects are innocent, but our hearts are unclean
and sinful. If you could get another heart, you would
look with another eye. The only way to make temptations lose their force is to decline occasions and to
cleanse the inward parts.

SECTION V

Another use which I would make of this is to try
ourselves what care we have of secret sins. I will give
unto you some reasons why I would have you to try
yourselves in this:

1. *Because there are many persons who wallow in secret
sins.* The Apostle complained of such in his time.
Ephesians 5:12, "It is a shame to speak of those
things which are done by them in secret." He speaks
of such as lived in secret fornication and unclean-

ness. Brethren, how many are there who apparel themselves in the secret thoughts of abhorred wickedness, but even in the secret actings of the same, as if there were no God to look on them, nor conscience to spy on them, nor judgment day to arraign them! Oh, how infinitely odious you must be in the eyes of that holy God, who dare to court Him in public, and yet dare to provoke Him to His face thus in private. You are like a whorish strumpet who dissembles marvelous affections to her husband abroad, and yet at home she will violate the covenant of her God before her husband's eyes. So you pretend so much for God before company, and yet in private you will presume to sin before His face. He sees you, and your conscience knows that right well.

There are at the least three horrible sins which now you commit at once.

First, that very sin which you would so conceal; and perhaps it may be a sin of the deepest dye. Yea, mark this, that usually the most damnable sins are such which are committed in secret, as Sodom's adulteries, and such fearful kinds of pollutions, and murders, and treasons, etc.

Second, hypocrisy, which is a screen to your sin, a holy cover for an unholy heart and practice, which makes the sinner so much the more vile in God's eyes, by how much the more that he not only sins against God, but wrests (as it were) something from God to cover and palliate his rebellion against Him.

A third is atheism. If there is not formal atheism, yet, there is a virtual atheism, as if God were not God in secret, but only in public, that He could see in the

light and not in the darkness; that His eye is as the
eye of a man only, whereas He is a universal eye, and
is a Light without all darkness.

2. *The principle of sinning is secret and common to every
man.*

The motions of sinning are not like the motions
of a bowl, which runs only by the virtue of an imprinted strength; they are not violent motions,
whose cause is only extrinsical, but they are natural
motions, whose principle is within the subject: "Out
of the heart (said Christ) proceed evil thoughts,
adulteries, fornications, murders, thefts, covetousness, malice, deceit, lasciviousness, an evil eye, blasphemy, pride, foolishness; all these evil things come
from within, and defile the man," Mark 7:21-23. The
nature which tempts you, that nature is in you. It is
the womb of many and infinite sinful corruptions
and imaginations. It casts out wickedness as the
fountain casts forth water. It is very true that outward
occasions, and Satan by his suggestions, may assist
and quicken original corruption, as the bellows may
enflame the fire, yet the fire has heat and an aptness
naturally to burn. So original corruption, though it
may grow monstrously active by temptations from
abroad, yet it can and does incline us, and can beget
private actings of horrible sins from its own native
strength; it can send out several forms of sinning
and incline us to contemplate them, yea, to contrive
the singular methods of transgression; yea, it can
feed the soul with wonderful delights in them, so
that in the eye of God, the sinnings are formed and
fashioned, and ripened with most odious perfections.

3. *There is a depth of hypocrisy in the souls of men, whose proper work is to have a secret way contrary to an open profession;* as a player who takes on him to act the part of a King, yet in his private and absolute way, he may be a person of most ignoble birth and unworthy qualities; so it is with the hypocrite.

Divines distinguish three sorts of hypocrisy:

One is natural, and has footing in every man. Even the most upright heart has in it some hypocrisy, and he sometimes seems to be that which he is not; he may be sometimes more full in his profession than he is indeed in his actions.

Another is foul and gross, which is when a man's heart is not at all what it seems to be unto the world. Christ compares persons guilty of it to whited sepulchres which within are full of dead and rotten bones; as when a man shall profess he loves God and Christ and His ways, and yet secretly condemns and hates holiness and resists the motions of God's Spirit, and is at defiance with all the heavenly rules of life and powerful obedience.

A third is formal, when a man not only deceives others with a show of what is not in him, but also deceives and cheats his own heart with a persuasion of his own happiness—partly from some specials which he finds in himself above others, and partly from the pride of his own spirit joined with an affectation of happiness; yea, all the while his heart keeps a haunt of some private lust and ungodliness; there is some sweet morsel under his tongue with which he will not part.

4. *Outward occasions can incline to secret sinnings.* Beloved, there lies a snare almost against us in all

society. We have such vile natures that as a spark of
fire will easily kindle a box of tinder. So but a word
spoken, many times, kindles a world of passion, of
malice, of revenge within us; yea, the misplacing of
a look begets in us secret disdain and discontent;
yea, the casting of an eye may enflame the heart with
excess of lust. Need we not then (putting all these
things together) to search our inward frame to see
what care we have about and against secret sinnings? But you will say, "How may a man know
whether he desires truly to be cleansed from secret
sins?"

I will give unto you some observations for this—
first negatively; then, second, positively.

The Negative Discoveries

The negative discoveries, those by which a man
may know that he does not desire to be cleansed
from secret sins, are these:

1. When the principal restraint of his sinnings is
terminated only in man. Beloved, really our conversing is either with God, or with ourselves, or with
men; and answerable to these, there are three several reasons of forbearing sin: either because of
God, whose will and holiness is injured; or else because of our conscience, because our secret quiet
and ease shall be interrupted; or else because if we
should adventure to sin, we should hazard our estimations and estates and safeties, and incur ig-
nominy, blame, shame, punishment, and loss with
men.

Now, mark it. When respect to man is the only

reason why I forbear sin, I am all this while loose and unconscionable in the inward frame. All my care is taken up about those actions and carriages which fall under the eye and judgment of man; and none but the visible and open actings of sin break out that way. If I forbear sin for man's sake, that men may esteem well of me and not censure or punish me, I therefore so far restrain sin as it may not be visible, but I do not strive against it because it is sinful; I say, not because the thing is sinful before God, but only because it is culpable before man. Now try yourselves in this: What is the restraint of your sinning? Suppose all men in the world were in a deep sleep, suppose that no eye saw you, suppose that no tongue of human justice would call you to account; would not your heart then, with full sail, spread out itself? Would you not now, like the lions in the night, wander about for your prey? Would not your heart turn out itself, drive out its secret inclinations? Would you not do that in any place which now you committed in secret corners?

2. When the hindrance of secret sinnings are a burden, they are crosses. A man does not desire to go out of the way for his delight. He is not weary of his affection, for delight is endless and unsatisfied: though the body may be wearied, yet the affection of delight is never wearied. Now brethren, a man may know his delights by his crosses. If I attain not that which I respect not, I am not moved; but if my spirit rise and swell and rage, or if I grieve and complain and am sad because of an impediment of something which has clapped in itself between me and my desires, this shows that I had a delight in it, that I

would gladly have had it. Now let me apply this to our business in hand. God, many times, hinders the sinner; He does step in by His providence and prevent him from increasing his guilt. He puts forth some accident, some impediment or other which stands between the intention of sin and the execution of it. The sinner has contrived and plotted the time and place and the manner of the sinning, but God (who overrules all) has disappointed him by the unexpectedness of other company or some other occurrence, or sudden sickness or misadventure. If now the heart grows into Ahab's turbulent fits, it is a sign it would have had Naboth's vineyard. If the hindrance of the sinful fact, whether open or secret, is a grief to you, this shows the bent of your heart to the sin; but I pass on.

3. When the nature of sin is no burden, but some particular actings are. As Joab said to David when he observed his sorrow for Absalom, "I perceive (said he, 2 Samuel 19:6) that if Absalom had lived, and all we had died this day, then it had pleased them well." So here, when the main trouble is for some actions irregularly starting out to the world, and not for the nature, which is a cause of that and all other sinful actings, this shows that our eye is outward and not inward.

Brethren, mistake me not, I do not mean that sinful actions should escape our tears; nay, verily all our sinful births and broods naturally call for sorrow and humblings; and the more sinful any explicit act is, the more dishonor God has by it, the more scandal religion suffers by it. Therefore, I say, the more sorrows and tears should we cast after it;

but then know, that according to the guilty quality, according to the proportion of it should be the answerableness of our grief and perplexity. Am I grieved for a rash and hasty word and not for a passionate and violent nature? Am I troubled for an unclean gesture or act and not for an unclean heart? Am I perplexed for a lie by my tongue and not for an evil and false heart? Verily then my eye is not on God, but man. It is not upon secret sins, but only upon open and manifest sins.

4. When we cannot abide the spiritual efficacy and inward searchings of the Word. Beloved, "the Word of God is quick and powerful, a two-edged sword, it divides between the joints and the marrow, it is a discerner of the thoughts and intents of the heart," Hebrews 4:12. You find it to be so, that it comes into your closet; it finds you out in your most secret way of sinning; it follows you into the most dark corners; it pierces into the imaginations and plots which you never yet brought out to the sun; it tells you of your very desires and affections, what you like most, crave most, do most. Now what do your hearts say? How do they bestir themselves when they find the Word haunt and pursue them, when they observe it come and close with the secret windings and turnings? Do you not strive to keep out the light? Do you not hold it off as they do the enemy in a siege in the out-works, that he might not break into the heart of the city? Would you not be spared, unsearched? Nay, you cannot endure the Word which comes to your private sinful gains and to your private sinful pleasures; you will not endure to be ordered how to think and how to desire. If it be so,

where is then in you the property of a holy David, who does not desire to guard and defend but to be cleansed from secret sins?

The Positive Discoveries

The positive observations by which you may know that you desire in truth to be cleansed from secret sins may be these:

1. Consider of what acceptance are secret temptations. There are open and broad temptations which carry some express prejudice into our names, and there are implicit and close temptations which carry a real prejudice to God's glory. Of this latter sort, there are again two kinds. Some temptations are those which the ingenuity of a refined nature may perhaps start at as too gross to yield unto them; as some kinds of blasphemy, and mockings, and revilings of God, or Christ, or the gospel, and those hideous excitations to self-murder or any unnatural villainy. Other temptations there are which may find a principle within the soul more intimate and apt to take and receive the impressions, if not opposed by the advertency and purity of a spiritual heart. Now assuredly, the heart desires to be cleansed from secret sins, which stirs up itself with all its might against those secret temptations, which deal for the sin within the soul, which lighten and quicken natural corruption by representation or by excitation, or by both! Oh, it is the heavy day of the soul when it is so inwardly assaulted and buffeted! The heart is so far from yielding that it is resisting with tears, with prayers. Observe one thing: the temptation to the

sinning is not only resisted, but it is made an occasion to the holy soul the more to labor against the corruption unto which the temptation would secretly incline (as if Satan should tempt to secret pride); not only not to admit the temptation, but now to go to God and pray more earnestly against a proud imagination and a proud spirit, yea, to be vehement for a more lowly and humble heart. Or, if Satan tempts to contemplative uncleanness or secret actings, not only to resist and abhor them, but to pray more earnestly for a chaste and pure heart and for chaste and spiritual imaginations and thoughts.

2. Consider how far forth you desire to approve yourself to God. God is the God of our spirits as well as of our bodies; and He not only ponders our paths, but also searches our hearts, that you send forth some words in prayer! Oh, this satisfies not because of so many distractions in the mind and of so many deadnesses in the affections! That man cannot accuse you for any habitual unevenness, this is not enough, if God cannot approve of you for a person after His own heart. If your heart were such as God would like, regard, approve, accept, then you would be better satisfied.

There is a twofold approving of ourselves, one in the consignable exactness of duty pertaining to our callings; hence the Apostle, 2 Corinthians 6:3-4, "giving no offence to any thing, that the ministry be not blamed, but in all things approving ourselves as the ministers of God in much patience, in afflictions, in necessities, in distresses."

Another is in the internal disposition of the soul, which is when the private frame of the spirit is so endeavored to be rectified, squared, beautified, and ordered, that the great and holy God may take delight and proclaim His gracious testimony of the same. Hear the Apostle, 2 Corinthians 10:18, "Not he that commendeth himself is approved, but whom the Lord commendeth." In the former respect is that phrase of Paul, Romans 14:18, "approved of men;" in the latter respect is that phrase of Paul, Romans 16:10, "approved in Christ;" and of Peter, Acts 2:22, "a man approved of God." Now verily, no man can sincerely desire to approve himself to God, to put himself over unto God's sentence of trial and decision so that he might find an acceptance in his eyes, but he indeed desires to be cleansed from secret sins. Why? Because God's sentence is righteous and according to truth. He does not weigh so much the actions as the spirits of men; not so much the outward expressions as the inward dispositions; not so much what they do, as what they would do; not so much that they do not, as this that they would do no iniquity. I remember that David is upon this very strain in Psalm 139:23-24, "Search me, O Lord, and know my heart, and know my thoughts, and see if there be any wicked way in me." Here he puts himself entirely upon God to try him, to search him, to see whether his heart is such as He would like and approve. Paul is in the same strain, 1 Corinthians 4:3, "With me it is a very small thing that I should be judged of you," that is, whether you approve of me, accept me, or condemn me. I tell you, this is not the main thing that I look on, verse 4, "But he that judgeth me is the Lord," that is, there is another Judge, a greater Judge, a better Judge, one who can canvass the secret and inward parts as well as eye the visible acts and motions; to Him do I look; to Him do I desire to approve myself.

3. Observe, where do you lay the sharpest edge of the axe? The axe, said Matthew, in another case, "is now laid to the root of the tree." Sin is like a tree; it has root and branches. That which we see of the tree is the bulk and branches; that which is the life of the tree we see not. It is the root which is moored in the bowels of the earth. Now as a man may deal with a tree, so may he deal with his sins; the axe may be employed only to lop off the branches, which yet all live in the root; and he may apply his axe to the very root, to cutting it up, and so he brings a universal death to the tree. So it is possible for a man to bestow all his pains to lop off sin only in the visible branches, in the outward limbs of it; and it is also possible for a man to be crucifying the secret lust, the very corrupt nature and root of sinfulness. Now this I say, he who bestows his study, his prayers, his tears, his cares, his watchings, his strength to mortify corruption in the root, in the nature, in the cause; how unquestionable is it that he desires to be cleansed from secret sins. Suppose a man has an ulcerous part undiscovered in his breast. If he applies such medicine as will carry away the spring of that ulcer, it is a palpable sign he desires to be cleansed from the secret ulcer itself. So it is in this case.

Beloved, we distinguish between these two things—the restraining of sin and the weakening of sin.

A man whose sins may crawl in him, like the

worms in a dead body, which may feed upon his most exquisite contemplations and dearest affections, with fullest and sweetest contentment, may yet curb and restrain the habits or sinful propensions from breaking out into act. The vigor of a natural and enlightened conscience and the ingenuity of a more nobly-bred disposition and the force of particular aims and ends, may be able to rein up and bridle in you. "Imperative Acts" (as the schoolmen speak), the notable or visible deliveries or actings of sin; but that which weakens sin is grace. That which purges out the sin is always contrary to it.

Again, we observe a difference between these two, namely, he who strongly desires to have another nature, another heart. Another nature or heart is a heart replenished with most holy qualities which stand in a present opposition to that of sin, and which in time will get the victory over it. Suppose a man is apt to much unbelief, secret mistrusts and distrusts, how know I that he would be cleansed from them? Not only by this that he complains, but also that he is day and night with God for the grace of faith and the strength of His Spirit to believe. And indeed it is the contrary grace which cleanses from sin, secret grace which cleanses from secret sins, forasmuch as the inward cleansing is not by outward medicines but by an inward principle, both in nature and operation, striving against the nature and operations of sin as the Apostle elegantly shadows it in Galatians 5 and Psalm 51. "Create in me a new heart," said David. The new heart is a new frame and temper to fill the soul with other inclinations and thoughts, and the life with other ways and actions.

SECTION VI

I now proceed to a third use which shall be for comfort to such persons whose desires are really carried to be cleansed from secret sins as well as public and visible; they may comfort themselves in many things.

1. *That their praise is of God, and He commends them.* See the Apostle, Romans 2:28-29, "He is not a Jew which is one outwardly, neither is that circumcision which is outward in the flesh, but he is a Jew which is one inwardly, and circumcision is that of the heart, in the spirit, not in the letter; whose praise is not of men, but of God." Now what a comfort is this that you are a person of whom the Lord will take notice, yea, whom the Lord Himself will praise and commend? To say of you, as of David, "I have found a man after Mine own heart;" and that your heart is perfect with the Lord?

2. *That conscience in a day of distress will acquit and clear them.* Beloved, there are two sorts of people:

Some daubing and dissembling and shuffling whose care it is not not to sin, but to be cunning in sin; these shall find that in the day of their distress conscience shall rip up before their eyes their most private vilenesses and that God will set their secret sins before the light of His countenance. Yea, and the more industrious and witty that they have been that way, the more shall conscience aggravate the hypocrisy of their souls.

Others conflicting and agonizing with secret motions, outward occasions, strong temptations: these persons in a day of distress shall find singular

testimony from conscience. For though now, while
their judgment is oppressed with variety of arguments and the mind is overladen with the heap of
temptations, they are not able clearly to judge and
decide their condition; yet when conscience (which
is the great umpire in man) shall arise to examine
fore-past actions and endeavors, it will then give
sentence for you, excusing you, approving you, that
in all simplicity and sincerity, you had your conversation both towards men and towards God; and that
it was the desire of your soul to fear the Lord, to do
no iniquity, but to walk before Him in all well-pleas-
ing. Conscience clears *as* the Word clears and *whom*
the Word clears.

3. *They may with confidence make their prayers to God
and shall be heard.* The hypocrite has Moab's curse,
that "he shall pray but not prevail," Isaiah 16:12. For,
said David, "If I regard iniquity in my heart, the Lord
will not hear my prayer," Psalm 66:18. But, said
Eliphaz, Job 22:23, 27, "If thou return to the
Almighty, and shalt put away iniquity from thy
tabernacles, thou shalt make thy prayer unto Him,
and He shall hear thee." Oh, how acceptable unto
God are the sacrifices of a spirit truly and uprightly
tempered!

4. *The Lord will more and more cleanse them.* He will by
degrees put more beautiful ornaments on the inward man and change their burdens. If Paul is troubled with himself, Christ will deliver him from himself; he has this comfort, that, for the present, God
observes his inward conflicts, and accepts his secret
uprightness; and for the future, that he shall have
the victory over his rebellions by Jesus Christ. There

are two things of which the soul which deals with
inward convictions (out of a pure respect) may be
confident; namely, one is grace to combat, another
is strength to overcome.

QUESTION. Oh, but can a man be truly holy
who has such vile inclinations, abhorred thoughts
and motions, such wonderful eruptions of sinful
abominations working yet within him?
ANSWER 1. You must know this, that a holy man
is a man, and a man is compounded of a nature, and
a nature is compounded of flesh and spirit, grace
and sin.
ANSWER 2. You must distinguish between the secret motions of sin, and the secret approbations
thereof. As grace does not utterly root out all the existence of natural corruption, so neither is it able,
absolutely, to suppress (though to hinder) the operations or workings of sinful corruption.
ANSWER 3. We distinguish of secret workings of
sin; there is a double secrecy:
One is natural, and it befalls any man, for sin
naturally carries shame with it and, therefore, has a
desire of secrecy.
Another is artificial, which is a cunning devising
of sin. This kind of secrecy is not so incident to holy
persons. They do not frame methods of transgressing, nor ways of dishonoring God; yet I will put forth
a distinction, I think it good. There is a twofold artificial secrecy:
One is antecedent and delightful, contrived on
purpose to enlarge the way of the vile heart out of a
deep love of the sin and to compass the continual

fruition thereof.

Another is a consequent and troublesome, and a kind of enforced artificialness, as was that of David, which arose from a sin secretly committed by him in the haste of a temptation. Now I think that even a holy soul may possibly touch upon an artificial secrecy by consequence, having been violently and preposterously carried unto some precedent sin, which that it may be hid from the eye of man, it therefore spins out some other methods of sinning. However, this is a very fearful course, there is no comfort at all it it, but a deeper aggravation of the former sinning; for as much as adding sin to sin is no remedy, but to repent of former sinnings is the only and best way of help.

SECTION VII

A fourth use of this assertion shall be for exhortation, to take heed of, and labor against secret sins. It is true that all sin is to be declined. But I therefore stir you up to beware of secret sins, because we are more apt to those than to the open ones. We sink ourselves sooner with these than with any other sinnings.

There are three things which I will handle here, and so conclude this point:

1. Motives to enforce our care.

2. Aggravations of secret sins.

3. Means which may present help against secret sin.

Motives to Enforce our Care

There are many arguments which may justly stir us up to take heed of and to cleanse from secret sins.

1. The Lord knows our secret sinnings as exactly as our visible sinnings, Psalm 44:21. He knows the secrets of our hearts. Psalm 139:2, "He knows our down-sitting and our uprising, and understands our thoughts afar off." Verse ll-12, "If I say, surely the darkness shall cover me; even the night shall be light about me, yea, the darkness hideth not from Thee; but the night shineth as the day, the darkness and the light are both alike unto thee." Ezekiel 8:6, "Son of man, seest thou what they do? even the great abomination that the house of Israel committeth here?" Like one on a high mountain pointing at the thief robbing a man in a thicket, so here the great and lofty God, whose seat is on high, beholds all the ways and motions of the children of men, even through the thickest clouds. Nothing can block out His observance whose eye fills heaven and earth. What is the curtain to Him, or the night, or the lock, or the chamber; or the whispering, or the thinking, or the imagination of that thinking? He does not need to have His understanding informed by the sensibleness of speech, or the visibleness of acting, Who made the frame of spirit, and searches into the depths of the soul and clearly observes all things in a perfect nakedness.

2. The Lord will make manifest every secret thing. Mark 4:22. "There is nothing hid which shall not be manifested, neither is any thing kept secret, but that it should come abroad."

There is a twofold breaking out of a secret sin or manifestation of it:

One is natural. As the child formed in the womb naturally desires liberty to come forth, and as the fire within to fly out and abroad; so the inward conceptions of sin naturally propend and strive to thrust themselves out into visible acting and view. The soul cannot long be in secret actings, but some one part of the body or other will be a messenger thereof.

Another is judicial; as when the judge arraigns, and tries, and screws out the close murder and the dark thefts, so God will be in the darkness, yet the judgings of sins shall be in the light. Though they are secret, yet these are open; though the times of theft are private, yet the places of judicature are open. Ecclesiastes 12:14, "God shall bring every work into judgment, with every secret thing, whether it be good, or whether it be evil." He does not say some work, but every work; and not only works but secrets; and not only secrets, but every secret; and not only secret good things but evil too; whether good works or ill works, whether secret or open, all must be brought to judgment, 1 Corinthians 4:5: "Judge nothing before the time, until the Lord come, who both will bring to light the hidden things of darkness, and will manifest the counsels of the heart." Though you may now cover your sinfulness with much hypocrisy, yet then all visors shall be pulled off, you shall be stripped of all counterfeit shapes. As you are, and as you have done, so shall you be made known to men and angels and to all the world. Your whole heart, and the whole course of your life shall be pulled to pieces before you.

3. Your secrets shall not only be manifested, but shall also be judged by God. Romans 2:16, "In the day when God shall judge the secrets of men by Jesus Christ." We read, sometimes, that God will judge our words, and God will judge our works, and here that God will judge our secrets. He will judge words and works as sin ripened in expressions; He will judge secrets as sins ripening and breeding. Job 31:26-28, "If I beheld the sun when it shined, or the moon walking in brightness; and my heart hath been secretly enticed, this also were an iniquity to be punished by the judge." Job 13:10, "He will surely reprove you if ye do secretly accept persons." Deuteronomy 27:15, "Cursed be the man that maketh any graven image, an abomination to the Lord, etc., and putteth it in a secret place."

There is a twofold judging to which secret actings of sin are obnoxious:

One is temporal and in this life; see this in David. 2 Samuel 12:9-12, "Wherefore hast thou despised the commandment of the Lord, to do evil in His sight, thou hast killed Uriah the Hittite with the sword (this was done in a secret letter) and hast taken his wife to be thy wife. Now therefore the sword shall never depart from thine house, because thou hast. Thus saith the Lord, Behold, I will raise up evil against thee out of thine own house, and I will take thy wives before thy eyes, and give to thy neighbors. Thou didst it secretly; but I will do this thing before all Israel, and before the sun." Ephesians 5:6, "Because of these things cometh the wrath of God upon the children of disobedience."

Another is eternal, that the Lord will judge them
with eternal wrath, for that is the portion of
hypocrisy. Though you may escape the judgment of
man, yet you shalt not escape the judgment of God.
Hebrews 13:4, "Whoremongers and adulterers God
will judge." He will sentence them Himself for their
secret abominations.

Secret sins are more dangerous to the person in
some respects than open sins, for:
1. A man, by his art of sinning, deprives himself
of the help of his sinfulness, like him who will carry
his wound covered or who bleeds inwardly. Help
does not come in because the danger is neither described or known. If a man's sin breaks out, there is
a minister at hand, a friend near, and others to reprove, to warn, to direct; but when he is the artificer
of his lusts, he bars himself of all public remedy and
takes great order and care to damn his soul by cover-
ing his secret sins with some plausible varnish,
which may beget a good opinion in others of his
ways.
A man, by his secrecy, gives the reins unto corruption. The mind is fed all the day long either with
sinful contemplations or projectings, so that the
very strength of the soul is wasted and corrupted.
2. No, secret actings only heat and enflame natural corruptions; as in shouldering a crowd, when
one has got out of the door, two or three are ready to
fall out after. So when a man has given his heart
leave to act a secret sin, this begets a present, quick,
and strong flame in corruption to repeat and multiply, and throng out the acts. Sinful acts are not only

fruits of sin, but helps and strengths, all sinning being more sinful by more sinning, not only in the effects, but in the cause. The spring and cause of sin will grow mad and insolvent hereby, and more corrupt, this being a truth that if the heart gives way for one sin, it will be ready for the next. If it will yield to bring forth once at the devil's pleasure, it will bring forth twice by its own motion.

3. A man, by secret sins, polishes and squares the hypocrisy of his heart. He strives to be an exact hypocrite and, the more cunning he is in the palliating of his sinnings, the more perfect he is in his hypocrisy.

Aggravations of Secret Sins

Will you give me your leave to make a short digression touching the degrees of aggravation of secret sinnings? Perhaps they may sink deep and quicken us to repentance and caution.

1. The more foul the sin naturally is, the worse is the secret acting of it. You know that some sins have a fouler dye in them than others; all are not alike, but some are more intrinsically vile. A blasphemous thought is worse than an idle thought; and the secret stealing of a shilling, though it is a sin, yet is not so great as the secret killing of a man.

2. The more relations are broken by secret sinning, the worse they are and more to be feared, for all relations are bonds and cords. They are a file of reasons why we should not sin. For a single person to commit folly is a damnable sin, but for one to break the covenant of her youth and God, for a per-

son who is married, this very relation trebles the
guilt. For anyone to murder is a sin of death, but for
the child to murder the parent secretly, this very relation increases the guilt.

3. The more profession a man makes, the worse
are his secret sinnings; forasmuch as he carries not
only a badge, but also a judge on his shoulders. He
not only wears a profession which is contrary to his
practice, but which shall condemn and judge him;
that he is not what he would seem to be, yes, his
contrary practice grounds and occasions the great
reproaches and blemishes, like dirt, to be cast upon
the face of religion; "and woe to him by whom offences come."

4. The more light a man has meeting him in the
dark and secret actings of sin, the more abominable
is the sin. When not only a discovering light, but a
checking light; not only a checking, but a threatening; not only a threatening, but also a troubling
light opposes and charges from the conscience
against the sinning, this makes it the more out of
measure sinful.

5. The more repugnant secret sins are to the
light of nature, the worse are they in their actings. A
sin is very broad when the light of nature, without
any aid of knowledge from the Scripture, shall make
the heart to tremble at the commission and to be
terribly amazed. The Apostle touches at these kinds
of secret sinnings in Romans 1, "unnatural lustings
and burnings."

6. The more art a man uses to effect his secret
sinnings, the worse they are; forasmuch (as about
the same sin,) it is ever worse when it is breathed out

by deliberation than when it is forced out by a mere temptation. And sin is not to be reputed an infirmity or weakness when art or cunning is the cause of it; forasmuch as art is sober and takes time to contrive and reason to place and displace, to help and forward its acts or intentions, all which are contrary to surprisals and infirmities.

7. The more frequent a man is in secret sinnings, the deeper is his guilt. When he can drive a trade of sin within doors; when it is not a slip, but a course; and he has hardly scraped out the bitterness of the former but he is exercising the sin new and afresh again.

8. The more gripes of conscience and resolutions a man has felt and taken against secret sinnings, and yet wallows in them, the more stain and guilt lies upon his soul. A wound to a sick man is worse than to a healthy man, forasmuch as the spirits are already wounded by sickness; no sinnings wound deeper than such as follow the woundings of conscience; a sinner thrusts the sword in again to the same hurt.

The Means to Prevent Secret Sins

But you will say, this is fearful to sin thus! What means may be used to get off and to keep off the soul from secret sins?

The rules of direction (which as so many means) I would commend unto you are these:

1. If you have been guilty of secret sins, be humbled and repent. A man shall hardly stave off a new sin who has not been humbled for an old sin of the

same kind. Future care seldom manifests itself without former sorrow. Have you been a secret adulterer, fornicator, thief, backbiter, oppressor, liar, drunkard, etc.? Oh, hasten, hasten in by speedy sorrow, by speedy repentance; bewail (if it is possible) with tears of blood your secret wickedness! If you do not judge yourself, God will surely judge you, and do not think that, because your sinnings were secret, therefore your compunctions must be small; no, you ought to abound the rather and the more in floods of tears and of bitter contrition, who dared to provoke God so.

2. Take heed of secret occasions and provocations. Why is it that you say, "O this nature! O this heart! O that Satan!" You have, I confess, shed many tears; you have felt many sorrows and troubles; you have made many vows and resolutions; you have put up many prayers and petitions, and yet you are in your secret sinnings. Why, what should be the reason? Do prayers do nothing against sin? Yea, do tears nothing? Do troubles nothing? Do vows nothing? Yes, all of those may do something, if something else is added, if the leak be stopped, if the windows be shut, if the doors be locked; I mean, if occasions and provocations are conscionably and carefully avoided. Otherwise they are nothing. If you pray, and then adventure your strength upon the occasion of your secret sinning, what do you do but seek God first and then rise up and tempt Him? Keep close to heaven, and keep off from the occasions, and then tell me whether God will not keep you from your sinnings.

3. Crush the temptations which come from the

roots. Though you decline occasions, yet you cannot decline yourself: and there is that in a man's self which can fetch in the occasion by representation, by inclination, by contemplation. Sometimes another provokes you to sin, and this is in society. Sometimes your own heart provokes you to sin, and this is when you are solitary. Now the thoughts steal out, now imaginations present and confer with the mind, with the will, with the affections. Would you now free yourself from secret actings? Then free yourself from secret thinkings.

The picture in the glass may enflame as much as that in the natural face. So sin, in the representation of the mind, may fire our corrupt hearts as well as the enticings of it by conversing occasions. Psalm 19:14, "Let the meditations of my heart be always acceptable in thy sight O Lord, my strength and my Redeemer."

There are two things which will never fail you in your suppression of secret sinnings:

One is to be digging up the intimate root of all sinnings.

Another is to stifle the first conception of sins, to make sin an abortive in the womb, that it shall never stretch out itself to actions. Beloved, to tie Sampson's arms was a vain thing. His strength did not lay there; but if the hair of his head was cut off, then his strength was gone, and he became weak. To tamper (only) with the acts of sin is not the way to be rid of sinful acts: but the singular way to be rid of bad acts is to be rid of a bad nature. The virtue of the effect always lurks in the cause and, therefore, it is the cause which gives life and death to it. If you could

once get a holy nature, which might be at defiance
with sin in its throne, know that a new nature and
daily combat would much help against secret sinnings. That sin is least of all acted with life which is
most of all combated within the heart, for sin has
least practice where it has most opposition; and of
all oppositions, those that are inward are most
weakening to sin.

4. Get a hatred of sin which will oppose sin in all
kinds, at all times, and in all places.

5. Get the fear of God planted in your heart.
There are three sorts of sins which this fear will preserve a man against:

First, pleasant sins, which take the sense with delight.

Second, profitable sins, which take the heart
with gain; but "what shall it profit me to win the
whole world and lose my soul?"

Third, secret sins of either sort. Joseph did not
dare to sin that great sin of uncleanness, though the
acting of it might have been secret, and though
perhaps the consequence of it might have been his
preferment. Why? The fear of God kept him off, he
had an awful regard to God; he knew the greatness
of His holiness, of His power. "How can I do this
great wickedness, and sin against God?" Genesis
39:9. Why, brethren, if we fear the Lord, it is not the
night which the thief takes, nor the twilight which
the adulterer takes, nor the seasons of secrecy or
places of obscurity that will prevail with us, etc. Yes,
but God sees me, the great Judge of heaven and
earth, the Holy One, the God who hates all sin,
whose eyes are brighter than the sun, and purer

than to behold sin: and who is mighty in power and just in his threatenings. He sees and beholds, therefore I dare not.

6. Believe God's omniscience and omnipresence; that the Lord is everywhere, and all things are naked and open to His eye with whom you have to deal. You cannot intend to think, you cannot whisper out your thoughts, you cannot finger the closest bribes, you cannot incline yourself to the most abstracted kind of secrecy in the world but God sees you clearly and perfectly. Now if a man could believe that God is still with us, and there are two which evermore go with us, the Judge and the register, God and conscience, that He is acquainted with all his thoughts, paths, ways, this would put an awe upon him. Would the wife be so impudent to commit folly and prostitute her whorish body in the sight and presence of her husband? Would the servant be filching out of the box if he saw his master's eye upon his hand?

7. Get your heart to be upright. Uprightness is an inward temper; and hypocrisy is an outward complexion. Psalm 119:3, "They do no iniquity." The inward man is the business of sincerity, to the forming and fashioning of that, it improves and employs itself. It knows that God delights in truth, and this, too, in the inward parts. It endeavors to please God in all things, and there to be most to God, where man can be least in observation, and that is in the secret and hidden frame.

2

"Keep back thy servant also from presumptuous sins; let them not have dominion over me; then shall I be upright, and shall be innocent from that great transgression." Psalm 19:13

These words contain in them David's second petition and request. Sins do not only differ in respect of openness and secretness, but also in respect of the degree of heinousness and greatness. Now because secret sins stick closest and are of a more easy and adventurous commission, therefore David prays much against them. "Lord, cleanse Thou me from secret sins." And, because presumptuous sins are of a more fearful efficacy (usually being a daring of God even to His face), therefore David prays as vehemently against them in this verse.

This verse may be considered two ways:

1. Respectively, as in connection with the former, by that word (also) "keep back Thy servant also"; as if David had said, "O Lord, I have prayed unto Thee to be cleansed from secret sins, and I beseech Thee let me be answered; but yet this is not all that I have to request; I have yet another request besides that, keep me also from presumptuous sins."

2. Absolutely, in regard of their proper matter, so they comprehend:

The Petitioner (thy servant).

The Petition, which respects sin's:

Presumption (from presumptuous sins).

Dominion (let them not have dominion over me).

3. The Petitioned, who is implied, and that is God, yet expressed by what He should do (keep back, etc.)

4. The conclusion or inference which he makes from the grant of all this, which is his uprightness and innocence; innocence, not absolute, but limited; innocent from that great transgression. There is more matter in these words than you yet will conceive of. I will touch some propositions, which might challenge a further prosecution, and then I will set down at large upon the main intentions and conclusions. From the words considered as a connection of a new request with the former request the following things might be observable.

SECTION I

First, there may and should be a conjunction, even of great petitions and requests (at once) unto God. As they say of graces and duties, that they are connected (and like so many pearls upon one and the same string) so we may say of requests to God, though they be many for kinds and number, and matter, yet they may be put up in the same prayer to God. David does not end at that request ((keep me from secret sins), but goes on, "O Lord, keep me from presumptuous sins." He multiplies his suits according to the multiplicity of his necessity and exigence.

There are divers qualities about our prayers,
namely:

1. *One is an urgent fervency; when the soul does not
nakedly commence the suit, propound it to God, and say,
"Lord hear me," but it enforces, as it were, an audience and
acceptance.* It strives with God and wrestles with Him
as did Jacob. "I will not let Thee go, unless thou
bless me," Genesis 32:26. And, "O Lord hear, O Lord
hearken and consider; do, and defer not, for Thy
name's sake," Daniel 9. This is a following of the
suit with God, as the woman did with Christ.

2. *Importunity: when a person renews the same suit, comes
often to the door of grace and knocks.*

3. *Patient perseverance.* "I will hearken," said David,
Psalm 85. "I will wait," said the church in Micah 7.

4. *A variety of multiplicity of matter, like a patient who
comes to the physician.* "Sir," says he, "such an ache is in
my head, and such crudity in my stomach, and such
a stitch in my side."

So, when we come to the Lord in prayer, we may
and should open not only one want, but all our
wants; and crave help not in one thing, but in every
thing. We should multiply requests. "O Lord," said
David, in Psalm 51, "I was conceived in sin, but
please cleanse that. I shed the blood of Uriah; but
please pardon that. I defiled his wife; please wash
that. I lost Thy spirit for these, but please restore
that. I weakened and wounded my graces, but please
renew them."

Or it is like Paul in Philippians 4:6, "In every
thing by prayer and supplication with thanksgiving,
let your request be made known to God." So I say, for
every thing let your manifold requests go up to God

by prayer. And I think that phrase (in Ephesians
6:18, "Praying with all prayer") will reach the point
in hand.

Why We Should Pray About Everything

All prayer extends itself not only to all the kinds
and forms of praying, but also to all the matters or
things for which we do pray.

Reasons hereof are these:

1. God can hear every request as well as any one.
A multiplied request as well as a single request, for
He takes not, nor observes things by discourse,
where one notion may be an impediment to the ap-
prehension of another; but all things (by reason of
His omniscience) are equally at once present unto
Him.

2. Nay, He can grant many and great requests as
easily as the single and smallest petition. The greatest gift comes as freely and readily out of His hand
as the most common mercy; even Jesus Christ, and
pardon of many sins, are of the same price with our
daily bread. Though the former gifts are (in comparison with the other) of a much more elevated nature and dignity, yet in respect of the fountain of
them, all of them come from the freeness of His
goodness and love.

3. Christ (by whom we are to put up all our requests, for He is our advocate and intercessor) is as
ready and able to implead many and great requests
as well as some and inferior. As He is our mighty
Redeemer, so He is our mighty intercessor; and His
blood is as efficacious and meritorious for many

sins as for some.

4. God has, for this end, made manifold
promises. Therefore, we may put up many and great
requests at once; the promises are called the wells of
salvation and the breasts of consolation. Now the
living wells will afford a plenty, as well as a scanting
measure of water. The child may move from breast
to breast and draw enough of either, if one alone
will not serve. If one promise comprehends not all
your wants, yet all of them do; and as God graciously
comprehends all our supplies in all of His promises,
so He has propounded them all unto us, that we
might then and there urge Him for the supply of all
our necessities.

5. Last, God is rich in mercy and plenteous in
compassion. His mercies are often called manifold
mercies, and His goodness is called an abundant
goodness; and His redemption a plenteous redemption; and His kindness a great kindness. Now mercy
is a ready inclination to pity and help; and multitudes of mercies are as a compounded and doubled,
and redoubled opening (as it were) of God's tenderness to do a sinner good.

Uses of this might be many, but I will briefly
touch only a few.

Then conceal none of your distresses from God.
The heart and life of man are full of sin, and as full
of want; there is not any branch of the soul, nor
limb of the body, nor turning of the life, but is replenished with some necessity or other. You have a
mind which yet needs to be enlightened, a judgment which yet needs to be captivated, a heart which
yet needs to be converted and humbled; how many

sinful commissions are there which need to be
bewailed; how many particular and vile inclinations
which need yet to be subdued! Besides all this, every
grace which you have (and there are manifold
graces in a holy soul) every one of them is in exigence and needs a more spiritual filling, both for
the habit, and acts, and degrees. Yea, and all our duties are but lame-handed motions, which need more
strengthening, or as mixed rivers which should run
more clearly.

In this case what should we do? To whom should
we go? Should we divide the principles of our helps,
and go for some to God and for the most to the creatures? Oh, in no wise, for all our help is only in
Him, who alone can help all! Or should we branch
out our helps and present them as a beggar does His
supplies, one day open one want and some distance
of time hereafter, open another? Oh, no! Come with
all, and with all at once to God, who is as able and as
willing for many sinners as well as for one sinner;
and for many sins in one man, as well as for one in
any. As they did with the impotent and sick man,
they brought all of him (bed and all) and laid him
before Christ; so should we bring body and soul, and
every distress of either, and present the whole bulk,
root and branches, all before the Lord at once for a
manifold supply. We should press upon Him for
manifold mercies, for abundant strength, "for God
is able to do exceeding abundantly, above all that we
are able to ask or think," Ephesians 3.

Beloved, as a man's own unworthiness should
not prejudice him from being a petitioner to the
throne of grace, so the variety of a man's necessities

should not discourage him to commence his suits at the throne of rich mercies. For as much as there is no reason in God which will dishearten us, and there is reason in ourselves to crave as earnestly and as simultaneously for all our helps as for some, you equally need the pardon of this sin as that, and mercy is as ready and able for both as for either. And if that corruption were more subdued, and yet this remained altogether untouched, you would have as many and more forcible suspicions of the truth of your estate from this division and inequality of your victory. Wherefore, as Abraham in his suit for those of Sodom and Gomorrah took up request upon request, descending from high to low, from many to few; so should we, in our requests, ascend from one sin to more, from more to many, from many to all. You know that confession of sins should not be particular only, but universal; and our sorrow for sin should respect the kinds, as well as the particular acts, all which import an amplitude of grants; so much mercy and supply answerable to the required latitude of confessions and sorrow.

'Tis true, some one sin may (upon special reason either of some guilt or present insolence) be more insisted on than another, (as one clause in the plea may be more urged than any other) yet not with the exception of the rest. Oh, that sin, Lord, by which I have dishonored Thee so much, and yet which rages so much; pardon it, subdue it, out with it! And not that only, but such sins; and not them only, but all my sins; blot them out cleanse me from them.

Another proposition which I will briefly touch on, shall be this.

SECTION II

Even a good Christian should have a fear of great sins as well as a care of secret sins. "Keep me also from presumptuous sins."

Reasons whereof may be these:

1. *The latitude of original sin, which as it is yet remaining in the best, so it is in them an universal fountain naturally apt to any vile inclination.* Though actual sins may be divided in the life, yet they are all united in their spring; that is, they are all of them virtually as so many potential effects involved and lurking in original sin, as their cause, which how far it may work, both from its own strength, and the assistance of temptations and occasions. If God does not actually prevent the interpose, if we do not put forth our fear and watch, we may with miserable experience both know and bewail.

2. *The instances of great transgressions.* Even those saints who have been as the highest stars have left behind them their twinklings and sad eclipses. Noah, his actual distempers by wind; Lot, his unnatural defilements by incest; David, his wounds and bleeding by whoredom and blood; Peter, his unkind and troubled denial of Christ against his knowledge.

Now when cedars fall, should not the tender plants tremble? If the sins of others be not our fear, they may be our practice; what the best have done, the weakest may imitate if they do not hear and fear: there being scarce any notorious sin into which self-confidence will not plunge us; and from which a holy and watchful fear may not happily preserve us.

An instruction from this, and so on: "Blessed is the man that feareth always," Proverbs 28:14. When we read of great sinners in the Scripture and see great falls and sins in others, as we should thereupon seek to recover them who are thus fallen by our counsel and prayers; so we that stand "should take heed lest we also fall," 1 Corinthians 10:12. If that Satan, who would deal with us, could be procured to shape our only mean and vulgar assaults and suggestions, to common and unavoidable infirmities and sinnings, this might somewhat abate the vigor and intention of our holy fear and circumspection; yet not altogether, forasmuch as he being a subtle enemy, trains and facilitates the heart by the frequency of small commissions, at length to the boldness of great impieties; or if Satan's suggestions were artificially laid, and pressing to great sins as well as small. Yet, if we had natures no way capable to receive the greatest impressions of sin, but were naturally averse and stiffly indisposed to such temptations, then our careful fear were not so requisite, but we are not shot-proof. Temptations (even to the greatest sins) have within our breast some principles which would presently shake hands with them. The actual light and acting grace do sometimes happily turn them aside from closing; though they keep them at the door, as the prophet caused the messengers who came from the king to take away his life; yet there is another principle of corruption which would let them in, and which would cooperate with those temptations, even to contemplation and inclination, and acting both inward and outward. Nay, this corrupt nature of ours alone,

(though it learns somewhat by temptations and occasions) yet it alone from itself can cast forth most
sore temptations to most abhorred sinnings.

Therefore, this we much do: Fore-past sins must
be eyed with grief, present inclinations with combat,
and future with fear. We must not in our war imitate
the Syrians, who were "to fight neither with small
nor great, but with the king of Israel." No, but we
must oppose all sins, those sins which encounter us;
we should force some out and keep the rest off. He is
a wise and sincere Christian who resists the smallest
and fears the greatest sins. "Keep back Thy servant
from presumptuous sins."

SECTION III

Another proposition which I might observe from
the words absolutely considered is this, that a good
man is God's servant ("Thy servant from..."). We
read of various servants in the Scriptures; some are
the servants of men who apply all their gifts and
parts and sacrifice the whole method of their beings
and expressings to claw and humour the itch and
pleasure of others. All flatterers are such, who are a
people of slavish bondage, having sold themselves
from themselves to some persons. Some are the
servants of the world, whose hearts and labors are
bestowed upon earthly things, and they make even
those noble souls of theirs to weary themselves for
very vanity; and to increase only in that with the
least toe, is too excellent to tread upon. Some are the
servants of Satan, in an instrumental activity and

readiness to entertain and execute his base and
hellish inspirations and motions. Some are the
servants of sin, who all that they are and can do is to
fulfill the lusts of their flesh. There is no servant so
obediently attending the command of his lord, as
they to receive and act the pleasure of their sinful
hearts. Some are servants to themselves, who, as if
they were born neither for God nor man, apply all
their will and strength and abilities only to their
own ends, without any real effectual consideration
to public good of church or country. And some are
servants to God. Moses was so, Simeon was so.
"Moses my servant is dead," said God. "Now lettest
thou thy servant depart in peace," said Simeon. And
David here ("Keep back Thy servant"). God's
servants differ from all servants in the world. Every
other servant loses himself by service; he is not *sui
juris,* in the law. But the only way to find a man's self
is to be God's servant. Every other servant loses his
liberty by his service; but liberty is then gotten when
we become servants to God. As soon as we enter His
service, we obtain our freedom. Every other servant
in strictness of rule, is below a son, a child; but every
servant of God is a son of God, and shall have not
gifts as a mere servant may have, but the inheritance
which the son who serves his father shall have.

There are two sorts of servants under God:

1. Some stubborn, who are *servi victi,* as Austin
says; the law of creation is upon them and so, will
they nill, they they are in some obediential and serviceable relation.

2. Others are servants, not of force, but of affection; not of compulsion, but of election. They have

chosen God to be their Lord, and have willingly re-signed up themselves (in the purpose of their hearts) to a universal observance and love of Him, and obedience unto Him, impartially and constantly to do His work. Such a servant to God was David, but this observation is very general; therefore I pass unto another.

SECTION IV

We who are God's servants should be used to move the Lord to help us against sins. You know that in all relations there are mutual bonds and duties: the wife owes much of subjection to the husband, and the husband owes also much of love, respect, and care to the wife. The child owes much attendance, reverence, and affectionate duty to the parents, and the parents owe much of instruction, reproof, correction, nurture, provision of estate for the child again. So it is between the Lord and His servant though, to a mere slave, there is no mutual obligation, or else it is in that which is weak. Yet to a servant, who stands in that relation, which they call ingenuous, as much is due from him to his lord, so there is something his lord ought to do for him: to feed him, to clothe him, to house and lodge him, to defend him against wrong and injuries.

This is it in the case of David, "Keep back Thy servant from presumptuous sins." It is as if he had said, "O God, Thou art my Lord, I have chosen Thee, to whom I will give obedience, Thou art He whom I will follow. I bestow all that I am on Thee." Now a lord will help his servant against an enemy, against an enemy who for the Lord's service is the servant's enemy. "O my Lord, help me, I am not able by my own strength to uphold myself, but Thou art all-sufficiency. Keep back Thy servant from presumptuous sins."

I observe in Scripture many singular methods to prevail in request upon God. Sometimes He has been urged from something in Himself to do things for His mercy's sake, and for His truth's sake, and for His goodness' sake, and for His holiness' sake. Sometimes He has been urged from something which He was very tender of, and at which He aims in all His dealings, namely, for His own glory and for His name's sake. Sometimes He has been urged, from some word or other which He hath let fall, at which the believing soul catches (as did Benhadad's servants from Ahab; thy brother Benhadad). "Remember Thy word (said David) upon which Thou hast caused me to hope," Psalm 119. "Thou saidst Thou wouldst do me good," said Jacob, Genesis 32. Sometimes He has been urged from the special relations between Him and His people; as from that of a father, Isaiah 64:8. "But now, O Lord, Thou art our Father;" and this is said of a lord, Isaiah 63:18, "The people of Thy holiness have possessed it but a little while. We are thine;" and in many other places, "remember Thy servant," and "remember Thy servants."

Beloved, it is a great thing to stand in near relations to God, and then it is a good thing to plead by them with God. For as much as near relations have strongest force with all, the servant can do more

than a stranger and the child than a servant and the
wife than a child, but though this urging of God, by
virtue of our relation, is an excellent point; yet because it is not the main intention of the place, I
likewise pass it over.

SECTION V

Another observable proposition may be this.

Our special relations to God should be special
reasons to work a care not to sin against God ("Keep
Thy servant from...").

"Thy servant..." There are many reasons against
sinning. The very nature of sin carries along with it
a condemnation of sinning, because sin formally is
a transgression and a rebellion, which alone is an
inglorious thing. Again, the laws and threatenings
of God should be as forcible cords to draw off the
heart from sin; and again, all the mercies and
goodness of God should exasperate the heart
against sin. Again, all the attributes of God might
hold us. Now with these this also may come in the
speciality of our relation to God, that we are His
children, and He is our Father. We are His servants
and He is our Lord. Though the common obliga-
tions are many and sufficient, yet the special relations are also a further tie. The more near a person
comes to God, the more careful he should be not to
sin against God.

"Let us who are of the day be sober, let us not
sleep as do others," 1 Thessalonians 5:6,8. "God hath
not called us unto uncleanness, but unto holiness,"

1 Thessalonians 3:7. "If you call him Father, pass the
time of your sojourning here in fear," 1 Peter 1:17. "If
I then be a father, where is Mine honor? If I be a
master, where is My fear?" Malachi 1:6. "I will be
sanctified (said God) of all them that draw near
unto Me."

There is a double drawing near unto God:

1. One is respect of office, as the priests of whom
he there spoke; who, therefore, because their calling
and office is more high and heavenly, should be
more religious and holy.

2. Another in respect of nature and change by
virtue of which our relation comes close to God.

How our Relation to God Should Make us
More Careful Against Sinfulness

Even this nearness should occasion more care
against sinfulness. Reasons whereof are these:

First, admissions of sinnings here do diffuse a
greater ingloriousness to God. Sin is more darken-
ing in a white cloud than in a black; as a spot is
more eminently disgraceful in a fair cloth than in a
foul cloth. Though the sins of evil men do prejudice
God's glory, yet the great sinnings of good men do
occasion much more, for not only the particular
sinnings send up a cloud, but other men by reason
of them, form out of them a smoke of blaspheming
and reproaching of the ways of God and the profession of grace.

Second, their great sinnings make them sorer
wounds and work. No sinning wounds so deep as

such which have more mercy and goodness to control them; and these only good persons most taste of. Much grace received, and much kindness conferred, will, in case of great transgressions, make the conscience eagerly to arise, and sting the offender.

What should this teach us, who profess more interest in God, more title to Christ, more purity of religion than others? Why, if we be light, then to walk as children of the light. If we do profess the gospel, then to walk as becomes the gospel. If we are the children of God, then to walk as "dear children, cleansing ourselves from all filthiness of the flesh and spirit." None needs to be more circumspect than he who is called to holiness. His very relation is of a tender (though high) nature; he cannot sin, but he grieves a father; yet this is as true, that none of our relations exempt us from temptations and assaults, which call upon us to be watchful and prayerful. If temptations do not drive you to your knees, they will drive you easily to the ground. No more but this; no man should sin, and no man should be more careful than he who is most good; for if he offends, then God suffers, Christ suffers, the gospel suffers, religion, profession, Christians, and all.

O then let us improve our interest in our God. "Should such a man as I flee?" said Nehemiah. So then, should such a man as I sin thus, walk thus, live, do thus? Why, God is my God, He is my Father, I am His child, His servant. If I should sin, sin would not only be my own wound, but His dishonor. I may not so abuse His love, His mercies, His calling, His honoring of me. Others look on me, but I must look on my God and on His honor.

Thus have you the general observations of the text. Now I come to a more punctual and intimate view of them, both in the petition and in the conclusion of them. Consider the words as a petition; they yield unto us two main considerations:

1. One of sin is presumption ("Keep back thy servant from presumptuous sins").

2. Another of sin is dominion ("Let them not have dominion over me").

First, for presumptuous sins; there are divers expositions of these words.

1. Keep me from those sins which by the suggestion or temptation of others I am enticed to; from another god or false gods, so that I do not serve them and am not captivated by them.

2. Keep me from acts of pride, which signifies to show pride or to behave proudly and recklessly. The Hebrew word in hiphel signifies to do a thing deliberately and audaciously. Before, David prays to be kept from sins of ignorance, and here from pride; from such sins as are done insolently and knowingly. Some translate it, "keep me from proud sins"; others "from insolent sins"; by which are meant manifest sins, open transgressions committed with contumacy, and with a high hand; but to hold to the expression in the text, presumptuous sins. And the observation begins in the following chapter.

3

Even the servants of God should pray to be kept from presumptuous sins.

Touching this, I shall inquire into these particulars:

1. What presumptuous sins are.

2. Of that strength which keeps regenerate persons from presumptuous sinnings, and what difference there is between the withholdings and restrainings of evil men and this keeping back of good men.

3. What reasons or causes of this desire to be kept back from presumptuous sins.

4. Then some useful applications of all this to ourselves.

SECTION I

QUESTION 1. What are presumptuous sins?

SOLUTION. Sin in general is any transgression of the law. The law of God is His revealed will for doing or forbearing, and it is the rule of nature and actions; whatever thing stands in conformity to it is good and whatever varies or swerves from it is sin.

Now sins are diversely distinguished, for all sins are not equal, either for matter or manner. For matter, some sins of themselves are more deep transgressions than others, as some diseases (in their own nature) are worse than others. To blaspheme and curse God is a sin naturally more vile than an idle thought or an empty word; and to commit idolatry is naturally more vile than to steal a shilling. To shed innocent blood is worse than to steal.

Again, sins may be distinguished in respect of the manner of committing; and thus it may fall out that even a sin in its own nature less than another may yet for the manner of commission be more heinous. And a sin, in its own nature greater than another, may yet for the manner of commission, be less guilting than a lesser sin which is more intensively raised by circumstances; as to gather a few sticks on the Sabbath was in itself not so great a sin as deflowering of a virgin, yet because the person did commit the sin with a contempt of God's express prohibition, it became more heinous and guilty.

Now here falls in that distinction of sin into "sins of infirmity" and "sins of presumption," which distinction is made not from the different qualities of sin, but from the divers qualification of sinning. The same sin may be committed through presumption which is committed through infirmity; yet the committing of it through infirmity is still much less and extenuating than the committing of it through presumption, forasmuch as all passive failings, (which arise from unevenness of strength) are not so high as the active trespassings which arise more from the ready contributions and concurrent assistances and furtherances of our own hearts. Now to the thing in particular.

Presumptuous sins are the bold darings and

proud adventurings of the heart upon things or ways known to be unlawful, against express threatenings, either upon a false confidence or upon contemptuous slighting or desperate wilfulness. I have in this description not only expressed the nature of presumptuous sinnings, but also included in it the several degrees and risings thereof, all of which give me now liberty to open and explain.

Consider, therefore:

1. *That presumptuous sinnings are proud adventurings of the heart upon sin.* There is a large difference between foilings by temptation, and adventurings by presumption. Temptation beats down that actual strength of grace resisting; but presumption tramples down the light of the word opposing. Therefore, presumptuous sinners are said to sin with an exalted or high hand. The sinner puts aside God's will and prefers his own. "Our tongues are our own," said they, "who is Lord over us?" Psalm 12. Yea, they are said to set their mouths against heaven. "What do you tell us of the Lord, of His displeasure or pleasure?" "As for the word which thou hast spoken in the name of the Lord, we will not do it," said they in Jeremiah 44. A man even tries it out with God, and provokes Him to his face and maintains the devices of his heart against the purity and equity of God's will.

2. *In presumptuous sinnings, a man knows the thing and way to be unlawful and, therefore, the presumptuous sinner is opposed to the ignorant sinner, Numbers 15.* Not that every sinning against knowledge (absolutely whatever) is a presumptuous sinning; the presumptuous sinner holds a candle in one hand and draws out the sword

with the other. My meaning is this, that he breaks
through the light of knowledge discerning the way
to be sinful; yes, and flaming upon his breast,
working in and checking his conscience;
notwithstanding all which, yet he will presume to
offend and proceed in transgressions. 'Tis true, even
a good man, in many particulars, may and does sin,
not only against habitual, but against actual
knowledge; but this is through infirmity, not
through contumacy. He approves that light against
the sin, and does not maintain the sin against his
light, yes, he yields not only by approbation of
judgment, but also by resolution and desire of will to
imitate the light. Yet, through the weakness of his
power, and from the force of a hasty temptation, he
may fall down even at noonday; but the presumptuous sinner sees light as an enemy and,
therefore, willingly breaks through it to the way of
his sin. Yes, he makes his heart to uphold the sin
against the force of his knowledge, and drives back
the arguments with a resolution, that however he
will have his sin.

3. *The presumptuous sinner (in that kind of sinning) adventures against express threatenings; thus it stands with a
man.* His heart and Satan incline and egg him to
sin, but God and conscience stand in the way
against him. As he said of the sword to Joab,
"knowest thou not that it will be bitterness in the
end?" So God said to him, "You shalt not have peace
in this way, it is the thing which I hate and abhor,
and I have revealed wrath from heaven against it."
But in presumption, the sinning soul steps over the
threatening to the committing of the sin. That

sword of God which may keep back another man,
though God sets the point of it to the breast of a
presumptuous sinner, it will not stave him off from
adventuring. Therefore, the presumptuous sinner is
said to bless himself in his heart though God
threatens a curse, Deuteronomy 29. This is a truth: A
presumptuous sinner is not changed by mercies nor
frightened by threats but, as the Leviathan in Job,
"laughs at the shaking of the spear." So the heart of
a presumptuous sinner puffs at all divine warnings
and menaces! "Come," said they, "let it come that we
may see him." As there is not a love to the goodness
of God, so there is not a fear of the greatness of God
in presumption.

4. *Presumptuous sins arise from a false confidence.*
There are two things upon which the presuming
sinner emboldens himself:

One is the facility of mercy. When a man sets
mercy against sin, he does well (because God's mercies should draw our hearts off from sin), but when
a man sets mercy against justice, now he offends.
Thus does the presumptuous sinner. Perhaps there
is not in every presumptuous sinner such a spirit of
atheistical madness that he is absolutely careless of
all that God threatens, nor is he so miserably prodigal of his soul that he rejoices to have it damned.
No, he may, and sometimes does apprehend threatenings so that his heart is caused to demur. It may
be stopping apprehension, that is, such as may
make him study how to pursue his sin, and yet to
wave and decline the edge of the sharp threatening,
and this he does by opposing mercy to justice. 'Tis
true, this is a sin, and divine justice will not take it

well, but I will adventure on it, hoping that divine
mercy will pacify the rigor of the threatening. I will
sin and offend justice, but then I will decline that
court by flying to the mercy-seat. God is of a gentle
heart, easy to be entreated, and will be presently satisfied and appeased. Just like a man who will break
his bones because he trusts to have them quickly set
by a skillful surgeon, or like a lewd child who adventures to outrages upon the scope and allowance of
his father's good nature. God fully intimates this
ground of presumption in Deuteronomy 29:19.
"When he heareth the words of the curse, that he
bless himself in his heart, saying, I shall have peace,
though I walk in the imagination of mine heart, to
add drunkenness to thirst."

Beloved, this is certain, that presumption disposes of mercy beyond all allowance and writes a
pardon which God will never seal. It will dare to run
in debt upon a conceit of a discharge, and clearing
however, as if divine mercy were nothing else but a
present untwining of all the knots which we make,
and a crossing of debts as soon as entered, and
served for no other end but that men should be bold
to sin, and cheerful after the commission of it; but
verily mercy is more precious than this.

Another is the self-possibility and strength of future repentance. He is one of the worst patients in a
way of sinning who is confident that he can be his
own physician. No soul wounds itself more than
that which vainly thinks that it can presently cure
them. Presumption is not always carried upon an
absolute hope of mercy, but the sinner being more
piercingly understanding, knows that mercy is a

special charter, and such a balm as is spread only upon a returning and humbling soul. Here it is that this presumptuous person will adventure to sin upon a confidence that he will (notwithstanding all this) fashion and polish his soul to a meet capacity of mercy by hereafter repentings and humblings. He foolishly deludes his soul with a fancy of such things which exceed his power. There are two things which the sinner cannot assure himself of.

One is the lengthening of his life, for this candle is lighted and put out, not according to our desires, but according to divine pleasure. All life has its limits from the Lord of life and death. He who sins today cannot be assured that he shall live till tomorrow. Now repentance is a work of this life; death binds us over to sentence, and then it is too late to return and, therefore, every presumptuous sinner adventures boldly upon that which cannot be his beyond the time present.

Another is the returning of the heart from sin. Though our natural principles can give the wound, yet they must be supernatural principles which give the cure. Our own hearts can cause us to fall, but God's grace only is that which raises us. Now God's grace is God's gift and not man's stock. Though we alone can fall off from God by sin, yet none but God can bring us back from sin by true repentance unto Himself. Presumption makes the heart bold, not only with time (which is in God's hand) but also with grace, which is only in God's gift. "Though I sin, yet I will hereafter repent", and thus the presumptuous soul, whose life may be instantly cut off, and to whom God may therefore deny His grace to repent because it before-hand presumed to sin.

5. *In many presumptuous sinnings there is a slighting contempt.* Therefore, in Numbers 15:30-31, presumptuous sinning is called a despising of the word of the Lord: "The soul that doth ought presumptuously, etc. shall be cut off, because he hath despised the word of the Lord." To despise the word of the Lord is to esteem of it as a vain thing, to disregard it in His authority and majesty over our consciences and hearts and ways. It is as if a soul should say, "What do I care if God speaks thus and thus? I will not be curbed and limited nor restrained." This is to condemn God, and it is called a rebelling against Him, Deuteronomy 1:26. "I spoke unto you, and you would not hear, but rebelled against the commandment of the Lord, and went up presumptuously to the hill." It is called casting God's law behind our back. God has hemmed and circumscribed the soul with precepts within which, if a man walks, he has God to be his security; but, in presumptuous sinnings, a man will exceed his limits and yet believe a safety. This very thing is expressed in Deuteronomy 17:11-13, "According to the sentence of the law, which they shall teach thee, and according to the judgment which they shall tell thee, thou shalt do: thou shalt not decline from the sentence which they shall shew thee, to the right hand or to the left. And all the people shall hear, and fear, and do no more presumptuously."

There you see that presumptuous sinning consisted in the slighting of the sentence of the law by the priest. The priest said, "This is it which God would have you do; this is it which He would not have done." Now the person who sinned presumptuously would not stand to this, but would break over this sentence and would go in his own way. He disregarded what God spoke; that should not be his rule, no, not his.

6. *Last, presumptuous sinnings may rise higher than all this, as when a man sins not only knowingly and wilfully, but most maliciously and despitefully against God and Christ.* The Apostle speaks of such presumptuous sinners "who tread under foot the Son of God, and do despite unto the spirit of grace," Hebrews 10:29. "And who crucify to themselves the Son of God afresh, and put him to an open shame," Hebrews 6:6.

This kind of presumptuous sinning is not only to sin, though a man knows it, nor only to sin because a man will sin; but it is also to sin on purpose to dishonor God, and to vex His Holy Spirit. The soul is grown into that abominable insolency, that a man even plots deliberately how to cross God and will, therefore, apply himself to such words and acts because he knows they will displease God. This is the very top and height of presumptuous sinning: when a man, in a sober and calm spirit, exempted from violent diseases and strong passions and insolently turbulent temptations, shall in sober circumstances desperately and of malicious and set purpose encounter God, adventure iniquity to provoke God. He knows that the worst which shall befall him is damnation, but he does not care about that. He will, however, have his pleasure in sin and will strive to despite that God who stands in a just enmity to his soul and sins.

SECTION II

QUESTION 2. What that strength is which keeps back regenerate persons from presumptuous sins; and what difference between the restrainings of evil men and this keeping back of good David.

SOLUTION. For a more distinct knowledge of this point observe a few particulars:

1. *Restraint is any kind of stop between the inclination and the object.* When the nature is inclined to such or such a thing, and a bar falls in to keep them asunder, this is restraint. It is as when God bridled up the fire from burning the three children, and the lion from devouring Daniel, Abimelech from touching Sarah, and Laban from hurting Jacob. The natural inclinations of the former, and the morally evil dispositions of the latter, were chained in. They were stopped, they were hindered, in respect of their actings and exercise. All creatures are capable of restraint because they are under a supreme power; only God cannot be restrained; but for all creatures, their natures, and inclinations, and operations are under His command by the law of creation.

2. *Restraint of any agent arises from a greater strength of a superior agent.* Whatsoever keeps a man back from a sinful acting, it is (at that time), while a restraint, of more actually strong force than the present inclination is. For example, in the stopping of a stone or water, that which is unequal in strength, a less force is not able to keep in the stronger. The cords wherewith Sampson was bound were no restraints to his motion and escape, for his strength exceeded them and he easily broke them asunder.

But God's decree and providence is a restraint to the raging sea, and His power is a restraint to gird in the malice and rage of man, because though sinful inclination be strong, yet God can overrule, and bound, and bind it in.

3. *All restraint presupposes an aptness, a disposition ready to run and get out.* The child whose desire is to lie in the cradle, is not there said to be restrained, and the tradesman, whose shop is his paradise, is not therefore restrained from going abroad; but when a servant would be gadding about, and yet is kept in, this is restraint. In every man there is too much sin; corruption is in us all, and it is with it as with a child in the womb who would be breaking out into the world. As with fire kindled within, which would be flaming abroad; such an aptness there is in our sinful inclinations to secret, and then to open, actings. Now the cohibition, the inclosing, the locking of them in, is properly restraint.

4. *All restraint of sin is from God.* That God whom David here desires to hold, or keep him back, also withheld Abimelech, kept in Laban, kept up Esau, kept off Saul; and it is granted that there are several means and ways of restraint, natural, moral, spiritual (as you shall hear soon) but it is God in them who causes restraint. He imprints such a vigor into those arguments, into those apprehensions, that they shall bind, and chain, and hold in the nature, which else would not judge so seriously, nor submit so easily to impedition or hinderance. As the horse rushes into the battle if left to his own swing and violence, so the heart of man, if left to itself, would put no periods to wickedness, but would grow from

evil to worse and fill up all the measures of iniquity.
There should not be one righteous Abel, but every
Cain would kill him; not a Jacob, but Esau would
pursue him; not a David, but Saul would hunt him;
not an apostle, but Herod would behead him. All
Christian religion would lie in blood, yes, and the
very order of nature would sink into confusion by
the efficacy of that sinful corruption which is
equally divided among all if God did not look down
from heaven and restrain the rage of sin in all.

5. *All evil men are not equally restrained by God, which
appears both in the matter and in the measures of sinning.*
Some evil men do not break out into all horrible
kinds of sin. Some, though they are at the same
school of particular sinning, are not yet in the same
form and height or degree of sin. Though they are
at the same trade, yet their skill and thriving in the
same sin is different. Every drunkard is not the
mighty man to drink, and every swearer lets not his
tongue loose to the highest blast of blasphemy.
There is no man so high in sin but, if God should
cease to restrain him, he would yet plunge himself
into a deeper guilt.

6. *The restraining of any sinner is an act of a merciful
providence unto him.* God's justice begins already to
smoke against a man when He totally leaves the
reins unto him, when He gives him up to himself, to
his own vile affections, reprobate mind, to his own
counsels and ways, and will no more strive with him,
but will cast him off to himself. But it is a great
mercy when He restrains. Though renewing grace is
the saving mercy, yet restraining grace is a great
mercy, when God will not let a man's sinful

corruption take its full walk, for restraint diminishes guilt, whereas, if this bridle were off, a
man would increase his sinful accounts by infinite
iterations and multiplications of sinning. Now he is
kept from enlarging his debts, yes, and it diminishes sin; whereas a man let loose would diffuse sin,
cast his fire-brands about, draw others to a consocia-
tion of evil, and so set up the trade. Now, by restraint, sinning is more contracted and narrowed,
yes, and it diminishes wrath and judgment for, according to the number and measures of sinning,
there shall be an equal proportion of vengeance and
punishment. The greater sinner shall have and feel
the sharper flames of hell: but now restraint keeps
in the sin and, at least, makes it less sinful (for as
sin sticking in the inclination is not so deep as that
which flies out of that into actings and consumma-
tions), and so, consequently, is a mean to lessen the
heat of future torment.

7. *God restrains the good and the bad from sin.* The evil
man is so wholly carried by a sinful nature that, if
God did not keep him back, he would bring all to
confusion. The good man is so weakly good that, if
God did not prevent and interpose and withhold, he
could not withstand so much evil as now he does.

How great a mercy did David acknowledge a restraint from sin to be! You may see in his own words,
1 Samuel 25:32-33, "Blessed be the Lord God of
Israel, which hath sent thee this day to meet me!
and blessed be thy advice, and blessed be thou
which hast kept me this day from shedding innocent blood."

The father has two children, one young and the

other old. If he does not keep in the elder, he will be like the Prodigal, sell all and be riotous. If he does not hold in the other, he will fall and be like Mephibosheth, lame on both feet.

Evil men have strong corruptions which God is pleased many times, many ways, to keep within the door. He will not suffer all their intentions, desires, projects, to see the light.

Good men have weak graces. Their own legs are not able to bear them up, and strong temptations and occasions may soon lay flat a weak defendant and, therefore, God is pleased yet to bridle in that remaining corruption, to keep off the soul, or something off from the soul, lest it should sin. We see it in experience, that grace alone is not able to keep off sin. Grace can keep us while God keeps the grace; but if God leaves us to the essays of our own best strength, we are unequal combatants in the field.

8. *God diversely keeps back or restrains men from particular sins and sinnings: sometimes,*

1.) By enlivening the conscience which, being strictly awakened, rises to such a height of impatience, anger, and rage that the sinner is willing to let go the sinning rather than to answer the scourging indictments and threats of conscience for it. He is like the luxurious patient. Though he likes the sparkling wine, yet he dares not drink it lest his spirit should be thereby inflamed and burn him up. Even an evil man, though he is not afraid of sin, yet he may be afraid of conscience and may, therefore, be kept from his sinning; as the collier from handling his coals, not because they are coals, but because they are burning hot.

2.) By self-reflecting apprehensions. The love that a man has to himself may be a means to keep him off from some sinful actings, for some sinnings have such infamy, and charge, and envy, and loss, and danger endorsed on them, that the very present arrearages of sin prevail and keep the man from adventuring. He will not strike the bargain for payment so sharp, and sure, and present.

3.) By legal imprintings. God is pleased, many times, to set up the flaming sword and the shadows of hell before the eyes of a daring sinner; tells him plainly that He will call him to an account, and wrath shall be his portion if he will not forbear thus to provoke Him whereupon he forbears.

4.) By denying and crossing opportunities. When a man has prepared himself for a sin, then God so secretly directs the ways and the eyes and the presence of other creatures, so that the sinner must keep in the cup which he has tempered, and dares not draw the sword with which he is girded, not act the evil which he before earnestly intended to prosecute and finish. The sinner does not always sin, not that he lacks a heart, but because he does not have a conveniency; as the ship rigged may be wind-bound. Though the greediness of sin thrusts on the sinner, yet the wisdom of the flesh will keep it in till the season of sinning may suitably match with the former contrivances of sin. Esau deferred to slay his brother Jacob till Isaac died.

5.) By denying or withholding of temptations. Beloved, though evil men are under the power of the Prince of the Air, yet I conjecture, not in this sense, that he may tempt them when and how he pleases; or that they must necessarily act every sin to which he tempts them. But as God is pleased, when Satan many times tempts them, yet sometimes to restrain them; so He is pleased, when Satan would tempt them, many times to restrain him, well-knowing that his temptations would easily draw out matter already prepared. A heart which has won itself to a sin may, without any more ado, by the very presence of a temptation and occasion, be instantly wrought unto it.

6.) By causing diversions, which may call aside the employment of the sinner another way. When Saul, in malice, raised a prosecution against David and had hemmed him in. God yet restrained Saul by letting in the Philistines upon his country, which drew back the execution of his rageful intention against David at that time.

7.) Last, by beginning, supporting, and enlarging the principle of sanctification, which is the sweetest restraint of the heart from sin, drawing it off, enabling it against inclinations and temptations. And such a kind of holding back David prays for in this place, namely, a sanctifying restraint, a renewing restraint, a subduing restraint.

9. *The restraining of good men is exceeding different from those of evil men.* Though the sins from which either are restrained may be common, yet the keeping back of one by renewing grace, and of the other by mere restraining grace, are very different.

How the Restraints On Evil and Good Men Differ

1. They differ in the fountain; for keeping off my mere restrainings proceeds from the care of universal providence, but keeping back by renewings comes from a special affection of God in Christ. God has an eye over all His works and a mercy over them, too. He does not totally leave, no not the sinful creature, but expresses a providence in permission of some things, contradiction of many things, and ordination of all things. Though men are desperately evil, as it were, the lords of sin, yet God will be known forever to be the Lord of nature by circumscribing, and abridging, and commanding it in its propensions. But the keeping back by renewing grace, this arises from a tender love, a most gracious affection which God bears to His servants, like the father withholding of his dear child from a sword which might hurt him or meat which might make him sick. The restrainings of evil men are from the wisdom of divine power, and the cohibitions of good men are from the goodness of special favor.

2. They differ again in their impression, for restraints of evil men arise only from argument, but those of good men depend upon nature as well as argument. In the former it is argument alone which makes the stop. In the latter it is argument and nature both, as Abner said to Asahel, 2 Samuel 2:22, "If I should smite thee, how should I look thy brother Joab in the face?" There was naked argument. "How can I do this great evil, and sin against God?" as

Joseph said to his mistress, Genesis 39:9. There was a divine argument and a holy nature. Bid a man to grasp a toad, his very nature shrinks back from this. Bid him climb a little rope to the top of an high mast in the midst of the sea, and here argument or reason may withhold him. It is one thing for a new argument to keep off an old heart; it is another thing for a new nature to keep back from an opposite corruption.

3. They differ in their entrance and seizure. The restrainings of evil men are but as locks upon the outer door: and the keeping back of good men is as the lock upon the closet. One is an impedite to the actions, the other is an impedite of the inclinations; one is a bridle upon the lips and hands, the other is a bond upon the heart and disposition. The one may seal up the lips so that a man does not swear; the other tempers the heart so that a man fears an oath.

4. They differ in their efficacy. Restrainings of evil men do not impair the state of sin any more than chains and prisons do the nature of thieves or lions. Look, as it was with the fire into which the three children were cast, the restraining of its burning act no way prejudiced either the nature of the fire or the faculty of it to burn. It only suspended the act. So it is with mere restraint about moral things. Though it does not give permission to the evil act (for the present), yet neither does it grant a restraining order. The body of sin is all one as before. But in the keeping back of a good man, there is not only an interlet of the act, but some measure of diminution to the sinful inclination.

5. They differ in the fairness of equality. Mere restraints do not deal justly with sins, they make a stop in one and leave open a gap for other sins. Like a vessel of many holes, though the water break not out in one place, because it is stopped, yet it freely flies out in the rest. So where a man is restrained only, though that sin cannot find a way in that vein, yet it will find a course (like the water which is hindered under ground) another way. But the holdings back by renewing grace indispose generally and evenly.

6. They differ in the fulness of duration, for mere restraints hold in the nature no longer than the things remain by virtue of which the mind was restrained. Let the fear of death expire, put aside the edge of the law, be sure that shame shall not follow, and the only restrained sinner breaks open school, so that he goes to the sin. But holdings back by renewed grace are cohibitions of the heart upon permanent grounds, namely, the perpetual contrariety between God and sin, between sin and His will, His holiness, His goodness, and His honor.

7. They differ in this, that the heart of a man only restrained, being at liberty, (like waters held up) pours forth itself more violently and greedily as if it would pay use for forbearance. It abounds in the sin and makes a more fully wicked recompense for the former restrictions. But where the soul is kept back by renewing grace, it does not multiply sin because of less practice now, but is laboring a fuller diminution of sin because of too much practice heretofore.

8. They differ in that an evil man is kept back as a prisoner by force against his will; but a good man is kept back as a petitioner. It is his heart's desire, "O

that my ways were so directed that I might keep Thy statutes: order my steps in thy word, and let not any iniquity have dominion over me. Keep back Thy servant from presumptuous sins."

It is an evil man's cross to be restrained, and a good man's joy to be kept back from sin. When sin puts forth itself, the evil man is putting forth his hand to the sin; but when sin puts forth itself, the good man is putting forth his hand to heaven. If he finds his heart yielding, he cries out, "O keep back Thy servant!" An evil man is kept back from sin as a friend from a friend, as a lover from his lover, with knit affections and projects of meeting. But a good man is kept back from sin as a man from his deadly enemy whose presence he hates, and with desires of his ruin and destruction. It is the good man's misery that he still has a heart to be more tamed and mastered. It is an evil man's vexation and discontent that still, or at any time, he is held in by cord or bridle.

And thus you see what David aims at in desiring to be kept back from presumptuous sins, not a mere suspension, but a mortification; not a not-acting only, but a subduing of the inclination; not for a time, but forever. Nevertheless, I think there may be something more added for the opening of this point, "Keep back thy servant from presumptuous sins." Take what I think briefly in this point: God keeps back His servants from sin.

How God Keeps Back His Servants From Sin

1. By preventing grace, which is by infusing such

a nature, which is like a bias into the bowl, drawing it aside another way, so that holy nature which God confers on His servants secretly draws off the soul from the consent, appetition and practice of sin propounded to the soul.

2. By assisting grace, which is a further strength superadded to that first implanted nature of holiness, like a hand upon a child holding him in. This divines call a cooperating grace, which is an addition of divine strength to that strength which God has formerly imprinted in preventing grace: which, whether it be an enlargment of habitual grace in the natural measure of it, (as when health is made to rise to a greater degree of strength) or whether it is an efficacious motion of God's Spirit, powerfully strengthening the inherent grace to the acts of aversation and resistance of sin and temptation. It is, I confess, an acute and disputable inquiry, yet whether the one or whether the other, the soul is by either more confirmed, and established, and upheld, and kept from sin.

3. By quickening grace, which is, when God enlivens our graces to manifest themselves in actual oppositions so that the soul shall not yield, but keep off from entertaining the sin. As when in the motions of sin, He inflames the heart with an apprehension of His own love in Christ, and then excites our love exceedingly unto Himself again whereby the heart is made marvelously averse, and to detest any closure with this sin by which so ample and gracious a love should be wronged and abused; or as when in the temptations to sin He excites that affection of holy fear which works that filial and awful

regard to a great God and a good Father so that the
soul is brought into Joseph's temper, "How can I do
this great evil, and sin against God?"

4. By directing grace, which is when God confers
that effectual wisdom to the mind, tenderness to the
conscience, watchfulness to the heart, that His servants become greatly solicitous of His honor,
scrupulously jealous of their own strength, and justly
regardful of the honor of their holy profession. And,
therefore, they decline all occasions of the sin
which may overlay their own strength, and dally not
with the temptations, or with the first motions. But
as they are in fear of themselves, so they are in defiance not only with apparent sins, but also with the
appearances of them. They shun not only the sins,
but the inlets and preparations to the sins; and verily he shall be much kept from the secrecy of sin
who, as a king, is wise to keep off parley with the
ambassadors of sin; I mean occasions which negoti-
ate with the soul and prepare it to lose its own
strength.

5. By doing grace, which is when God effectually
inclines the heart of His servants to the places and
ways of their refuge, safeties, and preservations from
sin, by enlarging the spirit of supplication which
carries the soul to its strength. Prayer engages God,
and thus we find that the praying Christian is more
kept from sin than the disputing Christian for,
though sin is stronger than reason, yet God is
stronger than sin by framing the heart to the reverend and affectionate use of His ordinances. A man
many times comes to the word a combatant but is
sent away a conqueror; he comes hither as a pursued

man, by sin and Satan; but here God gives him a
safeguard, a protection, and sends him away armed
with more holy resolutions, courage and defiance,
by strengthening his graces, by assuring his love
and strength, by making the sin more vile and odious.

SECTION III

QUESTION 3. Now I proceed to the third question. What causes or reasons should there be which
might move David to put up this prayer, "Keep back
Thy servant from presumptuous sins."?

SOLUTION. Reasons thereof are many. I will
touch them under a few heads: in respect of himself;
in respect of the sins themselves; in respect of others; and in respect of God.

In Respect of Himself

If he considered himself, there would be sufficient grounds for such a petition, because of:

1. His aptness, by virtue of original corruptions,
even to presumptuous sins. Beloved, I dare not tra-
verse the extent and compass of sin (in respect of
aptitude and possibility) even in a good man. Of this
I am sure, the least sin is farther than he should go
and, the higher he mounts in sin, the deeper are his
wounds. No man can be safely bad or comfortably
sinful. Nevertheless, this may be said that, though
there are some top sins, which perhaps a good man

does not commit; yet there is scarcely any sin for kind or degree which might not lay him flat if God did not hold him up and keep him back.

The reason whereof is this, because original sin (which cleaves to the best), is not only a corrupt, but also a universal corrupt inclination. What the philosophers conceive of the capacity and disposition in their first matter, that it is illimited, unbounded, infinite, not restrained to this or that form only, but in a general way lies open to all impressions; is most true of original corruption, even in all, that it is (for its part) a capacity, an aptness, to any actual villainy and wickedness, a womb of all uncleanness, a seed of all iniquity, not distinguishing between the vilest and the fairest transgressions. Paul complained in Romans 7:18, "I know that in me (that is in my flesh) dwelleth no good thing." The flesh, that is, the corruption of sinful nature, is an utter vacancy of any good; that is the privative nature of it, and then the flesh, that is, sinful corruption, is a diseased inclination, a filthy fountain, a lewd womb, a sinning sin, impelling, enticing, egging on the soul to consents and acts unlawful, and that upon all occasions, without any distinctions of great or little, and that is the positive nature of it. Though inherent grace much abates and keeps under that sinful nature (as a naughty servant may be held down by a good and stronger master), yet it is of a false, deceitful, and capable nature for the vilest impressions of actual sins.

2. His impotence and self-inability to keep himself from such sins. Beloved, it is true that grace is a sweet and enabling quality. He who receives grace,

with it, receives a measure of strength proportioned
to the degree of grace received, and no man is so
vain to conceive that a person receiving grace can
do no more against sin than he who was never
armed with such heavenly power. But then divines
have well distinguished that as there must be a first
grace (which they call "operating grace") to change
the nature within, so there must be a second grace
which they call "co-operating grace," to assist the
soul and the first grace against the insolence of corruption and of actual temptations. Grace can do
much, but (of itself) not always enough to keep off a
sin. It is true that the distance of the soul from sin
depends on grace, but that the soul keeps a distance
from such a sin; that is, that such a sin does not en-
gage and lay flat the soul, this does not owe itself to
the mere natural strength of the first created grace,
but to that grace as assisted and supported by an
higher hand from heaven.

So far as I yet conjecture, that principally effectual strength of created grace is more in its dependance than in itself. An arm is strong and able to do
much service, and to put off several assaults, but
principally by reason of its communion with the
head from which, if it were separated, it can do
nothing but fall down. The beam of light from the
sun moves, irradiates, pierces, and perhaps heats
and melts, none of which it could do if there were
an eclipse, an intercision, a cutting of it off from its
dependance on the sun. So grace does most and
more, as it is most and more assisted from above,
from its head, which is Christ, and from God who is
the Father of lights. Suppose grace were left entirely

and solely to itself. A person would be exposed to many and foul miscarriages. Though the water is well-heated, yet remove the fire and the natural cold will return and prevail over that accidental heat.

The natural habits of sin would easily have the better of the extrinsical habits of grace were not these held up and backed by a higher arm than that of itself or than that in corruption working against it. You know that all Adam's strength was not cannon proof against Satan's temptations. He assaulted and entered his castle and laid him flat and all the world with him. Peter, though a very good man and a very forward disciple (one qualified with much grace and high affections), yet was beaten down in plain field. He could not preserve and keep back himself, though armed beforehand with a warning from his Master, but denied Him three times, and that with some high qualifications, too. Nay, the great falls of the best men we ever heard of in Scripture show this much, that it was not their own sword and their own spear, that it was not their own strength which could keep them entirely back. And this points out to us not only the impotence of our own guard, but also the name by which we stand and, therefore, David prays, "Keep back Thy servant from presumptuous sins."

In Respect of the Sins Themselves

The mere consideration of sins as presumptions affords strong causes why David should pray to be kept back from them; for, though every sin contains a natural reason of dislike and forsakement (every sin carrying a foul quality in it and a condemning inconformity), yet some sins are of a deeper dye, and of a more crying guilt, and of a darker blackness, and of a more wounding sharpness, and of a louder vileness than other some are.

Among which higher ranks of iniquity are presumptuous sins and sinnings; which may appear thus:

1. The more shining light of grace is trampled over for to act the sin, the viler is the sinning; for if naked light makes the spot the broader (the sinner ever sins the more, by how much the more clearly he sees his way to sin), then shining light makes it much more heinous; that is, when knowledge, as it were, wrestles in the conscience, when it contends strongly with the soul by force of evidence and plain reasonings, to stay it. But now presumptuous sins and sinnings are the laying flat (as it were) of shining light. The soul (as it were) shuts its eyes and stops its ears; it breaks away to the sin against all the discoveries and clear impleadings of knowledge, gain-saying and withstanding it. The presumptuous person does not go to sin ignorantly, but he does, by imprinted light, see the sin as God's enemy, which yet he will embrace as his friend. Yea, the more inexcusable that a sin is, the worse it is, when little or nothing can be said on behalf of the sinner. Thus it is in presumptuous sinnings, the man cannot say "I did not know it, I was not warned."

2. The more pride of heart accompanies any kind of sinning, this makes it the more vile; for pride lifts up the point of the sword, it shakes the spear against God. When the will of God and the will of a sinner

come into a competition about sinning, then pride grows high. "Who is the Lord," said Pharoah, "that I should let Israel go?" Exodus 3. "Who is Lord over us?" said they in Psalm 12. When the heart goes proudly to sin, it will acknowledge no Lord but its own pleasure, and no rule but its own resolution. It can slight a precept and scorn a threatening. Now presumptuous sinnings are filled with pride. I think Austin had an aim at this, in his exposition of this verse, when he rendered the reading of it thus, "Keep back Thy servant from pride."

It is as if pride were knotted, folded, and doubled in presumptuous sinnings; there was pride and pride again in that heart which dared thus to sin; and verily, so there is in presumptuous sinnings a manifold pride: a pride of judgment to approve that which God has branded and condemned; a pride of will to rise up to that which God would have the sinner forbear, a pride of security to make a sanctuary for the soul, when God has threatened wrath, etc.

3. The more impudence and boldness attend a sinning, the worse it is.

There is a double impudency about sinning. One is of defense, when the sin has been committed, of which I am not now to speak, which is no more but to paint a whore or to cover a plain sore, to make that seem good which really is stark naught.

Another is of entrance, when the sinful soul lays aside all shame, and fear, and modesty, and restraints, and arguments. That man says, "Whatsoever may be said of it, whatsoever may come, yet I will go on. Let God take it well or take it ill, let Him beseech by mercy or warn by threatenings, nothing

moves me. Neither my peace, nor comfort, nor soul
prevail; nor my shame, nor trouble, nor misery keep
back." But thus it is in presumptuous sinnings, the
heart is bold and impudent, which can look so
much mercy in the face and yet will dare to sin;
which can look so many threatenings in the face,
and yet will dare to sin; which can look its own great
misery (in respect of the issue and end of the sinning) in the face and yet will dare to sin; nay, which
can (perhaps) look many former experiences of bitterness and anguish for the same sinful adventurings in the face, and yet will dare to sin: putting the
hand into the fire again which has burned it, and
venturing to swim in those waters, where (had not
God's mercy stepped in) the soul had long since
been drowned.

4. The more abuse of mercy concurs to the sinning, the more heinous it raiseth the sin; for mercy
is the sweetest stop of a sinner, and the kindness of
it should smooth off the soul from offending. What
is mercy but that unspeakable readiness in God to
forgive a sinner; a gracious willingness to sit down
with wrong offered, if yet the sinner will come in.
And the abusings of it are affronts to the highest
love; but now in presumptuous sinnings mercy is extremely abused.

First, in that it does not have its direct end. The
direct end of mercy is to awe and to keep off the
heart from sin. "There is mercy with Thee, therefore
shalt thou be feared," Psalm 130. But the presumptuous sinner is less fearful, because God is so merciful, and the mercies of God should lead to repentance, Romans 2. But the presumptuous sinner yet

dares to hold on the sinful trade.

Second, when it is made to serve and to encourage sin. Oh, this is the imbasing of that high and tender attribute of God, when we draw out from His goodness to embolden the heart to wickedness; as if that God whose soul abhors sin would let fall any expression to hearten a sinner! Yet thus it is with the presuming sinner, the very mercy of God makes him bold to sin against God. The confidence of that easiness in God to forgive occasions Him, therefore, to adventure and multiply transgressions.

In Respect of Others

David had good reasons to pray to be kept from presumptuous sins in respect of others, as well as in respect of himself, whether you consider his general calling (a man of goodness), or his particular calling (a man of dignity and place), but I will fold them both together:

1. Such sins would be exemplary and noted. There are three things which set a man upon the stage, which lift up his actions on high to the eye of the world.

One is his powerful and active sanctity. A very holy man is a kind of a wondrous sight, after which many eyes are gazing. Godliness is a very rare thing and, therefore, men look much upon him who professes it.

Another is his singular dignity. Lift a man out of the crowd, advance him to a place and seat of honor above others. How busy is the multitude to eye, and judge, and imitate him. The ways and actions of great persons are usually the present copies of the most.

A third is his notorious miscarriages, which are like the tail of a blazing comet. The great sinnings of good or great men fall instantly into common discourse and (perhaps) also easily into common practice. Therefore, David had great cause to pray against presumptuous sins which, by his practice, might prove a common snare, for who will not confidently write after that sinful copy which both goodness and greatness have begun? That which the great man does, the inferior person will do; and that which the good man does, the evil man thinks he may now lawfully do. If knowledge will venture, ignorance supposes that it may safely follow; and if holiness will adventure, why should profaneness be so nice as to stop? The way or fact is credited, either as not bad, or else not so dangerous, where both authority and profession are leaders.

Now this might be some cause to move good David to pray to be kept back from presumptuous sins, knowing how his actions were capital copies, wrote in text letters: and that the sinnings of great men are like the fallings of cedars, which bring down with them to the ground many lower shrubs: and that the sinnings of good men are easily snares, whereby other men would encourage and deceive themselves.

2. Such sinnings from him would be trophies to evil men. There are three things which flash evil hearts. One is the accomplishing of their own projects and lusts. Another is the distresses of the church. Aha, so would we have it. A third is the great

falls of good men. How like the dog they will bark
and insult over the wounded lion! A good man's
sins, which are his wounds and God's dishonor, are
their days of mirth and sport.

I observe that there are three mouths which the
higher sinnings of good men open.

The mouth of God. Oh, how His Word thunders
His displeasure against the soul of such an one who
is come so near unto Him, and yet has adventured
thus to sin against Him: "Dost thou thus require the
Lord?"

The mouth of conscience. If we do well and walk
uprightly with God, then the mouth of conscience
yields words of oil and peace (it exceedingly excuses,
comforts, acquits, upholds, etc.); but, if we wickedly
transgress and exceed informities, Oh, then the
mouth of conscience proves like the mouth of a
sword! It speaks with sharpness and woundings, and
terrible amazement. It breaks the bones of David,
Psalm 51, and it makes him roar, Psalm 32.

The mouth of evil men. Now their voice is set on
high, the trumpet is set to their mouth. Oh, what
ragings, railings, scoffings, obloquies, and blasphemies are instantly heaped upon religion and
profession! Yea, these are they, this is their holiness,
this is their profession, this their niceness, this the
hypocrisy of them all. Now, perhaps, this also might
move David to pray to be kept back from presumptuous sins, though not the immediate, yet the colateral reason, because he might not give occasion to
the adversary, that God might not suffer by him, nor
religion by him, that he might not sadden the
hearts of the righteous, nor weaken the glory of

holiness, nor stretch the mouths of them who can bless themselves in a course of vileness, and yet curse and accuse the godly for particular facts only.

In Respect of God

Here also might David frame strong and singular reasons to be kept back from presumptuous sins. I know there is nothing in God which a good heart might not urge as a sufficient argument against sin, but I will contract my thoughts and matter.

1. What God had been to him might cause him to pray against presumptuous sins.

For His temporal kindness. That was exceeding great; He raised him from the crook to the sceptre, from the shepherd's tent to the king's throne, and now, after all this, to answer so great goodness with great sinfulness would be a high degree of odious unthankfulness.

His spiritual kindness. That was more than the former, He set his love upon him, and made him a person after His own heart, gave unto him His good spirit of grace and joy, comforted his soul in many adversities, compassed him about with favor as with a shield, heard his prayers, granted him the desires of his soul. Oh, then, how should David do such great wickedness and sin against his God! God forbid that David should put forth a hand to such a high kind of sinning who had received, from the hand of his God, such high kinds of mercy and goodness. Mercy should make the greatest distance between us and sin, and cause the purer walking between us and God.

2. What he was to God. Why, David was His servant, (see the text) and presumptuous sinnings are high oppositions to our service of God. David was His child, His son; and presumptuous sinnings are great incongruities to the way of filial obedience. "Should such a man as I flee?" said Nehemiah. So here, should such a man as David, one to whom God was so near, one who was so near to God, should he break out into the ways of rebellion, into the acts of an enemy, into the paths of hostility? not only sin, (which may befall the best) but sin presumptuously, which befalls the worst, not only to be surprised by temptation, but also to dare one in a sin by a proud presumption? What! For a child to take arms against his father, for a holy David to sin with so high a hand against so good a God, and so loving a Father? No marvel that he fears and prays, and that earnestly, "Lord keep back Thy servant from presumptuous sins."

No other might be expected from men professing themselves haters of God, and lovers of sin; but, for a friend, for a servant, for a child? How can my God take such vile dishonors from me? And who will honor Him if his own should adventure and presume thus to disglory his name, and wrong His and their relation?

SECTION IV

Now I shall descend to the useful applications of this point to ourselves. There are four general uses which may flow from this prayer of David: 1. Of instruction; 2. Of Examination; 3. Of Exhortation; 4. Direction.

USE 1. OF INSTRUCTION
1. To see our own danger. As the prayers of holy men for good things should teach us faith and hope, so their prayers against great sins should teach us fear and watchfulness. There is a story of a heathen man who prayed to Jupiter to be saved from his enemies. One who heard him so petitioning willed him to mend his suit and to desire Jupiter to save him from his friends, for he trusted them more and, therefore, they might do him most hurt. I would add one thing more to have mended that petition also: He should have prayed to have been saved from himself, for there is more danger in ourselves than in all enemies or friends.

Oh, brethren! We carry about with us vile natures and treacherous hearts! Even those abominations which sometimes we would have trembled at, unto them will our wicked selves deliver ourselves, if God does not keep us back. Natural corruptions will bid fair for the foulest commissions; and that the match is not finished and acted is not because we lack hearts, but because God restrains and hinders. "My soul is even among lions," said David, in another case. Assuredly our soul dwells with such a nature as will not distinguish between small and great, but is then most like itself when it is boiling in the vilest degrees of sinning.

The temptations cannot be so black and foul, but our corrupt hearts would easily kindle by them, and we should embrace them unless there were a God to stay and stop us. You know that Hazael said, when the prophet wept and told him of that savage and barbarous cruelty which should break from him in ripping up the women and butchering of the children, "Is thy servant a dog?" Said he, "I abhor the thoughts of such unnatural villainy;" and yet, being left to himself, he soon acted that which he now seemed to abominate. Even those sins which made a cry to heaven, as Cain's murder and Sodom's uncleanness, and the mighty sins which the prophet touched at, yes, and the highest and stoutest rebellions, all have, in all men, a natural foundation, and seed and principle.

2. Not to boast ourselves of our standing. Learn Paul's counsel thoroughly, "let him that stands take heed lest he fall," 1 Corinthians 10:12. Even you, who have heretofore bitterly judged another for his sinnings, are now in the same transgression, and your conscience is all over running with blood. Either thus you are or thus you may be.

There are four things which the great falls of others should work in us:

One, great compassion. It is an ill heart which can rejoice at other men's sins, and it is never right with us until we can hate our own sins and shed tears for others.

Two, humbling fear. "Considering thyself, lest thou also be tempted," Galatians 6:1. Your glass is made of the same brittle metal, and that it falls not and breaks is because of the hand that holds it, not because it keeps itself. If God should permit Satan to winnow you, you would, perhaps, more readily deny

Christ and His truths than ever Peter did. Many a
man has sound limbs because he was never in the
field at battle.

Three, earnest prayer for continued assistance;
forasmuch as though our combats and dangers are
here below, yet our guards and safe-comes are there
above, and only there.

Four, tender jealousy. When others fall into sin,
it is good for us to fall upon our knees and watch,
since our forbearance depends not on the better-
ness of our nature or the greatness of our strength,
but on the efficacy of God's preventing and assisting
grace.

3. You may here learn what weakness there is in
the strongest Christian. All his own strength is not
sufficient for him against temptation or sin. If anything could keep off sin it is grace, but grace needs
help as well as sin needs a bridle. "Hold Thou me
up," said David, "so shall I be safe," Psalm 119:117.
Look, as it must be a divine power which implants
grace, so it must be an Almighty hand which must
maintain it. We can neither form our own hearts
nor conquer our own lusts. What would become of
the child if the nurse did not hold him? And where
would the ship be driven by a tempest had it not a
pilot to steer and order it? None can say what ship-
wrecks would befall even a good soul were it not
continually preserved and looked unto by a good
God. Our strength and safety is more in the name of
God and Christ than in our own defense. Hence it is
that our Savior commended that petition even to the
best, "Lead us not into temptation;" not that God
tempts any man to evil but that Satan would easily

lead us into sin did not God lead us out! His suggestions are crafty, his temptations strong; our hearts
deceitful, our graces weak, our hands feeble, our
resolutions insufficient, so that we may all cry out in
this case, as Peter in another, "Help Master, or else
we perish."

'Tis true, we must resist, and we must handle all
our weapons, and we must seek, and we must resolve,
and we must study, and we must hear, and we must
read, and we must decline; but in all these, yea, with
all these, yea, above all these, we must take in the
Lord and depend upon His help. "Lord, keep back
Thy servant," or else none of these (without Him)
will keep off the sin. That soul is most kept from sin
which keeps most to God. None can keep up a soul,
keep off a sin, keep back a temptation as God can
do.

SECTION V

USE 2. OF EXAMINATION

Now let us come yet more closely to our own
hearts. David's care is here against presumptuous
sins, but how does it stand with our soul? Are we in
the shallows only or have we adventured into the
deeps? It is true that there are some presumptuous
sinnings which are past all shore; they are out of the
reach of all recovery, therefore, I meddle not with
them. But then there are other degrees which are,
though very fearful, yet recoverable. Consider:

1. Presumptuous sinnings arise more from the

manner than the matter. It is not always so much what is done as how the soul behaves itself in the sinning which makes it presumptuous. A little sin committed with a high spirit may therefore prove a high sin.

2. Again, in times of much light, either there is much formal and explicit presumption or else virtual and interpretative presumption. For where so much is afforded to lighten and keep back, it must be reputed as presumptuous yet to adventure on.

3. There is a habitual presumption when a man will hold on in a course and way of sinning; and there is a particular presumption in respect of this or that fact. Now one of these most men do touch upon.

I know you do not like to be handled roughly in this thing—such are our hearts. We would rather have our sins concealed than uncased and still conceive that we are not so bad as the worst. Therefore, let me propound these things unto you more generally.

Presumptuous Sinning

1. What do you call that kind of sinning when we ourselves venture upon the same sins which we condemn in others? Romans 2:1, "Thou art inexcusable, O man, whosoever thou art, that judgest: for wherein thou judgest another, thou condemnest thyself, for thou that judgest doest the same things."

2. What kind of sinning do you call that when the heart will maintain its way against the revela-

tions of wrath, (that is) though God proclaims
vengeance and death against such a sinning way, yet
the man will adventure on in the commission. I say
will adventure, for through weakness a man may be
trodden down; but it is stoutness when he will break
through the army. When a person will go through
the pikes, he will not give up his worldly and fleshly
lusts though the heavens are darkened about his
soul with threatenings. Is not this presumptuous
sinning?

3. What kind of sinning do you call that when
the soul suppresses truth and holds back the light
for unrighteousness' sake, when it knows the fact or
way to be sinful and yet will not be held back?

4. What is it for a person to bless himself in his
way and to protect himself when God has cursed his
facts, to say, "None of this evil shall befall me, but tomorrow shall be as today? The prophet is a fool and
the spiritual man is mad. God will not do as He reports, therefore, soul, take your ease, your course, let
us eat and drink, and to our sins still."

5. What is that when men will not repent till they
are old or ready to die? Till then, they will continue
upon that score of sinning, upon a presumption
that sin will be easily discharged and mercy
presently had?

6. What is that returning of the soul to a fact or
way which it has found to be bitter already? And,
though it has found hell in the conscience for the
same sinning, yet it will break out again upon a
hope of great mercy.

OBJECTION. Yes, but alas! The best have their
infirmities and escapes. We think no hurt, and God

knows our hearts. We do sin but who does not? But it is not through presumption but through infirmity. The spirit is ready but the flesh is weak. We still carry flesh and blood about us; it is our weakness, and God, we trust, is merciful.

SOLUTION. It is most true that the best are sick and the strongest are weak; but then it is as true that the heart is deceitful and sin is subtle and men are apt to raise themselves in a false opinion of their safeties and to extenuate the height and parts of their sinning.

But to the objection. I will briefly reveal unto you, whether your sinnings fall from infirmity or else proceed from presumption. This must be granted in the general. There are sins of infirmity as well as of presumption.

Two Sorts of Infirmities

Infirmities are of two sorts:

First, mere infirmities—sins arising from mere weakness, without any deliberation of the mind or choice of the will, as sudden evil thoughts, words, deeds, dullnesses, defects, shortness in good, etc.

Mixed, which have a tinge of presumption, but not enough to make the sin to be presumptuous; a knowledge but not a practical judgment; some apprehension, but not a perfect deliberation; sudden passions perplexing the judgment, and dazzling of it; inadvertencies, inconsiderations. But more particularly:

1. Acts owning themselves to infirmity depend

most upon outward strength. They have not such an entire causality from the subject, but are produced from unequal power. It is granted that even a good heart may yet be found in the dirt, it may be overtaken with some particular facts which are stark naught; but this irregular action arises principally from a strength of temptation which exceeds the actual strength of the renewed heart. It is like a man in a crowd. Though he strives another way, yet he is overborne, he is overset, he is carried down, for all his strength cannot shoulder off the crowd, he is too weak. So, when a man sins through infirmity, there is a nature which resists. Paul had a law in his mind, warring against the law of his members, Romans 7, yet the strength of that sinful law did overbear the resisting strength of his renewed mind, in respect of particular facts and, therefore, the acts were acts of infirmity. But what is this to him whose heart is set on wickedness, who imagines sinful devices, who shapes and contrives his way of sinning, who tempts even sin itself to sin, whose sinnings arise from affection, not from temptation, who provokes his corruption to get out, who is a devil to his own heart, inclining and stirring it to sinful commissions? Were our sinnings springing from a full principle, from a nature giving out itself, and that alone, I cannot judge them to be infirmities.

2. Acts of infirmity are not habitual but particular; they are rather transient than permanent acts. They are acts, but not continued acts, like a land-flood, not like a river; and the reasons of it are these:

1.) Partly because they spring from temptation which, though it may now and then over-reach the soul, yet the renewed heart observing the slight of Satan, and the imbecility of itself, provides, therefore, for stronger defense and strength to resist. And,

2.) Partly because they flow from passion and sudden distemper, which is not a constant inclination, but only a fit, a present violence.

David, in a sudden passion, will kill Nabal and every mother's child. But when Abigail met and assuaged him and made him understand reason, he was quite from his projects. But now where things fall into a habit, into a course, into a common practice, when a man is every day at his sin, when it proves an haunt, this cannot be called a business of infirmity. When our actions run and fall into a kind of naturalness and custom, so that a man is always tippling and always swearing and always filching and always lying, when the way of his sin is a trade, why, this is no more to be reputed an infirmity than for a mariner to be in his ship or a tradesman to be in his shop!

3. Acts of infirmity are involuntary acts. The man does them but the will is against them. "The evil which I would not do, that do I," said Paul in Romans 7. As the fact opposes the law, so the will opposes the fact. It is that which a man's judgment disapproves and which his will is averse from. The traveller's will is to go the right way, and in that to stand, yet he may stumble and fall down, and this may be called an infirmity; but if he is himself, and should put off his clothes and lay himself down in the dirt, this would be an act of voluntary madness. So when a man sets himself to sin, when he will go

and wallow in the mire; when, with Ahab, "he sells himself to work wickedness," so that he bargains away his soul for a sin. When he gives up himself to uncleanness with greediness, this is not infirmity; it is a height of proud presumption. But through infirmity of prevalent resistance, a good man may be sold under sin; as Paul, he may be led captive, being over-surprised; he may be led with Peter that way, or to that fact, which yet he would not willingly do.

4. Acts of infirmity are not a state of quietness or consistence. That is, if a man sins from a weakness of withstanding grace; though the temptation has been his conquest, yet his sinning shall be his trouble. Weak strength in grace, though it is not always actually sufficient to prevent sin, yet it will be able to melt the soul for it. If temptation has surprised the soul to sin, grace will then surprise the soul to mourn; neither will it lie with sin upon it. Even a weak child thrown down, will be scrambling up or crying for some to raise it; but if the places of our fall be the places of our peace and of our rest, it is a bad sign that our sinnings exceed infirmities. When the sinning is to us as the sea to the fish, or as the center to the stone, or as the bed to the laboring man, this is no infirmity.

5. In sinful acts of infirmities, the heart, as it intends no sin, it condemns sin. The heart is more sensible, watchful, prayerful against it, and exceedingly strives to mortify it and subdue it.

SECTION VI

USE 3. OF EXHORTATION

A third use shall be to exhort us to imitate holy David in a care against presumptuous sins and to be kept back from them.

Consider seriously a few things:

1. *It is a great judgment to be left to ourselves, to be given up to a man's own heart, to be given up to Satan, to be given up to vile affections, to a reprobate sense, to our own counsels and ways.* It is as if God should say to a person, "I have dealt with you by My mercies, but you will be unrighteous still. I have dealt with you by My Word and counsels, but you will proceed on in your sinning still. I have dealt with you by My Spirit in many convictions and motions, but you will sin still. I have dealt with you by reproofs, and checks, and troubles of conscience, but your heart is set in you to sin still. Since you will be unrighteous, you shall be unrighteous still. Since you will be filthy, you shall be so still. I will leave you unto the hands of Satan, who works mightily in the children of disobedience, and he shall take you captive at his pleasure. I will leave you to the vileness of your own sinful nature so that, since you will not hearken unto Me, you shall (as you desire) with all greediness, fulfill the lust thereof, but I will withdraw from you My mercy and My loving care. Go on and fill up the measure of your iniquity and of wrath."

Why, brethren, this is a sad and forlorn condition. What is the estate of the patient when the physician gives him up and relinquishes him to his own sick palate, to his own vain appetite and diet?

Why, says he, medicine will do him no good; it is in vain to prescribe him rules. Let him go on, take what he wills. I see well he is a dead man. Thus it is with him whom God leaves unto himself.

Surely there is not a more direful judgment than for God to give over His keeping of us. Whither will not our wicked hearts carry us? What will not sin (left to itself) dare to do? How outrageously will it swell? How irrecoverably will it sink the soul! All helps are little enough to bound and keep in sin but, if it be left to its own force and violence, then, like the sea without a shore, what a deluge it makes!

2. *To sin upon presumptuous grounds, upon a presumption of mercy, is the next way to cut us off from mercy:* "Knowest thou not, O man, that the kindness, and longsuffering, and mercy of God should lead thee to repentance; but thou through thy hardness and impenitency of thy heart, treasurest unto thyself wrath against the day of wrath," Romans 2:4-5. God will not be merciful to the wicked transgressor, but He will wound the hairy scalp of such a one who goes on still in his sins. Mercy is a sweet city of refuge to the penitent sinner, but justice will tear off the presumptuous sinner even from the horns of the altar. God never yet said that He would forgive him who will not leave his sins. Do not flatter yourself, you forsake your mercies; unless you will forsake your sins. God will not spare you nor pity you.

3. *Presumptuous sinning makes high work for the soul.* The pricks of a pin, the cut of a knife, may do much hurt, but the gash of a sharp sword forcibly followed will open death in your sides. Every sin fetches blood in the soul, but presumptuous sinnings even

cleave the conscience asunder. If you are good or bad, you who mount up in an high kind of sinning, good Lord, how it will (in a day of judicial sense) make your very sinews to crack and your joints to tremble.

Of all sensible rackings in the soul, there is not any one comparable to that of despair. Oh, despair! It is the death pang of the conscience; it is the soul in the extremity of amazing throes. It sees no heaven and no shore, but lays the soul either in hell or ready to be cast quick into it. Now presumptuous sinnings prepare the way for despair. When the soul would have its sinful course, it would not be beaten off by any method and warning of heaven, but goes on in a secure confidence of the easiness and largeness of mercy.

When God will not take these proud braveries any longer, but arrests the stout transgressor and sets his sins in order, both for the greatness of fact and the height of pride and darings, and that against all light and goodness, and warning and threatening, and the sinner sees himself fallen into the hands of a terrible and glorious God, from whose fierce displeasure it cannot now rid itself, "Oh!" cries out the miserable man, "what shall I do? Woe to me that ever I was born. I have shut up heaven against myself, I am rejected forever. As I have dealt with God, so now He deals with me. I would not hearken to Him, and now He will not harken to me. Oh, I shall never have mercy! I have adventured on so presumptuously that I have cut off myself from any hope and possibility of recovery. I was entreated, but still I would sin. I was warned, but still I would sin. I saw it to be sinful, but I would do it. I felt some trouble for it but I despised counsel and scorned reproof. I slighted mercy. I quenched motions, and these so often. Oh, Lord, now Thou hast met with me; now shall I never rise any more. I would have my sins, and I have them still, and I shall have Thy just wrath and hell with them, too."

Thus the presumptuous sinner makes way to the despairing sinner, for what is it which causes despair? When the soul sees justice to be exceedingly great, and a cloud over the mercy-seat, now it sinks apace, and what darkens the mercy-seat more than the greatness of sinning? And why does divine justice seem so terrible but because the person hath been so audaciously sinful? "Now," he says with Cain, "my iniquity is greater than can be forgiven," Genesis 4. "No, no, there is no balm for such wounds; there is no mercy for such great transgressions as I stand guilty of."

SECTION VII

USE 4. OF DIRECTION

The last use of the point shall be for direction, guiding us to the observation of some particular rules so that we may be kept from presumptuous sinnings.

1. *Beware of little sins.* The stirrup, though it is low and small, yet it serves a man to mount. The great flames of fire took their beginning from a coal or a spark. And men usually have been first wading in lesser sins who are now swimming in great

transgressions. Sinnings (supposed as little or inconsiderable) have not only this happiness that they are not so much regarded, but this unhappiness, that they are more often committed. And then this is certain, that the frequent commission of small sins is great in itself, and also disposes and prepares to greater commissions. Many drops make a current; he who makes no conscience of many little sins will shortly take the boldness to assay and act some great sin. For:

The more any sin is committed, the more is the judgment blinded and corrupted.

The more are the affections inclined and seduced.

The more is conscience benumbed and seared.

The less force have divine arguments with the soul, being surfeited with the pleasures of former sins, and then it must well follow that the heart, being thus qualified, may easily be wrought upon to a foul commission. This I find, that the way to be kept from a high sin is to fear the least sin, for little sinnings are not like a little inch of candle which goes off in an absolute period, but they are like a train of powder which takes fire from corn to corn, till at length the barrel is burst asunder; or like a little sickness, which is a humour disposing to a stronger distemper, or like a little circle in a pond, which begets greater and greater.

Observe three things:

First, Satan has a strange hand over that soul which can bear with any sin. He may, by lesser things, maintain his command. It was said that the little child commanded the land for the child prevailed with the Queen, and the Queen with the King, and he over the land. Satan can prevail for a little sin, and a little sin can prevail with the heart, and the heart with the whole man.

Second, little sins are breeding sins. No sin will keep its bounds, but naturally would greaten itself. Though it seem modest at first, yet it will, by degrees, become familiar and impudent.

Third, they are enticing sins. They are the advocates in the bosom for greater. They do not only labor for their own lodging, but will deal strongly with the heart to embrace greater, as occasion and temptations present themselves.

Therefore do this, give the water no leave; no, not a little. Little streams make way to the ocean. And you study the present way to become a great transgressor, to rise to presumptuous sinnings, who will allow yourself to be an habitually immoderate sinner.

2. *Take heed of the repetitions of any sin; do not do a sin over and over.* Of all transgressions which dispose the soul towards presumption, the repeated have a special influence, and I will give you a reason for it.

Because presumptuous sinnings depend much upon the boldness of the heart, when the heart becomes bold and fearless, it will then venture through thick and thin. It will presume far. They were men who *sinned with both hands,* and as high as Sodom, who came to this pass, that "they knew no shame."

Now repeated sins frame a boldness in the heart (as repeated blows do the anvil), and, the more hardened the heart is, the more bold it grows—

partly because they delude the heart. They work false principles in the mind; forasmuch as we have gone on in these courses again and again, and no evil befalls us; therefore tomorrow shall be as today, let us eat, drink, and sin.

It was a sweet prayer that of Elihu in Job 34:32, "That which I see not teach Thou me: if I have done iniquity, I will do no more." For all sin grows strong by practice, and the often going over it is like the motion of the feet from one round of the ladder to the other, still rising, or like the manifold turnings of the wheel, which mount the weight still to a higher pitch. What Job therefore spoke in another cast ("Once have I spoken, but I will not answer: yea, twice; but I will proceed no further," Job 40:5), that I say unto you. Once you hast sinned, thus, and thus, yea, twice, and yet conscience is tender, there is yet fear and sorrow, but proceed no further, lest you become mighty to sin. This is certain: The stronger sin grows, the more easily will a sinner presume. Now repeated sinnings wedge in the sin with strength, as the more often the scholar writes after the copy the fairer he writes and the more he is enabled to write. So often sinnings make the soul more strong in that kind, and then more fit for a worse.

3. *Do not stifle or reject the frequent checks of conscience.* God has appointed several things to give the sinner a touch, like cords to twine him in, to keep him from sinnings: the voice of the Word, the voice of judgment, the voice of men, and the voice of his own conscience.

Now mark it, there are two of these voices more

especially which, if a man will neglect and slight, a thousand to one he will fall to being a presumptuous sinner.

The voice of the Word. Proverbs 29:1, "He that being often reproved, hardeneth his neck, shall suddenly be destroyed, and that without remedy."

The voice of conscience. When the conscience shall concur with the Word in its informing acts, and in its directing acts, and in its warning acts, and in its restrictive acts, and in its corrective and judicial acts, it shall point out the way, or fact, in the evil, and unlawful quality of it, and strive, and reason, and fret, and reprove, and threaten, yea, and speak bitterly, yet a man will go on, I say, this man hastens to some great sin, to presumptuous sinnings.

I will give you a reason for it: because the Lord will forsake this man, He will leave him to himself. He will give him up to his own heart. Since he will not hearken to the counsel of the Word, nor to the advices of his conscience, God will strive with him no more, but he shall be left to himself. This is the usual course of God's righteous and judicial proceeding.

Now what can the heart do, being left to itself? As it has no strength against a great temptation, so it has sufficient strength and desire for the greatest methods of transgressing. If restriction is a merciful bond to corruption, then wrathful desertion, a desertion of the creature, a denial of preventing assistance against temptation or inclination, or acting, why, it is as the unmuzzling of the mastiff or the untying of the lion. Not that God sets the heart to sin, but that the heart will, in a moment, be mighty in sinning which is judicially deserted or left by God for former sinnings.

Therefore, I beseech you, take heed of scorning divine admonitions and reproofs. Consider that place well in Psalm 81:11-12, "But My people would not hearken to My voice, and Israel would none of Me. So I gave them up to their own lust, and they walked in their own counsels." If your heart can rise above the Word, it will rise above your conscience, and if your heart rises above your conscience, your next sinnings will rise above the former. He will not be modest to sin who grows impudent against the Word and violent against his conscience.

4. *Do not secure your heart because of God's present silence.*

Beloved, I observe that God is silent (often times) when men are in either way, in the good and in the bad. A man may repeat his seekings of God and yet God may be silent. "O my God," said David, Psalm 22:2, "I cry in the daytime, but Thou heardst not, and in the night season"; and a man may repeat his sinnings against God and yet God may be silent. Psalm 50:21, "These things hast Thou done, and I kept silence." But then this silence is not an infallible testimony either way. Though He is silent to the many prayers of His servants, yet the vision will speak at length for, as you have a time so seek, so God will find a time to answer. And, though He is silent many times at the sinnings of men, yet this is but forbearance; it is not an acquital. If you take your times to sin, God will take His time to punish, Psalm 50:21, "These things hast Thou done, and I kept silence, thou thoughtest that I was altogether such a one as thyself, but I will reprove thee, and set them in order before thine eyes."

OBJECTION. But, you will say, what is this to the preventing of presumptuous sinnings?

SOLUTION. Very much, for presumptuous sinnings depend much upon security. A man secures his facts and ways from this, that God is silent and does not presently draw the sword. He does not send for the arrest and, therefore, the man presumes to a second or greater sinning from God's connivance and patience toward former. Solomon insinuates it clearly. Ecclesiastes 8:11, "Because sentence against an evil work is not executed speedily, therefore the heart of the sons of men is fully set in them to do evil." There is now no fear. they make no bones of it, they will venture yet again. But brethren, take heed. If you sin and yet prosper in the world; if you sin, and yet conscience is quiet; if you sin, and yet God presents not a present testimony of His displeasure, yet do not presume; for if you do evil, sin lies at the door. First or last, when you open it, your sins shall flee in your face. Though the punishment of the sinner is not present, yet it is certain. "It shall not be well with the wicked, though he prolong his days," Ecclesiastes 8:13; yea, "the sinner of an hundred years shall be accursed." And this is observable, that God's silence towards a forward transgressor is made up at length not only with certainty but with number and measure. Perhaps He will take such a time to account with you for your sinnings that He will break you suddenly all to pieces. He will break your estate, your conscience, your body, your soul,

and all irrecoverably forever. When a man emboldens his heart to sin because of divine patience, God
usually does two things:

He rises suddenly to the vengeance.

He curses the sinner without all remedy, and so
fully vindicates His silence and glorifies His justice.

5. *If you would be kept from presumptuous sinnings, then
both study and improve mercy aright.* Mercy is the sweet
savor to a sinful soul, that gentle voice which speaks
hope to a trembling spirit, that tender hand which
supports and relieves a fainting soul. And yet even
from this sweet flower, presumption sucks the vilest
poison, corrupting and enflaming the heart to the
greater boldness of sinful adventures from the
greater goodness of exceeding mercifulness in God.
But then mark it, that upright apprehension of
divine mercy would serve to keep off the soul from
presumptuous sinnings if a man considered two
things.

Mercy, the very intent of it, the pulse of it, is to
draw a man off from sin. It is true, mercy is a harbor,
but not for the traitor to thrust in his ship. It is a city
of refuge, but not for the audacious man-slayer. Oh,
no! Mercy is the tenderest goodness but, with all, it
is a special goodness, and is set up not as a light by
the sea, that a man may know thereby how to sail
more freely, that a man should therefore sin more
violently, but as a proclamation from a prince to
draw in the rebel to sheath his sword, and to fall
down on his knees. "There is mercy with Thee,
therefore shalt Thou be feared," said David. "And
knowest thou not, O man," said the Apostle, "that
the goodness of God should lead thee to repen-

tance?" Romans 2:4. Has God mercy to pardon me?
With what heart can I then presume to provoke
Him? Has He mercy to pardon me? How can you
then, Oh, my soul, hold on in your sins, and not return when mercy sends a message after you! It is the
last, and most prevailing motive, for a sinner to repeat even this, that God will be merciful to him.

Mercy misimproved is both justly denied to the
sinner, and also intends his sin. The only way to forsake our mercies is that we will not forsake our sins.
God will never show you mercy if you will not return
from sinning against Him. If we will not return, iniquity shall be our ruin.

OBJECTION. Oh, but God is merciful though we
are sinful!

SOLUTION. Yea, but He is merciful only to the
penitent, and, if you will is impenitent, you forsake
your mercies, "and treasurest up wrath unto thyself
against the day of wrath," Romans 2:4-5. Nay, more
mercy so infinitely upbraids you that the very devils
will hiss at you. In the day of judgment they may cry
out against you, for the most abominable wretch living, yea, in this respect, is worse than they. "Lord,"
they may say, "we have sinned exceedingly against
Thee, why, what should we do? We had never any
hope or proposition of mercy, it was never offered to
us, nor assured us; but here's a wretch that, though
he were a sinner, yet Thou didst beseech him by Thy
mercies to leave his sins. Thou assured him of free
pardon if he would return, and he not only refused
the pardon, but because of Thy goodness in it,
therefore grew more proudly bold, and presuming
to sin against Thee."

6. *Consider this: It is a difficult thing to repent, and the more a man sins the harder it is to repent of his sins.*

OBJECTION. Why, will you say, what of this, to the prevention of presumptuous sinnings?

SOLUTION. I answer, this conduces much because the presuming sinner leads on his soul to sin upon this ground and confidence, that if the worst comes to the worst, he will yet at last put off his sins, and repent; whereupon his heart adventures far.

Now if a man were thoroughly convinced of two things, this ground would sink and, perhaps, his heart might be taken off from presuming.

One is that it is a difficult thing to repent. Why, repentance is the new setting of the heart and life; it is the very contradiction of a man's former love and practice. It is the undoing of all his doings. It is the shifting, as it were, of his nature and the trans-planting of himself, the divorcing of the affections, the new bent and edge of the soul for all holy and pious obedience, and is this an easy thing? Is it easy for a man to become an enemy to himself, to lay down his sweet delights, his precious profits, his closer nature, to judge and condemn his heart and ways, forever to forsake his own counsels, his own inclinations, his own courses? Don't you know that to sheath up an idle word and form of language is not so facile an act? How much more, then, to put off root and branch? Do we not stick in the same sins after many threatenings of wrath, after many executions of judgment, after many invitations by mercies, after daily counsels and directions by this Word, after instances of punishment, nay after particular and personal experiences of the deceitfulness of our sinnings? Does not this show that it is a difficult thing to repent?

Nay, take an assay of your heart; begin the study of yourself. Remember your doings which have not been good, your ways that have been evil, summon up all the matter of repentance (for if repentance be true, it must be a universal turning), and then set upon the work of repentance, and tell me whether former sins cannot plead hard for future and constant possession, whether they cannot work mightily and deceitfully? Tell me how willing and ready you shall find your heart, which comes to this duty as a thief to the executioner? Tell me whether Satan will easily give up his title and interest, and will give Christ possession quietly without many fervent suits to heaven, yea, without bitter and strong conflicts, yea, unless the Almighty God Himself comes in, and turns him out of your heart, and turn your heart to Him.

Another thing is that the more a man sins, the more he disables himself to repent. Tell me, seriously, does not the debtor weaken his ability of payment by greater engagements? Does not the disease consume the powers of nature by its increase? Why, what is that which spoils us, and disarms us of strength? Is it not sin? Then the more sinning, still the less strength to return from sin. Nay, sin not only corrupts our strength by multiplied sinnings, but withal increases its own strength. The more a man sins, the weaker and weaker he becomes, and sin, thereby, becomes stronger and stronger. Now tell me, if it is hard for you in strength to turn from sin, will it not be harder for you in weakness to conquer strength? If you cannot step over the brook, why, do you imagine it easy to stride over the ocean? If you cannot stand before the child, do you think in a moment to cast down the strong man? Surely by your continued and multiplied course of sinning, your mind is more blinded, your judgment more corrupted, and your love is more enflamed, and your heart is more hardened; and are you not then more disabled?

Once again, by your more sinnings, the counsels of God are more despised by you, the Spirit of God is more grieved and resisted by you, and the mercies of God are more abused by you, and the patience of God is more profaned and injured by you; so that God, in justice, may forsake you and deny His hand forever unto you, and then, what wilt you do? What can you do?

I beseech you, lay these things to heart. They may check and hold off your hearts from presuming. "Why," thinks the soul, "here is a temptation to sin, yea, but I must repent, and it is not so easy to do that. If it is, let me try about my former sins, without a new addition now." And then this I am sure of, that the more sinnings will make the work of repentance more hard; forasmuch as they wedge in the sin more into the affections and provoke God more; therefore, it shall suffice me to have sinned already. I will adventure no more nor no further.

7. *Consider that your life is short and your account is sure.*

You sin this moment, and are not sure to live till the next day, and have not assurance of life till tomorrow, for what is our life but a lease of time which

God lets to man, the date of which is only known to God, and commanded by Him? James would not have us talk of tomorrow, and Christ would not have us think of any more than for two days: and Paul said that the present time is the acceptable time, and the day of salvation. "Thou fool," said Christ, "this night shall they take away thy soul." Death attends you every moment; it is even laying hands on you in the womb; and you are never going to sin but death says, "Lord, shall I now strike him, arrest him in his very rebellion?"

Now, if a man were effectually persuaded of this, perhaps he would not presume to sin, for presumption is usually confident of longer life and, therefore, emboldens itself to stronger sins. That is a foolish error and vain, for, were it true that in a natural probability, you might yet live long, yet in a judicial course this is most true that great sinnings shorten the life. The thief goes to the gallows in his youth because of this theft; and the sinner is suddenly laid in his grave by reason of his sinnings. And, then, woe unto you! Better that you had never been born if you live and die in your sins. To the judgment seat of God must you be brought with sin in your bones and presumptuous iniquity in your heart. You who now dare to out-face the ministers of God, shall not then dare to look the holy, and just, and terrible God in the face; but He will fill your breast with confusion, and all the veins of your soul with flames of hottest vengeance and indignation.

8. *Get knowledge sanctified.* Knowledge is like a sword: it may defend a man and it may hurt a man; it may both arm him and kill him; or like the light of

a candle which may both direct and also burn. And so accidentally, even knowledge itself may prove a great addition to our sinnings. That which serves to give us light against them may yet improve the guilt of them upon us.

There is a two-fold knowledge:

One naked, which shows the evil.

Another sanctified, which keeps from evil. The former is good at the object, but the latter is good with the subject. That looks upon what is to be done or not to be done; this looks down to the heart and inclines it strongly to embrace the good and to resist and abhor the evil. This is certain, that not all the spirits of speculation are a sufficient rescue of your soul from presumptuous sinnings.

OBJECTION. "Why," says a man, "I will not sin so. I know better than to do so."

SOLUTION. Alas! The bullet strikes down the soldier for all his head-piece. Naked knowledge is at best but a head-piece (and that not of proof either), but sanctified knowledge is a breastplate, and that keeps off the dart.

9. *Last, renounce your own strength of nature, of parts, of gifts, yea, of graces, yea, of services.* He shall be brought far in sin who goes far upon his own strength. Your own strength will deceive you; it is not enough to keep you good nor preserve you from being bad. If you could get a trembling heart, a bended knee, a believing eye, and a humble spirit, then your castle would be impregnable.

4

"Keep back Thy servant also from presumptuous
sins; let them not have dominion over me."
Psalm 19:13

Having handled David's prayer against sin as lying in presumption, now I shall touch on it as it respects sin in dominion, "Let them not have dominion over me." There may be several conjectures
about the connection and depending sense of these
words.

First, as if they were a distinct petition. "Lord, I
pray unto Thee against high kinds of sinning, and
perhaps I may sometimes be laid flat by them; but
then I desire of Thee that, though they strike me
down, yet they may not rule over me. Though I
stoop, yet I may not serve; though I fall, yet I may not
lie and rest. Though they may be sometimes so
strong as to overcome, yet never so full as to reign,
let them not have dominion over me."

Second, as if they are but the same petition
greatly enforced, "O Lord, I beseech Thee to keep
back Thy servant from presumptuous sins. All sins
are bad and inglorious, but none so foul as they;
that are high transgressions. Therefore, I beseech
Thee, let them not have dominion; that is, never suffer them to prevail over me, never let them enter
into my soul or life. Let them never overcome me,
let them not overtake me, let me never commit

them."

Now, whichever way you conjecture the sense of the words may be aimed at, it requires accuracy to determine and cut the thread. For my part, I think that both may be commodious and are pious, though the latter to me seems more genuine; yet in this I easily submit to better judgments.

––––––––––

For the words themselves, this is evident, that they express the spirit of holy David as vehemently carried against presumptuous sins in dominion. For the better discussing of them, I shall inquire these particulars:

1. What dominion of sin here may import, and wherein it consists?

2. Whether sins in dominion may befall a David?

3. Why David prays so against it?

4. Then some useful applications.

SECTION I

QUESTION 1. For the first of these, what dominion of sin imports?

SOLUTION. Dominion is given sometimes to God, sometimes to Christ as Mediator, sometimes to man over man, sometimes to Satan over man, sometimes to death which is said to rule, and sometimes to sin, when it is between sin and the sinner, as between a king and his subjects. As a reigning king has dominion, so does sin. It acts in all things like a king: (1) It has possession of us; the original sin of

our hearts and the actual sin of our lives; (2) It has a
title: our forsaking of God, and voluntary election
and compact; (3) It has a throne, our souls; (4) It has
servants, our members; (5) It has a council, our carnal wisdom and corrupt reasonings; (6) It has power
to give laws and see them executed. Paul speaks of
the law in his members, and the law of sin, Romans
7:21-22.

But more distinctly, for the better understanding
of this, observe these particulars:

1. *Dominion is the right and power of a lord over a
servant.* It is a word implying superiority and subjection, one who has authority to command and another whose condition is obediential and to serve.
So that in the dominion there is one who rules and
another who is ruled; one who commands, and another who yields, at least *virtute juris,* (he is to yield
and obey) and *ratione facti,* where dominion is exercised, there is actual command, and actual obedience. The centurion who had authority and dominion over his servants "said to one go, and he did go;
to one come, and he did come; to another, do this,
and he did it."

2. *Dominion is twofold.* It is either:

Original and absolute, and this is when the lord
has a natural, prime, and irrespective title. It belongs to him to command and impose obedience,
merely from his absolute right, and according to his
own pleasure. Such a dominion belongs only to
God, who made all the world, and is Lord of all. All
the creatures are His servants, and are set by the law
of their creation to the obedience of His will. He
rules the nations, and has power to order, limit, ap-

point, to require, to bind both bodies, and souls, natures, consciences, and acts.

Derivative, depending, and limited: Such is the dominion which God has given man over the creatures. The great Lord has made man a lord over the works of His hands, a *pro-rex,* a deputy, as it were. Yea, and He has derived dominion to man over man, to one man over another, to the king over his subjects, to the parent over the child, to masters over servants. I say, He has derived dominion unto them, that is, a power to command and order, yet this is a restrictive dominion and not absolute. It must not be against God but for God, and according unto God.

3. *There is a twofold dominion:*

One is lawful, that is, such a dominion and subjection which the Word and will of God does or will warrant, as that of persons over persons, or of God and Christ over all persons and creatures. God may command us for He made us; and Christ may command us, for He redeemed us. Both our persons and our services fall unto Him, we are not our own, for we are bought with a price; therefore, serve or glorify God in your body, and in your spirit, which are God's, 1 Corinthians 6:19-20.

Another is unlawful and, as it were, usurped, which is when command is exercised and obedience given without any just title or right; and this dominion is either assumed by Satan (who is called the prince of the air, the prince of darkness, a ruler, and one who works mightily in the children of disobedience), or else it is exercised by sin. Sin is said to have a dominion, a law, a rule over a sinner, and the sinner is said to obey the sin, to serve it, to fulfill the lusts of it.

4. *Consider that the dominion of sin implies two things:*
One is singular power and strength, joined with
authority. The authority of it consists in this, that it
commands the man (as a King does his subjects)
and the strength of it consists in this, that it is able
to make its commands to be obeyed and followed.

Another is quiet, willing and totally yielding subjection to that authority, law, and command of sin;
when a man is as cheerfully and readily prepared to
obey his lusts as any subject is to embrace the commands of his prince, or any servant is to follow the
will and pleasure of his lord and master.

The former of these is sometimes called in
Scripture the power of darkness, Colossians 1:13;
sometimes the strong man, Luke 11:21; sometimes
the law of sin, Romans 7:23; sometimes the power of
Satan, Acts 26:18; sometimes the efficacy of the
prince of the air, Ephesians 2:2. All of these phrases
imply that where sin reigns or has dominion,there
it is of singular power, not only to stir and assault,
not only to tempt and provoke, but also to command
and incline, to rule and dispose of the heart and
ways, so that the will of a man is but, as it were, the
will of his lusts; and the desires of the man are but,
as it were, the desires of his lusts. He is taken captive
at the pleasure of Satan, and sin needs not use any
violent compulsion or strength of argument to draw
on the sinner, only if sin speaks the word, it is
enough; that is law enough.

The latter of these is expressed sometimes by ful-
filling the desires of the flesh and by having the
conversation in the lusts of the flesh, Ephesians 2:3,

by being servants to unrighteousness, Romans 6, by taking pleasure in sin, by sinning with greediness, by selling of a man's self to work wickedness, and by giving ourselves up or over to uncleanness. It is when a man, as it were, by a proper and voluntary act, surrenders up his soul to the obedience of iniquity, as the servant passes away himself, when he takes such a one to be his lord, that all his faculties, and strength, and designs, and main intentions shall submit themselves to the service of his lusts and sins.

So that dominion of sin, on sin's part, comprehends strong and complete power, a commanding and disposing power and, on the sinner's part, it comprehends resignation, and complete subjection. A molesting power does not constitute its dominion (for sin may molest as an enemy where it does not rule as a king), nor does attempting and suggesting power (nakedly considered) constitute its dominion (for sin may be a tempter where yet it is not a ruler). But where the dominion of sin is erected, there it sits in the heart as a king on the throne, and gives forth its laws and commands to the soul and body, as to its proper servants and instruments; the which commands are as cheerfully entertained as they are unjustly prescribed.

How Sin May Have Dominion

But a little more to wade into this point, sin may be said to have dominion, or to reign, in a threefold respect:

1. In respect of assent, when the understanding

subjects itself to its motions. I say subjects itself, for there are two acts of the mind about the motions and commands of sin: one is *apprehension,* another is *subjection.* A man may apprehend sin as working, and yet he may not embrace, but resist, the working of sin, and then it is not sin in dominion. If I see an enemy approaching, and rise up to oppose that enemy, he is now an enemy encountering but he is not a king ruling. So that it is not mere apprehension, but subjection, which puts up sin into the throne, into a dominion. That is, when sin gives the command, and the sinner yields thereto, renders up himself to the obeisance, freely gives way unto, and entertains the motions of sin.

And hereto we must again distinguish of that subjection of assent which denominates dominion, that it is not a mere passive subjection (as when a man is taken prisoner), but an active subjection, a subjection of approbation, as when a servant hears the will of his master and he likes it. So where sin has dominion, the sinner does not give a naked assent, but an approving assent. He allows his sin and approves of his sinful course.

Neither is this all, for every active assent is not sufficient to denominate dominion. A man may be, all of a sudden, circumvented. He may be under the quickness and strength of a temptation; he may be so over-born by sudden passion that, possibly, he may assent and approve a sin in respect of the fact in this or that particular, for this and that time, as a true subject (suppose one of David's) not understanding all things aright, not pausing, was drawn to the conspiracy on Absalom's side. So a Christian, in whom sin does not have a proper dominion, may, all of a sudden, be so ensnared by sin and temptation that he gives way unto it; yet, afterwards, he returns to himself and condemns his own act by sound repentance.

Therefore, know that the assent which sets up sin in dominion is double.

One is *antecedent,* and this assent is such a work of the mind wherein sin is not only not rejected and condemned, but yielded unto and approved. What Abraham answered in another case to Isaac calling out, "My father," he presently answered, "Here am I, my son." So, when sinful corruption thrusts out the sinful inclination or motion, the sinner presently answers, "Here am I, I am ready to do thy will; I like it; I allow it."

The other is *consequent.* This is an assent not only when a sin is to be committed, but after it is committed, and that too, not while the heat of sinful deceit or temptation remains and lies upon the soul, but when that is gone off. When matters grow quiet, and sober and calm, then a man likes his fact; he likes his course; he does not only antecedently devise mischief on his bed, and abhors not evil. He sets himself in a way that is not good, as David speaks, Psalm 36:4, but he "rejoiceth when he hath done evil, and delights in the frowardness of the wicked," as Solomon speaks in Proverbs 2:14.

Even a godly man, by temptation and infirmity, may yield an antecedent assent, but then as soon as he comes to himself again, as soon as he recovers his judgment to be clear and his affections to be calm, he will then set upon himself and reverse his own acts. He will judge and condemn both his deed and his assent ("such a fool was I," said David) and he will hate himself and his sinful yieldings; (such a beast was I, said David again), and he will not rest in such an estate. Peter goes out and weeps bitterly, so that even his understanding will condemn his understanding. His understanding, by a subsequent act of judiciary sentence, will condemn and disallow, yea, and disavow the antecedent act of the understanding in assenting and yielding. The serious judgment will condemn the rash judgment. It is like a man who has foolishly yielded to the bond, if he can get it into his hands he will now blot out his name, and tear off his seal. So it will be in this case.

But where sin is in dominion, there is not only antecedental permission, that is, a free and favorable leave given to the committing of sin, but consequently there is adhesion to the sin and defense of it. The man approves and upholds that which was committed. There is not a revocation of the fact; a man does not put in and sue out a writ of error against himself, that is, that he was circumvented by deceit and mistake, nor does he make protestation against his sinful commissions, but still owns them as being ready to proceed and advance on forward. He gave his bond before that sin should be done, and now, the sin being drawn out, as it were, into a deed of his own approbation, he further confirms the same, by adding thereto his seal. He approves it still, and says, "Tomorrow shall be as today, and much more abundant."

2. In respect of the consent of the will, when the will declares itself expressly as a party for sin.

Beloved, the disposition of the will is the fairest throne of sin's dominion, and as we judge of the dominion of grace far better by the will and affections than by the workings and reaches of the understanding, so, on the contrary, we may more safely judge and determine the dominion of sin by the frame and bent of the will than by any other faculty. Whatsoever may be discoursed about natural actions, for their prime and principal causation, whether by the will or by the understanding, yet this is most true in morals that the greatest domination is from the will, either for good or evil, and this holds in the case of sin's dominion. The will has (in a sort) the casting voice; it is one of the chief of the royal arms and supporters of the sinful throne. Sin is strong indeed, when it has taken seizure and possession of the will. The more corrupt a man's will is, the more strong is corruption in the man. Sin is high when the sinner will sin, and will go on.

Three Things About the Will

The schoolmen observe three things which appertain to the will, and all of them demonstrate sin's dominion.

Consensus. You know that the consent of the will is that which makes the match between person and person (in law, the canon law, *consensus, non concubitus facit matrimonium*), so here the consenting of the will is the espousing and contracting of the soul and sin together.

"I will be a lord to you," says sin.

"And I will be a servant to you," says the sinner.

"I will give you pleasure and profit," says sin.

"And I will give you my heart and obedience," says the sinner.

Electio. This is such an act or work of the will in which a man prefers one thing before another, or one way before another, and where sin is in dominion, the sinner would rather be sinful than godly. He would rather go on in his sins than forsake them. They love darkness rather than light, John 3:19. "Thou lovest evil more than good, and lying rather than to speak righteousness," Psalm 52:3. As it was with the Hebrew servant, when the year of jubilee was come, liberty was propounded unto him, he might go free if he would; it depended upon his own choice, but the servant (sometimes) loved his master and would not go free. So, when the Lord comes to a man in whom sin exercises dominion, and propounds unto him several things and several ways, here is heaven, and here is hell; here is life and here is death; here is holiness and here is sin; here is the way of duty, and here is the way of disobedience; why, as Esau made choice of the poor mess of pottage, or as the Jews of Barabbas; so the sinner makes choice of his sins and sinful ways. I would rather keep my drunkenness still, my uncleanness still, my covetousness still, etc.

Imperium or *propositum.* The will is the chief wheel of the soul, it is that which, in a sort, commands all the faculties and all their acts. Now, where the will is chief in sin, if sinning is the fruit of its lustful commands, a man has set up his resolution. It is the purpose of his heart to be as he has been, and to do as he has done. He will not learn to do good, he will hold fast his wickedness. Here sin is in dominion.

Nevertheless, for the clear discovery of this part of sin's dominion in respect of the will, be pleased to observe several things.

There is a twofold will.

One is altogether single in its workings. It does not partly incline to good, and partly to evil, but either only to good, or only to evil. Where the created nature (which is reasonable) was never morally deformed, or where the rational nature is gloriously reformed, there the will inclines only to good (as in the angels and blessed souls). So again, where the nature is totally deformed (I mean in respect of spirituals), where it is entirely corrupted, there the bias of the will draws the will only to evil. The whole weight and strength of the will is for sin, and the sinner (without any intrinsical opposition of another nature in the will) will yield and surrender up himself unto sin. Now such a will as this plainly argues dominion of sin, where the will, what it is and can do, that it is and will do, for sin; when we may say of the will as John said of the world, "the whole world lies in wickedness," 1 John 5:19. So the whole will (the whole frame and bent of it) is universally obediential or serviceable, where the whole nature of the will vents itself into an habitual and plenary consent; this is of itself manifest that sin has dominion.

Another is mixed and compounded. When the will is divided within itself and, consequently, its consents and dissents (embracings and refusings) are likewise opposed one to another and opposing each the other in the same man, you must know that original sin (which yet in part remains) is diffused through the whole man, and into every faculty. And so renewing grace (which is opposite thereto) is a universal temper, dispersed into every faculty, too. Neither is it able utterly to dislodge sin in respect of being on some actings, so that a regenerate man (as Austin spoke) has in him an old man and a new man. His flesh is like a dead man and his spirit like a living man. The living man moves up, the dead man hangs down. The living man's breath is sweet, the dead man's savour is loathsome. As far forth as the will is renewed by grace, so far it rejects and denies sin's consent, but as far as it is affected and disturbed by remaining and working corruption, so far forth it is willing and ready enough to consent to sinful actings.

Now, when we say that the dominion of sin depends upon the will, this is not to be understood of the compounded will or of the assent and actions which arise from a nature and will imperfectly renewed and cleansed in respect of degrees, but of the single and corrupt, and so complete will, wherein the consent is total and plenary. Now the plenary consent of the will consists properly in the full and natural, and longing inclination of the will after sin, when the will embraces an evil, sets the heart upon it, bends after it, and that without any resistance or striving so that it is the embracing of sin with an unstriving consent of the will, which sets up the dominion.

QUESTION. Here now falls in a subtle and deep enquiry whether all resistance impairs dominion, and no resistance always infallibly argues it?

SOLUTION. I answer briefly to the first.

All resistance does not prejudice dominion. A man may hold a firm league with sin in his heart, he may be a servant to it, though sometimes, in some particulars, he may skirmish and quarrel.

There is, therefore, a double resistance, or denying, or disputing with sin.

One is colateral and accidental; which does not arise from an immediate contrariety of nature, but from a contrariety of effects. For example, a man in whom sin has dominion, his sinnings may be sent back with such bitter writs of attachment that he may stand at defiance and be at some forbearance (awhile) from sin; or he may have such affecting apprehensions of death and hell, and shame and terror, whereupon he may resist sin as penal and painful, as a thing so bitterly vexing and galling, and this grieves him too.

Another is natural and immediate, which depends on a holy nature implanted in the soul which opposes sin as a thing formally evil and displeasing to God. This resistance, I confess, prejudices sin in its dominion, but the former does not.

No resistance implies the consent to be plenary and, therefore, sin to be in dominion. When the estate of the soul is such that no contrary quality stands between the command of sin and the obedience of a sinner, it is easy to point who is lord of the house. And, indeed, what more palpably demonstrates dominion than a quiet subjection.

It is not all the commandings of sin alone which argue dominion infallibly (an enemy may command much, and highly, as Sennacherib, and yet not be obeyed), but it is consent, and the more full and quiet kind of consent (which is that where no resistance is made), which shows that the strong man possesses the house.

QUESTION. But yet another question is raised and to be removed as to whether a good man, in whom sin does not have dominion, may not yield a plenary consent of will: which if he does, then, does not his plenary consent argue dominion?

SOLUTION. I will tell you what I conjecture about it in a few propositions.

It is possible that he may sin willingly. Two intensive aggravations of sin (in respect of particulars) may befall a good man. He may sin knowingly and he may sin willingly, the cause whereof is this: because his will is but in part renewed and, therefore, may be a willing principle. Neither does this set up sin in dominion, though it greatens sin in the commission; forasmuch as not every particular willingness, but a habitual and a complete willingness, assures sin of its dominion.

Observe that there is a double concurrence of the will's consent to sin.

One is real, when in truth the whole composition, and all the inclination of the will, is for sin; the bent of it, and bias, all runs that way and, where it is thus, there sin is in dominion.

Another is sensible; which is an observed acting of the will as embracing and leaguing with sin, when all (which may for the present be observed) is a corrupt inclination and consent. Now here I con-

jecture that possibly sin may not always have dominion where yet, for the present and for a particular,
the whole sensible part of the will seems only for
sin.

My reason for this is that the resistances of grace
are secret and more hidden; and again, when the
soul is hurried to a sin in the heat of temptations
and passions, it is not easily able to observe every secret and transient regretting and opposition.

You must distinguish between dominion of sin
and a strong inclination to sin. Dominion of sin is a
thing more natural, but the strong inclination may
be preternatural: as a stone by strength may be vehemently carried upward or an arrow out of a bow,
and yet the propensions of their nature are quite
contrary and downward.

A man in a violent temptation and under the
strength of a seduced judgment, like a captive, may
be exceedingly haled. He may put on eagerly for a
sin, yet with some little reluctancy, with some strivings on the other side, with some dissentings,
though faint, though feeble, though not able to put
by the actually greater strength of the temptation, so
that the will may be strongly inclined when yet it is
not totally inclined. The violent flying out of the
soul may be but the hurrying strength of an enemy
which marches in haste; against which the regenerate part of the will may put in its exceptions and,
though unable to stay the soul, yet it may be able to
appeal to heaven against this rash and strong working.

Last, you must distinguish between facts and
courses; between particular and general intentions;

between too much yielding and a plenary yielding
and resignation.

The will may come on to sin where it has no dominion, in respect of facts; and by a particular intention, and by a partial yielding. But where the will
comes on as to a course, and with a general intention, and with a plenary yielding, there is dominion.
Thus of the dominion of sin in respect of the will.

3.* The dominion of sin may be considered in respect of the work or service. The working of sin, and
obedient acting of it, also includes and expresses its
dominion. Hence they in whom sin has dominion
are said to serve sin, and they are said to to obey sin
("his servants ye are to whom ye obey"), and they are
said to commit sin (to do it as a man would follow
his trade), and they are said to do the work of the
devil, John 8:44. It is as if the sinner had nothing
else to do but to follow and serve his sins, which we
may evidently see in persons under the dominion of
any lust. Their whole and main designs are to fulfill
it. The drunkard, it is his work and life to sit and
drink; the covetous person, it is his work and course
of life to be scraping and getting. Where grace is in
dominion, why, the main work is to serve and please
God, to learn his will and obey it. So is it on the contrary where sin has dominion. The service of the
sinner is given up to sin so that obedience to sin
(which is the doing of the work of sin) evidently
demonstrates the dominion thereof.

Nevertheless, you must wisely understand this as

---

* Point 3 follows point 2 on page 138.

you have the other parts respecting sin's dominion; therefore consider:

First, that there is a twofold obedience unto sin.

One is material: when that thing is done or acted which is sinful. The work is repugnant to the will of God, yet this absolutely does not constitute dominion; forasmuch as it may be with the soul as with a captive, who may do the same work which the subject does, yet not with the same mind, and not in the same form of service.

Another is formal: when the work of sin is not only done, but it is done after the manner of sinning. For example, when a servant or subject expresses service and obedience, they do it with the hearts of servants and subjects, and as to a master and king. So where a man obeys his lusts, where he does the work as covenant-work, as the work of a servant, as a proper work, as a ready work, and as a hearty work, this indeed argues dominion.

Again, We must distinguish of obedience to the commands of sin.

One is simple and absolute, which is when to sin, though it is not every particular thing which a man does, yet it is a principal thing unto which he applies himself. It is as if that is a man's trade, not which he presently looks upon or deals in, but which he principally and chiefly deals in, unto which he applies the current and strength of his stock. So it is here. Sin is a man's absolute work when it is his main work, and he is besides his calling (as it were) when he is beside his sin. Such an obedience is a respect unto sin in dominion.

Another is cursory or transient. A bee may light

upon a thistle, but her work is to be gathering at flowers. A sheep may be in the dirt, but its work is to be grazing on the mountains or in the meadows. An honest traveller may be besides the way in a wood, or in an house, but his work is to go in the king's road. So is it possible for a man in whom sin does not have dominion to touch upon sinful facts; but his main way, his principal work, to which he applies the intentions and strength of his heart and spirit, is obedience unto God and His holy and righteous will.

Therefore, in the third place, observe another distinction which, though it holds some correspondency with the former, yet it says a little more and gives yet a further light.

There is an obedience of course, which is a continued applying of ourselves to the work of sin. It is our trade which we do drive, the mire in which we wallow, the mill which we help going on.

There is an obedience of fact, which may be but some particular and intervenient acts; not a thread spun out and drawn, but a sword drawn and sheathed again and laid down. There is something which steps in, interrupts the progress, and takes off the soul from service, and then it is not sin in dominion.

QUESTION. I know that it is a notable case, whether all interruptions of sinful facts impeach sin's dominion?

SOLUTION. For my part I think that all absolutely do not. There are two kinds of abruptions or interruptions; that is, working causes, which do, if we do not untwine the thread, yet respite and hinder the finishing of it.

Some are political: when the interruptions depend upon politic and private respects, as upon the wisdom of the flesh, the stingings of conscience, the defect of occasions, the safety of our names and credit, etc.

Others are natural, which depend upon a contrary nature, touching the heart for its particular trespassing, humbling it, recovering it again out of the snare of the devil. And this interruption is not only a mere limit or politic halt for a while, where the sinner takes breath and makes a pause before he will go on, but it is an undoing of a particular illdoing by an holy nature now recovering the soul.

Once again observe that the work or obedience to sin is twofold:

Either by surprisal, and compulsory, and this work owes itself not to the intention of the heart nor to the approbation of the judgment, but to the deceitfulness of sin and the strength of temptation.

Another is cheerful and, as it were, of nature. Now remember that acts of surprisal do not testify sin in dominion. Indeed, this they may testify that sin in its inclination, or Satan in his temptation, is (at that time) very strong; but yet, not that they rule. Dominion, in this case, is not when a man is vanquished and made captive, but when he yields himself and willingly follows.

Though sin is acted, yet it is not therefore sin in dominion unless it is a willing doing of the work of sin. Though force and compulsion may be sufficient to testify that there is a tyrant, yet ready obedience is that which testifies homage to a king.

Thus, have you heard a little in the general about the nature of dominion, and about the nature and manner of sin's dominion.

I conjecture that it is fit to add one thing more in general about the dominion of sin as respecting its powerful commands.

Sin is habitual. Where sin in the course behaves itself as a king, it rules and commands, and disposes of the person to its base services and lusts.

Sin is actual, and this is not properly its dominion, though it is miscalled so; yet to give a little scope to freeness of language, I will call it an actual dominion, which is a particular prevalency of acts rather than a sovereignty or dominion in the nature; when, though the heart and nature have surrendered themselves to Christ as the only Lord, and to his will as the only law yet, in many particulars, sin gets the better over grace. Though it cannot be said to rule, yet it may be said to conquer. It makes the man to fall down; it is too strong and prevalent for all the actual improvements and particular resistances of grace and prayer at that time, and for that fact. Against which, if I mistake not, David here principally bends himself when he prays, "Let not them have dominion over me"; that is, not only let them not rule but, which is beyond that, let them not so much as prevail over me. Though I may meet with temptations to presumptuous and high sinnings, though I may find a false nature ready enough to break forth upon a vain confidence; yet,

Lord, then so effectually aid and assist me that I may not only resist but repel them; though they may attempt, yet let them not once conquer nor overcome me; let me never yield to them, nor act them. Yet if any thinks that he aims at the habitual dominion of those sins, I will not enter into the lists. Let him enjoy his opinion, but I think this of actual dominion is more pertinent to the place.

SECTION II

QUESTION. Whether sin in dominion may befall a David, or regenerate person?

For the resolution of this question, remember these particulars:

1. *There is a difference between a conquest by sin and the dominion of sin.* A conquest is when sin prevails; dominion is when sin rules. The conquest respects power; dominion respects the will; in conquest the person resists, but his strength is too weak, in dominion the person yields up himself to the will, and the law, and power of another. Sin may overcome a regenerate person, but it does not have dominion in him.

2. *There is* dominium tyranni, *and* dominium domini. A tyrannical dominion is by force and constraint; a regal dominion is by consent and choice. The former is incident to the regenerate. Paul complains that he is sold under sin, Romans 7, but Ahab sold himself to work wickedness. Paul is brought into captivity to the law of sin, but Judas willingly offers himself to betray Christ. In tyran-

nical dominion, there is unwillingness, hatred, dislike, conflict, weariness, trouble, and desire to be freed; in regal dominion there is chief contentment, delight, and rest, etc.

3. *The dominion of sin may be taken either:*

Strictly and properly; where sin is absolute and full, uncontrolled, and the sinner freely and totally resigns up himself to the lusts, will, and commands of sin.

Largely, and in some respect; when as to some particular act of sin, there is not (for a time) any actual or prevalent present resistance. Even the will itself is surprised by carnal affections, but yet, in the event, and at length, it is revived, and grace resumes its *imperium,* and recovers the person again. In this sense sin may be said to reign, or to have dominion in a regenerate person; but it is as a thief or robber reigning and ruling in a royal castle, which shortly he is forced to quit and leave.

But for a complete, uncontrolled, habitual, final dominion of sin, this cannot befall the regenerate.

The dominion of grace and Christ is eternal. True grace is an immortal seed; it cannot be totally lost. It is a well of water springing to everlasting life.

The union with Christ is inseparable, and insuperable, which could not be, if a regenerate person might fall under such a dominion of sin.

The promise of grace must not fail, sin shall not have dominion over us, Romans 6:14. "I will subdue their iniquities," Micah 7:19.

The covenant of God is, "I will put my fear into their hearts, that they shall not depart from Me," Jeremiah 32:40.

Jesus Christ has conquered, as well as other enemies, our sins.

QUESTION. If sin in dominion cannot happen to the regenerate, why does David pray?

SOLUTION. Three things may be said of this.

1. If David, or any regenerate person, should be left unto himself, sin would have dominion over him. Therefore, he prays, acknowledging that it must be a strength greater than his own.

2. Prayers are a means to fetch us out of the dominion of sin and keep sin from having dominion over us. Upon Paul's prayer, the answer was, "My grace is sufficient for thee."

3. Although habitual, universal, and final dominion of sin is incompatible or inconsistent with the state of grace, yet actual and particular dominion is possible. And there are great reasons for a regenerate person to pray if it were no more than against particular and temporary dominion of sin; but of this more distinctly in the next section.

SECTION III

QUESTION. Why does David prays against sin in dominion?

SOLUTION. Remember that precedent distinction of actual dominion, which comprehended a particular prevalency over the soul for particular acts of sinning, and of habitual dominion, which intimated the full resignation of the heart to the commands of corruption.

In both respects there may be great reasons why

any man should pray against the dominion of sin.

Against Actual Dominion

First, because though actual dominion does not infallibly testify the person to be bad, yet it is ever a breaking forth of what is very bad. The action in this case is but sin acted. Now consider:

1. Every sin (as acted) is, therefore, the worse. You know that sin, though it is a vile thing, yet it tends towards a perfection (in its kind). "Lust, when it hath conceived, bringeth forth sin, and sin, when it is finished," James 1:15. He alludes to a child in the womb which, in the conception, is not so perfect and complete as in the birth and life. Sin is naturally bad. If it is at all, it is evil; if in inclination, it is evil; if in thought, evil; if in acting, then much worse. When it is brought forth, then it is more ripened and, therefore, the more sinful. Now where sin has but actual dominion, there it prevails; though not always to a full consent, yet to a sinful service or act. The person does the thing which is evil.

2. The acting of the greater sin is always a greater kind of sinning; I mean, *caeteris paribus,* if things are equally set together.

A high sin, a presumptuous sin in temptation, is not so guilty as the same presumptuous sin in dominion; for all sin in service is ever worse than any sin in conflict. Though sin may trouble a man more when it inclines and tempts, yet it wounds a man more when it prevails and overcomes.

Second, actual dominion, though it does not always conclude the absence of grace, yet it always impairs and weakens the strength of grace.

There are two things which sin, prevailing to act, does not necessarily infer:

One is privation of grace, for even a good man may stoop and fall. A good man may yet do that evil which he would not. An honest traveller may be struck down and a faithful soldier may be taken captive. Though to sin is the evil man's work, yet it may possibly be the good man's action.

A second is annihilation of grace. There is a great difference between sickness and death. Though sickness removes health, it does not remove life; it is death which does that. Particular dominion, or prevalence, may lay flat, wound deeply, leave a man in a swoon (as you shall hear presently) yet it is the habitual dominion which denies life.

Nevertheless, particular dominion even weakens grace; that is, any sin (much more a presumptuous sin at which David seems here to touch) prevails and wins ground on the soul to yield to act. There the corrupt nature improves itself, it has the better. And this is certain, that sin is never improved but grace is weakened; weakened much in its measure, and in its strength. As all health is weakened by the prevalency of sickness and all heat by the victoriousness of cold, sinful actings abate the vitality of grace, the edge and the spirit of it, and lay it in a swoon so that a man may now have little heart to pray. Infinite distrust toward God and, which is as bad as the rest, if he does not take heed, actual prevalencies (at the least) incline and tempt him shrewdly to habitual actings. So a man shall hardly do sin any one service, but sin, to recompense him, will impose thereupon many commands for more.

Third, because actual dominion, though it does not always cut off the union, yet it may and does disperse and check the comforts. It is an eclipse, though it be not a night. He who had the leprosy, though he did not lose the right to his tent or house, yet he was denied the use and benefit of either. A child who offends his father, though he does not therefore presently cease to be a child, yet his offense turns and changes the countenance of his father. Though it does not break off the relation, yet it does break off the respect. He shall not easily be admitted into his father's presence; and then he shall see bended brows instead of smiles, sharp rebukes, and upbraidings, instead of kind and wonted welcomes. So shall even David himself find if great sins get dominion over him, if they prevail. If he acts them, though God does not cast off his person, yet He will draw off His countenance, "Why hidest Thou Thy face?" He shall quickly find the difference between the service of God and the service of sin.

When he goes to pray, his sin shall meet him; and when he goes to hear, the ordinances shall cast his sin into his face. When Sampson lost his hair, he could not do as formerly as at other times. So even actual dominion of sin, though it does not nullify the relationship, yet it wonderfully varies the condition. The sun seems to be darkened at noonday, the air is filled with tempest and thunders, which lately was overspread with beautiful light. God looks in terror and displeasure, and the conscience wounds with closest bitterness. All former comforts seem to take leave of us. Sometimes we are so distressed that we fear we are lost for ever. One such sinning may cost us many years of cruel vexation, and of this we may be sure, that till we are soundly humbled and renew our repentance, we shall never see a smile in God's countenance, nor hear a good word from conscience. Now this is a doleful case, that a man shall hear the same promises from which he sucked much comfort, and yet he may not taste; now he cannot rejoice, and that God, whose communion was so sweet, now, through his sinning, becomes so bitter and heavy.

Fourth, because actual dominion (especially of great sins, and over a David), is accompanied with great prejudice to divine glory. They say that fevers are usually worst in the strongest constitutions, and spots are usually the greatest blemishes in the fairest garments. So we may say of sinnings: the better the man is, the more dishonorably foul his offendings are. God loses more honor in the eyes of the world by the slips of the good than by the wallowings of the bad. Evil men are hardened, good men derided, Satan and sin advanced and, by all these, God is infinitely dishonored. Therefore, David has a good reason David to pray, "Let them not have dominion over me."

Habitual Dominion

But then, in the second place, if we interpret the dominion here of a habitual dominion of sin, the reasons of prayer against sin, as in such a dominion, are very strong and urgent.

1. Habitual dominion decides the estate. The question of a man's soul is whose servant he is;

whether he belong to God and Christ, or to sin and
Satan.

Now particular failings do not determine this,
but the dominion of sin does; his servants we are
whom we obey. You know what the Apostle has said,
Romans 6:16, "Know ye not that to whom ye yield
yourselves servants to obey, his servants ye are to
whom ye obey, whether of sin unto death, or of obedience unto righteousness?" If sin rules, and the
sinner yields up his heart to the love and obedience
of it; he professes this much, that Christ is not his
Lord, and the law of Christ is not the law which he
will obey; as these rebels spake of David, "What portion have we in the son of Jesse?" So here the sinner
says, "I do not belong to Christ; sin is my lord. The
servant of sin am I, that is the thing which I have
chosen, and that is it which I will serve."

So that one may, without any scruple, conclude
that if sin has dominion, the man has yet no interest in Christ, not one degree of true grace. He is a
most wretched sinner; sin is his Lord, God is his enemy, hell is his portion, unless he gets from under
this dominion.

2. There is no dominion in the world so vile
whether you consider it, first, in the commands of
sin, or, secondly, in the service of the sinner.

First, the commands. The commands of sin are
the vilest commands, for:

They are illegal. Any command which finds
ground and title may be defended, but sin has no
reason to command. A condemned man loses all
command; sin is the only thing which God's law has
condemned. And again, it has no title to the soul.

The soul owes not itself to it, either by a natural or a purchased subjection. We owe a natural subjection to God because He made us and a purchased subjection to Christ because He redeemed and bought us; but sin's commands are merely usurped and insolent.

They are purely sinful. All its edicts and desires are but rebellions, that a man should transgress a righteous, supreme, good, and holy law. There is not any one thing which sin at any time commands, but it is that which God forbids and for which God will judge the sinner.

They are extremely unreasonable. A command may be esteemed unreasonable when one service runs contradictory against another, as to command a man to run and yet to stand. So is it with sin—it commands a man to such a service as is opposite in particulars; for as all sin is opposite to grace, so some sins are opposite to others; though not in the fountain, yet in the actings. A command may be esteemed unreasonable, when any service tends to the ruin of the obedient. It would be an unreasonable thing, and unjust, to command a man to run into the fire and burn himself; but the commands of sin tend directly and intentionally to the destruction of the sinner. Sin enjoins a man to much service and pains, and all this is to dishonor God and to damn his own soul.

Second, the service of sin is the most disloyal service in respect of God, renouncing Him, denying Him His due, and conferring it on His only enemy.

It is the most injurious service to our souls.

It is the basest service. If a man served a dog or a

toad, this would be a vile abasing of himself; but it is
far baser to serve sin, for those creatures have some
goodness in them, but sin is naturally bad. Nay,
though we cry out at the devil as vile and base, yet
the devil himself is better than sin, for it is his sin
only which makes him so base, and he has an absolute being which he owes to God; but sin has no relation to God, and it is that which degrades all beings.

It is the most drudging service. A man who is a
servant to sin is at the command of every lust, and is
taken captive at its pleasure, and there is no hope,
nor measure, nor end. All the day will not serve, nor
will the night satisfy. An age of years is spent, and
when a man's strength fails him, yet sin sets him to
work still. The cruelest tyrant wearies himself sometimes by his unwearied commands, but sin never re-
lents nor spares. Nay, that which shows the extremity of this vassalage is that the sinner continues service there, and then, where he sees and knows his
misery, he has felt the fruits, the bitter fruits of sinning, yet sin still commands and easily puts him
upon the same service afresh so that he often tires
his thoughts, spends his estate, consumes his
strength, breaks his sleep, and loses his friends, his
God, his soul, his all, to drudge at the commands of
his own base lusts.

It is a most unprofitable service. Though in some
service there may be but an uncertain gain, yet in
the service of sin, there is a most certain and great
loss. "What profit had ye in those things whereof ye
are now ashamed," Romans 6:21. Therefore, sinners
are said to sow the wind, and to reap the whirlwind;

they deal in vanities which shall not profit, and every sin is a lie. Let it pretend much, yet it advantages nothing. Suppose a man had an estate worth £10,000 and he should receive a baby for it. Tell me, what did he get?

Oh, that precious soul of man, which is worth more than a world, is utterly lost by sin! What, then, does the service of it profit him? For what is a man profited (said our Savior) if he gains the whole world and yet loses his own soul? You get a little credit by your sinning, yea, but with whom? And what is that, while the great God disgraces you, and your own conscience often shames you? You get a little wealth by your sinning, yea, but what is that treasure of wickedness but a treasury of wrath against the day of wrath? You get a little pleasure by your sinning, yea, but what are these short minutes of joy to those eternal nights of darkness in which they must end and be swallowed up? One fall breaks all the glass to pieces, and one anguish of conscience, or peal of death, blasts and sinks all the vain triumphings of a sinful heart. Sin may pretend fair and promise much, but the wages thereof, that is, that which you must expect for your service, is death: yea, that death which is opposed to eternal life, Romans 6.

It is a most uncomfortable service. How often is the servant of sin in the depths of fear and in the heights of trouble? His very sinnings are more his torments than his joys. He is many times vexed with thoughts how to sin, and afterwards he is hewed in his conscience for his sinning. Though he does not have grace to make him grieve, yet he has a con-

science which can make him tremble. The very sur-
feits of his sins are distasteful to his soul, and make
him oftimes weary of his very life. He is ashamed of
company, and dares not yet to be solitary. The night
is many times a terror unto him, and the day renews
his anguish. Though the servant of sin (in the transient flash of his spirit) outbraves all counsel, yet he
ordinarily feels infinite gripes within. Either he is
utterly insensible of his misery (which is one of the
greatest judgments), or he is sensible, and then he
feels a hell of horror for his lewd obedience. Nay, so
exceedingly high do the distresses sometimes prevail that he is forced to despair of all mercy and,
thinking to ease himself of some flames, greedily
throws himself away into the very gulf of hell-fire.

What shall I say more? Where sin has the dominion over a person, a man is a slave to the devil, and a
servant to that which will vex him, wound him, and
damn him. He never enjoys himself, nor shall he
ever enjoy God, unless that yoke of service is broken
and, therefore, there is good reason for any man to
pray against the habitual dominion of sin.

SECTION IV

Thus for the explication. Now something for the
application thereof unto ourselves. First let me begin with inquiring what we think of the dominion
of sin within our *own* souls?

You will say, "We trust there is no such thing." I
remember the Jews said as much to Christ in a case
not much unlike this one. "We are Abraham's seed,"

said they, "we were never in bondage," John 8:33. But
Christ replied, "Verily, verily, I say unto you, whosoever committeth sin is the servant of sin," verse 34.

I will premise a few things at this time.

1. *There is no man living but he is born a servant to sin.*
Sin is his lord before he can tell who is his master.
Sin does not require age to set on the crown, but
even in the very womb it begins its reign, and poi-
sons and impairs our whole nature. Therefore the
Apostle said that by nature we are the children of
disobedience and wrath, as well as others, Ephesians
2:2. It is the disposition, sway, and bent of us to sin,
and to walk on in sin.

2. *It is a hard thing to get off the dominion of sin.* Sin is a
strong man; it has possession, and goes not out by
entreaty or bribe, but it must be by force, by one that
is stronger. I assure you that the Almighty God must
reveal His own arm and He must cast down
strongholds. He must work a kind of miracle or else
sin will still be a lord and the sinner will be a
servant to his lusts. A man may change any master
soever, and with more ease than sin.

3. *It is very manifest that sin has the dominion in many
persons.* I will present unto you such instances which
you shall confess do evidence so much.

What do you think? Does not sin have the dominion, where no kind of arguments and dealings
are able to disengage the heart and to turn it? When
no kind of merciful arguments, and no kinds of just
threatenings, and no sense of bitterness, can yet
discovenant and disservice the soul; but still it holds
the league, keeps the agreement with sin? Now
then, how often has God come to many persons and

offered unto them His pardoning mercies, and the
blood of Christ, and eternal life, if they would leave
such a sin of drunkenness, such a sin of filthiness,
such a sin of worldliness, but unrighteous they were,
and unrighteous still they are and will be. How often
has God set the point of the sword upon the breast
of a sinner, revealing His wrath, threatening death
and hell, if he will not leave the service of his sin.
Nay, scourged his estate for his sinning, nay,
scourged his body, nay, his soul, and conscience,
and all this to renounce his sinful lord, yet men
hold fast their wickedness. They yet give over themselves to sin with greediness; they study how to fulfill
their lusts, and rejoice when they have done evil.
Does not this show that the heart is indeed en-
deared, and totally mancipated, by a strong and elec-
tive subjection unto sin?

What do you think of such whose hearts cannot
endure the dominion of Jesus Christ, and the service
of righteousness? It is even a tormenting slavery
unto them, even the imaginations thereof are so.
The soul of a man cannot serve two masters, and
there are but two of them upon which our service
can be bestowed, either sin, or Christ. The Apostle
intimated as much in Romans 6:16, "Know ye not
that to whom ye yield yourselves servants to obey, his
servants ye are to whom you obey, whether of sin
unto death, or of obedience unto righteousness?";
so that these divide the soul. If a man yields obedience unto righteousness, he is then no servant of
sin; if he yields obedience unto sin, he is then no
servant of righteousness. If he is an enemy to sin, he
is then a servant to righteousness; if he is an enemy

to righteousness, he is then a servant of sin. Yet, many persons are enemies to righteousness. "We will not have this man to reign over us," said they in the gospel. They cannot endure the dominion of Christ either in His word or in His spirit. The rules and precepts of the word are the cords which they will break asunder, Psalm 2:3. "They cast the laws of Christ behind their backs, and hate to be reformed," Psalm 50:17. There is nothing more unacceptable to them than to serve the Lord Jesus Christ in holiness of heart, newness of spirit, and righteousness of obedience.

What do you think of those who are still overcome of their lusts, and are willingly entangled? The Apostle Peter conjectures that sin has dominion in such, "while they promise them liberty, they themselves are the servants of corruption, for of whom a man is overcome, of the same is he brought in bondage," 2 Peter 2:19.

There is a twofold overcoming of a person; one is only in respect of the action, another is also in respect of the affection.

It cannot be denied that even a holy man (who is heartily the servant of Jesus Christ) may be overcome in respect of particular actions. Relapses are not impossible to him who is truly good, and they consist with (though they weaken and disconsolate) the service of grace. There is the same natural principle of sin in the best after repentance as before. There is the same Satan to suggest and incline. There may be the same occasions and provocations, but then there is an overcoming in respect of affection, and this shows the dominion of sin. Now this overcom-

ing is either when a man through policy forbears, or
else in passion seems to bid defiance to his sin, being either in sickness and apprehension of death or
in pangs and distress of conscience (to which the
Apostle seems to allude in 2 Peter 2:22 ("The dog is
turned to his vomit again"). Now he cries out
against sin, and thinks he detests it heartily and will
not, for a world, act the sin now; yet, when this tempest is off, when the water grows cool, when circumstances are free, when the bitterness either of death,
or cross, or conscience, is over, and sin tempts and
wooes him again, he yields up himself. He gives over
his heart and affections; he loves the sin and wallows in it as much as ever. "He turns from his holy
commandment" (as the Apostle speaks), verse 21. All
his good moods of holy profession are gone off, and
he is more entangled, and renews his bondage with
ardent and excessive delight, even with greediness,
as the Apostle Paul speaks in Ephesians 4.

Now, if this is an argument of sin's dominion,
namely, the willing and affectionate re-entering of
our hearts to the service of sin, then certainly many
of us have just cause to fear, and to suspect ourselves
"who return with the dog to the vomit, and with the
sow to the wallowing in the mire"; who are not only
surprised in action but in affection. Nay, and our affections are more eagerly carried to the sinning now
than heretofore. Our minds are more on them, and
our desires, yea, and the measures of sinning in the
same kind rise in a higher strength. We are more
mighty to drink, more inglorious in swearing, more
unsatiable in earthliness, more vain in conversation, more obstinate in our sinful courses against

the reproofs of the Word, the checks of our conscience, the shame of men, the fear of hell, and the hope of heaven. We grow worse and worse.

What do you think of those who make choice of sin to be the lord they will serve?

There are but two sorts of people in the world—good and bad—and both of them choose their lords.

The good choose the Lord to be their God, Joshua 24. They choose the things which please them, Isaiah 56:4; they choose the way of truth, Psalm 119:3, and they choose the good part, Luke 10:42.

The bad are also said to choose their own ways, Isaiah 66:3, and evil, Isaiah 65:12; that in which God delights not; yea, and they are said not to choose the fear of the Lord. When several things are propounded, and a man prefers this before that, this is called an election or choice. There is laid before the sinner Christ and His way and sin and its lusts. Now, when he prefers the latter before the former, he is said to make a choice, which many do. They prefer their sinful lusts before the commands of Christ, as appears in all the times of competition, and in the courses of action, yea, and when they may go free, yet, with that Hebrew servant, they will not, for they love their master.

Last, what do you think of many who love their sins? Love is that which bestows the soul and service thereof. The whole strength of man goes that way which his love goes, for it is of a constraining and most serviceable nature. Now there are many who love sin. There is, as it were, a conjugal match and

union between their hearts and their sins and, be
sure of this, that sin has the whole man if it has won
the love of the heart.

4. *A person may possibly delude his own heart, and deceive himself about the dominion of sin and, therefore, it is
convenient to try ourselves whether sin has not dominion indeed.*

There Are Six Erroneous Deceits

DECEIT 1. One is the unsensibleness of its
power; when a man feels no violence of sinful inclination, no stirrings, no opposition, no com-mands,
but there is a calm and quietness in his spirit and in
his way, which could not be, as he thinks, if sin had
dominion and rule in him.

Now this is a deceit; for it is most probable that
sin has the strongest dominion where the heart is
most insensible of the law and commands of sin.
When the strong man keeps the house, all is quiet,
said our Saviour; where subjection is peaceable,
there dominion is (in all likelihood) most absolute
and complete.

Nay, this is certain, that where Christ sets up His
sceptre (which casts down the dominion of sin),
there is the greatest stir. The law of the mind will
war against the law of the members, Romans 7:23,
and the Spirit will lust against the flesh, Galatians
5:17.

This insensibleness and quietness may arise
partly from the oneliness of sin, and partly from the
ignorance of a sinful condition, and partly from the
habitual custom of sin. Whether the sun shines or

not, there are as many atoms and motes flying in the room, there they are really, though not sensible till the light comes in to manifest them. When a man is in a deadly disease, he may be void of all sense of it. His life may be dropping out, and his disease may rule in his body, though he does not feels any aches, or pain; for this insensibleness depends upon the strength of his disease, which has not only pierced his natural temper, but his senses also. So may a person be utterly insensible of sin for want of all saving light, and holy experience, which arises from a new nature.

Nay, and as we see men in bondage and slavery, when they are long in the same, grow insensible, and the hand which is used to iron and nettles, is not sensible of them; so the frequent actings of sin may suppress the inward sense of sinning; this being an easy observation, and most true, that much sinning adds to the strength of sin, and disables the sense of a sinner, sears his conscience, and makes his mind reprobate, and as it were without sense.

DECEIT 2. Another deceit may be a freedom from many courses of sinful actings. When a man is not like every whore who prostitutes her body to every lover, so he does not rage and live in all sorts of wickedness. Nay, his ways seem to keep clear of divers iniquities.

To this I answer, though a man does not commit all evil, and his ways or courses are not universally spreading in all the kinds of sinning, yet sin may rule in that man. It may have dominion; forasmuch, as:

Particular subjection is sufficient to set up dominion. Though a servant has but one master, and does not serve every one in the parish, yet he is a true servant in respect of that one master. And, though a subject does not obey every prince in the world yet, if he obeys any one, it is enough to prove that he is a subject. So, though the sinner is not at the command of every lust, yet if he is the servant of any one lust, sin has the dominion over him; for it is not the multitude of sins which absolutely and necessarily concurs to dominion, but a subjection to the power of any one.

A man may do all that service to one sin, which others do to many sins. He may devise and study to fulfill it; he may cheerfully and greedily receive its commands. He may heartily love it, and go on in it, and, for its sake, oppose the sceptre and dominion of Christ; he may consecrate all his strength to the obedience of it. Now, as they observe in politics, there are several forms of government or dominion, as democracy, and aristocracy, and monarchy, sometimes the dominion is exercised by many, sometimes by one alone, yet the subjection to any argues dominion.

DECEIT 3. Yet again, another deceit may be not only declination of some sins, but also opposition, which a man thinks cannot possibly consist with dominion; for a kingdom is not, or should not be, divided against itself.

To this I answer, there may be notable deceit in this also; forasmuch as to that of exemption from great and gross sins, it is not the greatness, but the power of sin which makes it reigning. The princes in Germany have dominion, though the dominion of the emperor is more large. The least sin acknowledged, loved, or served suffices to dominion. The dominion of sin is most within the heart.

As to that opposition, there is a double opposition of sin; one depending upon office, another depending upon nature. A person advanced to some office in the commonwealth may oppose a sin with respect to his office, which yet perhaps he favors and dearly loves in respect of his private nature and practice. A justice of peace may oppose many sins upon the bench, which yet he lies in at home, in his own house and dealings.

Again, there is a twofold opposition of sin; one because it is sin, another because it is shame; and this latter may befall him who is under the dominion of sin.

Once more, there is an opposition of a sin either because of the opposition which the sin has to God's will, or because of the opposition which the sin has to another sinful way and inclination. For though it be true that all sin has a contrariety to the rule; yet it is as true that some sins have a contrariety among themselves, as prodigality to covetousness, etc. And a man may oppose the one, not from a respect had to its natural vileness, but from a respect had to his private and personal inclination; this other being such a way of sinning, as he likes not, but it would overthrow that other sin, which he has set up, and which he loves, and in which he is resolved to walk.

In a word, it is not particular but universal opposition of all known sin which denies dominion. A man may oppose many sins for one sin's sake, as well as act sin for its sake, and both show sin to be in dominion.

DECEIT 4. A fourth deceit may depend upon the troubles which a man may feel after some sinful actings. His soul may be grievously heavy and perplexed, and hereupon a person may conclude that sin does not have dominion because he conceives dominion of sin to exclude all trouble for sin.

Nevertheless there may be error in this, for, though hardness of heart after sin is as ill a symptom of wickedness as impudency before sin, yet all trouble for sin committed, is not an infallible argument of indominion, which I clear:

1. By instance. If the worst of men may have after-troubles for former sinnings, then it is not an infallible argument (because if sin has dominion in any, then surely in the worst of men), but even they may have after-troubles.

As it is with the most honest wife, and with the most dishonest strumpet; both of them, after their childbirth, may have their after-throes; so the most ingenuous Christian and the most lewd sinner may, after their sinnings, partake of great anguish and troubles of conscience. I refer you to Ahab and to Judas, and to those of whom he speaks in Job, "that the terrors of God did drive them to their feet."

2. By argument. Trouble for sin, in respect of the conscience only, is but a judicial act; it is but a part of the wages of sin. Indeed, trouble in the affections (which divines call godly sorrow) is an act or effect

of grace; but mere trouble in the conscience, which consists in sense and accusation is that which God brings upon the sinner for his transgressions. He awakens the conscience after sin to accuse for sinning, whose directions and checks could not avail to keep off from sinning, so that a person whose heart is in no measure changed by grace (and therefore of necessity is under sin's dominion) may be filled with extreme wrath, and bitterness. Yea, the very terrors of hell may shake, amaze, and confound his soul. Why? The reason is because, though grace is required to raise godly sorrow; yet conscience only awakened and actuated by light and divine command, is abundantly sufficient to accuse, condemn, vex and trouble the sinner.

DECEIT 5. A fifth deceit may be in the vacancies, or spaces, or interims of sinning, because a man does not every moment, or every day lie at his sin, but there are often times some pauses and distances of time between sinning and sinning. He therefore conjectures that sin does not have dominion over him. Why? Because where sin has dominion, there a man sells himself to sin and wallows in sinning, and makes it his trade at which he spends his life and strength.

To this I answer that sin may have dominion, though there are some respites and breathings between sinning and sinning. For:

Some respites do not arise from a nature which will not subject itself to sin, but only from the defect of occasions and opportunities of sinning. A thief does not always steal because he may be sometimes

sick, and because there is not always an open conveniency for his hand. The like may be said of any
sins which are capable of visible and corporal actings.

Again, the dominion of sin does not absolutely
consist in an uninterrupted propagation or service
of sinful acts; that is, that a man does not do other
particular acts, but sin. The drunkard is under the
power of drunkenness though he is at other times
sober; and the filthy person is under the power of
uncleanness though he does not every day see and
embrace his harlot. But the dominion of sin is to be
judged by the diposition of the heart and the main
part of the course; if sin is the main thing which a
man intends, and the singular thing to which he resigns and yields up his heart. Whether he is always,
or sometimes, in the actings is not material.

Nay, for a man to give no respite to sinful actings, this would be against that wisdom of the flesh,
which concurs to make up the dominion of sin.
Though the propension to sin may be constant,
though the love of the sin may be great, yet the actings of sin may often vary and be suspended upon
private reasons and respects, either of safety, quiet,
profit, or pleasure.

DECEIT 6. A sixth deceit may be from the practice of some actions which are contrary to all outward sinnings, at least in respect of exercise, because a man is, perhaps, a constant churchman and
has a course of duties (such as they are) in his family, and he is much in vowings, and can condemn
sin to purpose. Now surely sin has lost its dominion.

I answer that, notwithstanding all this, sin may yet be in dominion for the dominion of sin is within.

It may consist with many visible acts of piety. I will clear this unto you by propounding one case. What do you think of a hypocrite? Does not sin have dominion in him? You will confess it has, and verily it has; but now even a hypocrite may step forth into all outward conformities. I know no visible act of piety which a hypocrite either does not or may not perform.

Second, though those material good acts are formally opposite to sinful acts as acts, yet as the denomination of a Christian, so that of a sinner, is more from the affections than from the actions. And indeed, this defines and decides the dominion, or indominion, of sin immediately, namely, the disposition of the heart which may be really rotten and false, and the true harbor of sin, though the person gets out to the acting of some visible duties of piety. There must be more than externals in duty to evidence that sin does not have dominion.

How Can a Man Know That He is Not Under the Dominion of Sin?

Having delivered unto (in the useful application of the point already) the natural community of sin's dominion, the difficulty of release from it, the probability of its rule in many men's hearts and the erroneous grounds by which men deceive and flatter themselves as free and exempted persons, I now pro-

ceed to set down some instances or trials by which it
may appear that a man is not under the dominion of
sin, or that sin does not have dominion over him.

1. If Christ is his Lord. The Apostle has a sweet
passage in Romans 6:17-18. "But God be thanked
that ye were the servants of sin, but you have obeyed
from the heart that form of doctrine which was
delivered you, being then made free from sin, ye become the servants of righteousness"; that is, you
chose Christ to be your Lord and resigned up yourselves to His service. This is a most undoubted truth.
If Christ is my Lord, I am not, then, a servant to sin;
sin is not my master. Christ's dominion is destruc-
tive to, and inconsistent with, sin's dominion. It ever
stands alone.

OBJECTION. But you will say, "How may a man
know that Christ is his Lord?"

SOLUTION. This is a great point, and much depends on it, so I will touch it a little.

You know that one may be a Lord in a double respect. One is in respect of title and right; another in
respect of authority and acknowledgement. It is certain that Christ is the Lord of all the world. All the
nations of the earth are given unto Him and are, in
respect of His title and right, to stoop and bow
themselves down; but He is not acknowledged as a
Lord, He is not embraced (as so) by His enemies, yet
there are some in whose heart Christ sets up his authority and rule, and who do acknowledge Him, who
do make choice of Him to be the Lord of their
hearts and lives. That is, they prefer the government
of Christ; they consent unto Him that He only shall
rule them, and they resign themselves up to His will.

They bestow their hearts and service on Him.

Beloved! When a person makes a choice of Christ to be his Lord, he considers the several kinds of dominion (of sin, of the world, of the devil, of Christ); he considers them seriously, and compares them, and then he finds that no dominion, for a man's soul, is like Christ's; none so sweet and profitable. Christ has the only right to the soul, and His government is infinitely best.

Now the person, hereupon, makes choice of Christ and comes unto Him with humble tears, and beseeches Him to reign over him. "O blessed Jesus! (says the soul) Thou art the only Lord, and there is none like Thee or besides Thee. I have been a rebel, an enemy unto Thee. I have been disobedient and have served divers lusts and pleasures. I have served the world and the prince of darkness, but now I renounce their service and condemn my slavery, and come unto Thee to be my Lord. Thy title is just and proper to my soul; it is Thy purchase and, therefore, the service of it belongs to Thee. Thy precepts and commands are righteous and holy, therefore doth Thy servant make choice of Thee, and love them. Thou wouldst have my heart, my will, my affections, my life, and who should have them but Thyself. Upon Thee do I bestow myself, and most gladly do I consent to Thy holy will, and resign up all the strength and powers of all that I am, or have, or can do, to the service and honor of Thee. Though sin rages, yet I will serve Thee; though the world frowns or fawns, yet I will serve Thee; though Satan tempts, yet I will serve Thee.

"My heart I bestow on Thee as well as my safeties.

My service I bestow on Thee as well as my hopes. Thy honor I desire sincerely to intend; my love I set on Thee. My fear is of Thee, my greatest care shall be to obey Thy will, and my only joy is to bring Thee glory."

Such a choice of Christ to be our Lord infallibly argues that sin does not have dominion, forasmuch as this cannot be without the change of the heart and whole man, which change cannot consist with sin's dominion.

2. If sin and we are enemies, then sin is not our lord. Sin is an enemy two ways. Either really: thus it is an enemy to him who yet dearly loves and faithfully serves it. Though it gives unto a man the wages of unrighteousness (many sinful pleasures and many sinful profits) yet, in all these, sin is an enemy to the person. It works his soul off from God, happiness, and holiness, and exposes it to death and hell.

Or sin is an enemy practically: thus sin is an enemy when a man looks upon it, and deals with it as with an enemy. He judges it as a vile thing, and hates it, and abhors it as the only evil thing, an enemy to his soul. Beloved, when sin has dominion, there is then a confederacy between it and the soul, the prophet calls it "a covenant", and the Apostle calls it a contract, or espousal or marriage; that is, such an agreement and conjunction where the soul bestows its choicest love on sin. But when the dominion of sin goes off, then the covenant is broken, the knot is dissolved, and the affection of love is displaced. As it was in another case, Amnon's love turned to the cruelest hatred.

So here, though a man loves his sins, yet now his

love is changed into hatred, and this hatred infallibly argues the indominion of sin; for:

Hatred includes separation. It is such a quality as draws off the soul. Love is that which draws the soul towards its object, and hatred is that which draws it off. "Get thee hence," said they in Isaiah 30:22. And "what have I to do any more with idols?" said Ephraim in Hosea 14:8.

Now sin's dominion consists in the cleaving and united subjection of the affections. The soul makes sin its center unto which it wholly inclines. It and the soul are one when sin reigns, and, therefore, the separation of the affections (which is done by hatred) argues that the yoke is broken asunder.

Again, hatred includes perfect opposition. The greatest defiance, contradictions, and warrings arise from hatred. We oppose and cross most where we hate most. And this cannot be where sin has dominion, for there our weapons are edged, for we love our lusts much, and defend them most, and are careful to preserve and keep them.

Hatred inclines to destruction. Ruin is the scope of hatred. We seek the death of him whom we hate, and all the evil which befalls a person hated is the joy of him who hates. So is it where sin is hated. A man seeks the death of sin and, therefore, such persons as hate sin are said in Scripture to mortify the flesh and crucify their lusts; that is, the killing, subduing, and rooting out of sin is that which they desire and endeavor. Now this cannot stand with sin in dominion; where a man is so far from offering any deadly violence to his reigning sins that he reputes him as the greatest enemy who draws forth any crucifying weapons and applies them to the casting down of his strong holds.

3. If holiness or grace has our love, then sin does not have dominion over us. Beloved, it is granted that:

The dominion of sin may consist with the naked profession of holiness. A hypocrite (whose heart is in the deepest, most affectionate and elaborate service of some one particular lust), he may yet wear the livery, garb, and profession of greatest sanctity. Nay, he therefore seems good that he may (the more inobservably and fully) follow his sin.

The dominion of sin may consist with the knowledge of holiness. As great parts and intellectual speculations of holiness may depend upon foreign causes without grace (namely, upon mere study and frequent hearings, and a natural desire of knowing, and looking into all intelligible objects, and also on a humour of pride, that a man will be accountable to say something in every thing); I say, as those intellectual parts may depend upon weak and vain causes, so they may consist with an ardent love of reigning corruptions; for learning does not alter the nature, nor does more knowledge overthrow sin. A man may be a learned sinner and, by his knowledge, grow more accurately and inexcusably sinful.

The dominion of sin may consist with some visible actings of holiness. A man may be a traitor when he yet seems to do something of the service to a prince. So sin may be a man's lord though he does many things which seem good. Herod loved Herodias, though he heard John the Baptist and did many things gladly. There is scarcely any man (where Christ is professed) who is so universally bad but he may (now and then) do something which may be particularly good, at least materially considered.

But yet, fourth, the dominion of sin cannot consist with the love of holiness for, where sin is in dominion, there sin has the love of the soul. Now it is impossible for a man to love sin and to love holiness. I grant that many things may be the object of love, though there are a numerical variety of them, yet there may be an objective unity. They may all meet in one common reason and natural course of love and, therefore, may be loved. But then opposite and contradictory things cannot be both loved at once. The reason is because you cannot reconcile them into an objective unity. That which is a reason of love in one is a reason of hatred in the other. Now sin and holiness are opposite; they are at the greatest distance in spiritual contradictions. Their natures, courses, and effects all are opposite, so that a man cannot, at once, posssibly love them both. And, therefore, if holiness and grace have your love, truly sin does not have dominion.

I must not insist at large on this, only observe whether you love holiness precisely and purely for itself. What is it you esteem most? Which do you desire most? Is the lack of it your greatest grief? Is the prosperity of it, either in yourself, or others, a true and singular joy unto you? At what pains are you to purchase and increase it? What are your thoughts of them who are holy? Of those ministers who edge and work on your heart most unto holiness? These and such like things will show whether you love holiness which, if you do, then sin is not your lord.

4. A fourth trial is this: whose laws do you approve and delight in? According as a man's lord is, so are his laws; and according as the man is, so is his mind and affections towards those laws of the lord. You shall find that when sin has dominion, there sin has several laws, several commands, the obedience of which is delightful to the sinner; and, therefore, such a one is said to fulfill the lusts of the flesh, to commit sin with greediness, Ephesians 4:19. and to yield himself over unto sin.

Thus it is on the contrary. Where sin is broken off from its dominion and Christ rules the heart, His laws have a marvelous suitableness with the spirit of that man. His law is written in their heart, that is, there is a powerful and answerable inclination stamped in the heart which gives way to the command. "In the volume of Thy book it is written of me, that I should do Thy will; lo, I come," Psalm 40:7-8. "I delight to do Thy will, O my God, yea, Thy law is in my heart. Thou saidst, Seek ye my face, my heart said unto Thee, Thy face Lord will I seek," Psalm 27:8. "Lord, what wilt Thou have me to do?" Acts 9:6.

OBJECTION. It is true that sinful corruption (yet abiding in the best) will make head against the holy commands of Christ, it will be backward enough, cross enough, unwilling enough, resisting and striving.

SOLUTION. But yet three things will more habitually appear in a person whose soul is governed by Christ and not by sin.

One is approbation, that is, his judgment highly

esteems the commands of Christ. Paul counted the commandment holy, righteous, good, and tending to life, Romans 7:12.

Another is consent, that is, his will yields unto it as to a rule most fit to be obeyed, "I consent unto the law that it is good," Romans 7:16, and, therefore would obey it.

A third is inward delight. Romans 7:22, "I delight in the law of God after the inward man." The Apostle from this (though he found a contrary law in his members warring against the law of his mind, and much evil present when he would do any good) concludes against sin's dominion. Romans 7:25. "So then with the mind I myself serve the law of God, but with the flesh the law of sin."

Why, brethren, this is a great matter, and a great discovery of our hearts, to observe what law that is with which we take part; which we set up as our rule, whose authority we justify. Sin will command in him who hates it, that is, it will be prescribing to our affections and our actions, but then if Christ rules us, we war against those commands, we resist them, we defy them, we pray against them, we take no part in them. We acquit that law of Christ which we would follow, but sometimes cannot (as fully as we should). We justify it as a most righteous command, and strive to conform our hearts to that, and to order our lives by that.

5. A fifth trial may be this, what is the disposition and course of our hearts under the passive captivities of our souls by particular sinnings?

There is a twofold captivity of the soul to sin.

One is active, wherein a man (as Ahab) sells

himself to wickedness, or as Judas, who offered himself to betray Christ (he went to the high Priest, "what will you give me, and I will betray Him").

Another is passive, wherein (as Paul complained) he is sold under sin, like a soldier overpowered and by strength taken captive and led away prisoner. I confess that this is most true, and a good man may sin, nay, he does sin. Sin may have many particular victories where yet it does not have a kingdom or dominion. As there may be antecedent differences before sin is committed, and as there may be concomitant differences when sin is committed (which may be as so many lively testimonies against dominion), so there are consequent differences.

Three Things That Show Sin Does Not Have Dominion Though it Prevails and Overcomes

There are some things afterward which show that yet sin does not have dominion, though it did prevail and overcome.

Three things:

1. One is hearty grief. Though a good man does not always have sufficient strength to conquer a temptation, yet he has sufficient grace to bewail his sinnings. Though he cannot always rejoice that he stands, yet he can heartily grieve that he falls. Either sin is his conquest or else it is his sorrow. Though you do not see David cast down by his pleasures, yet you shortly see him cast down himself by his mournings. Though you see Peter untrusty to his master, yet you shall presently find him bitterly weeping for

his miscarriage. Whereas the servants of sin do the work and take the wages, they sin and rejoice when they have done evil: but the servants of righteousness actively afflict their hearts, for that which has deceived and prevailed upon them.

OBJECTION. It is granted that terror may grip an evil heart for evil doing, but there is a great difference between a sword which wounds and a fountain that runs.

SOLUTION. Conscience may be wounded in the good and in the bad but, besides this, acted sins are a good man's wound, they are also his great grief of soul.

2. Another is earnest desire of recovery. It is a singular and observable matter, when a man has sinned, to whom he holds out his hand upon it. The servant of sin works sin, and his hand stretches itself out as a servant still, ready to advance and finish the service. Sin is his work and delight; it is the lord and captain after which he would yet march. But a holy man (not under dominion, but surprisal; not under service, but captivity) is not himself till he has recovered his liberty and strength. There is such a high displeasure with himself and with his facts, that he will go free; he will not have his ear bored to serve such a master as sin.

Good Lord! How his heart trembles, how his heart meditates, casts about, works, strives. Sometimes he cries out, "Ah wicked, ah deceitful heart!" Sometimes he condemns himself, "What a beast was I thus to sin?" Sometimes he looks up toward heaven and sighs bitterly, "Ah! What a God have I provoked? What mercies have I wronged?" Sometimes he looks

in and weeps, and says, "Ah! What motions did I
withstand? What a spirit have I grieved? How unlike
myself is myself?"

Sometimes he is down in prayer, "O Lord forgive,
blot out, heal, help, recover my heart again unto
Thee." One way or another his soul is working like a
fountain in which dirt is cast, till it has purged out
the filth. He is not at rest till sin is more subdued,
his heart more changed, his affections more preserved, his peace more confirmed, his soul not only
recovered but also bettered. Yea, thus it will be with
such a heart (which makes it clear that sin does not
have dominion) that, though sin prevail to action,
yet it shall not to affection. "Though I did the evil,
yet I hate it; though it prevailed, yet I will not serve it;
though it has beat me down as a tyrant, yet I will not
follow it as my lord. Nay, I am not at quiet till I can
recover the sight of my Lord Christ again, and have
made my peace, and strengthened my heart for
more loyal service unto Him."

3. The third is strong hatred and conflict. The
war is more increased; by victory, revenge is more
raised, 2 Corinthians 7.

SECTION V

A second use from David's prayer against the dominion of sin shall be for thankfulness to such in
whom this dominion is broken off.

Though there is so much of sin remaining as
may keep you humble and watchful, yet if dominion
is gone there is so much done as may challenge you

to be heartily thankful. Give me leave to put on this a little.

Six Reasons to be Thankful for Being Delivered From the Dominion of Sin

1. Deliverance from the greatest evil is reason enough for great thanks. It is more than if God had delivered you from hell if He has delivered you from the dominion of sin. No hell is like sin reigning forasmuch as torment in strength is nothing to sin in strength. That is indeed a very miserable thing, but this is a very evil thing. Sin is worse than all punishment, and reigning sin is the worst of all sin.

2. None but God could deliver you and, therefore, if He has done it, bless Him. A man may deliver his friend out of prison by paying his debt; a father may deliver his child out of captivity by sending his ransom; a country may be delivered from the oppression of an invading tyrant by great strength of its own. But there are two hands out of which none but God can deliver: one is Satan's, another is our own. As David spoke in another case, "Thou hast loosed the bands of my distress," and "it is the Lord who subdueth the people under me," and "it is not my bow nor my sword." That is what I am saying here. It is not your own arm which has gotten you the victory. It is no other hand but God's high hand which has delivered you from the powers of darkness, which has kept sin from dominion, which has cast out the strong man, which has cast down the strongholds. You were not so much as sensible of

your own vassalage, or of sin's dominion; you did not have the power to feel, much less to conquer and deliver. And when you were sensible of sin, your heart did not behave itself as an enemy, but as a friend most willingly bowing under the yoke, readily embracing the lusts and motions of the law of sin when you have been called upon to put off the yoke, and to come out of the house of bondage.

The Hebrew servant (who loved his master) was never more unwilling to part from his house than your heart was to come off from your love and service of your sins. And yet the Almighty God (in compassion to your soul) has delivered you. He has dethroned sin, He has drawn off your heart to a better lord, and would not suffer sin to rule you. By the mighty power of His grace, He has made you free from the house of most heavy bondage.

Therefore, not to your good nature, nor to your free-will, nor to your abilities, nor to your wit, or parts, or reason, but to the Lord be all the glory. The victory is His; therefore let the praise be His.

3. It is special grace and mercy. Paul calls it rich mercy, great love, and riches of grace, Ephesians 2. It is mercy to be rid of a disease, more a mercy to be rid of a sin. To resist a temptation, much more to take off dominion, the spirit of Christ alone does it. The more singular a mercy is, the more thankful should we be. Titus 3:3-5, "We ourselves also were sometimes foolish, disobedient, deceived, serving divers lusts and pleasures. But after that the kindness and love of God our Saviour toward man appeared... According to His mercy He saved us."

"Thou hast in love to my soul delivered it from

the pit of corruption," said Hezekiah, Isaiah 38:17.
Oh, then, what a mercy is it to be delivered from the
power of sinful dominion! If you were rid of a hard
master, that would seem a mercy; if of a cruel tyrant,
that would seem a mercy; if of a desperate enemy, if
of bonds, if of sickness. What, then, is it to be rid of
the rule of sin, which is infinitely worse than all
these!

4. No lord is so bad, and no commands so vile, as
those of sin in dominion. Therefore, bless God for
your deliverance, you whose souls are (through the
mighty graciousness of a good God) rescued from
the powers of darkness. Tell me, what are your
thoughts, what are your judgments, what are your
troubles for the workings of your vanquished enemy? If the weakened corruptions appear yet so vile,
what were your reigning corruptions? If sin is so
monstrous unto you now only in temptation, what
was it heretofore in dominion? If the finger is so
heavy, what were the lions? If a particular action (as
you imagine) exposes you so dangerously, what does
the service of sin do? Under what displeasures of
wrath lay your souls, when sin had fullest affection
and complete obedience?

Rebekah seemed weary of her life because of the
presence of the daughters of Heth. If the presence
created such an affliction, what might the conjunction and union have done? Verily, if sin is (as it is)
bad and troublesome in combat, oh, it is infinitely
worse in the throne and absolute empire over the
soul, wherein every faculty serves it with all its
strength and madly strives how to dishonor God. It
breaks His law and resists His spirit to fulfill lusts,

please the devil, and damn the soul.

Oh, bless the Lord for His goodness to you, that yet the dominion of sin is put off. 'Tis true, corruption yet remains, but yet it remains not as a lord but as a tyrant; not as a king but as an enemy. Time was that sin had your love, but now you hate it. Time was that sin had your mind to devise for it, but now those imaginations are cast down. Time was that your will was espoused to sin, but now a divorce is sued out. Time was that your members were ready enough to fulfil the lusts of the flesh, but now they are made servants of righteousness. Time was that you sold yourself to wickedness, and were never so joyful as when you were sinful, but now it is not so. You are a drudge, a slave, a vassal no longer. Your former ways amaze you, and the present commands of sin are an affliction to you. O bless the Lord!

5. Again, if the dominion of sin is off, then assuredly the sceptre of Christ is set up in your soul. Beloved! The soul stands not, abides not in a middle estate; it must have one lord or other. It is necessarily under some one dominion (either of sin or of Christ) and this know, that the dominion of sin cannot be taken off in the soul but by a contrary, by a better, by a stronger dominion, but that of Christ who dispossesses the strong man. It is He who has changed your heart, who has made your heart to change its master, who has drawn off your love, your service.

Now, no dominion in the world is like that of Christ.

None so holy. He is holy, He loves holiness, and all His commands are righteous.

None so gracious. He does not exact beyond what He gives, and will yet mercifully pardon our true endeavors of service wherein they fall short.

None so peaceable. His very service is a kind of wages to the obedient. A vassal to sin is like a man laboring all day about thorns and nettles (the more abundance of them grasped by him galls him with the more wounds and pains). No man can be long cheerfully sinful. Either terror or fear accompanies most sinnings; but the service of Christ has warrant from the Word and peace of conscience.

None so assisted. His commands are accompanied with strength and spirit. He bids us to do the work, and gives us His own hand thereto, imposes duty, and imprints ability, writes the law to the ear, and writes it also in the heart.

None so rewarded. No man serves Christ too much or for nought. Though all our work is but duty, yet He pays us rich wages. We owe unto Christ all our strength and the use of all our graces. Neither do we bring in so much of these in full service as we should, yet our good Lord and Master will give us (if we are faithful servants) at night our penny, and at the last our crown.

6. Last, be thankful, for if dominion is off, then damnation is off. "There is no condemnation (said Paul) to them that are in Christ Jesus, who walk not after the flesh but after the Spirit," Romans 8:1. A man is not damned merely because he has sin (for then no man could be saved, for who is he that sins not?), but because sin is his lord, and he is the servant of sin. Not so much because he is bad, but because he will be bad, not only for the act, but for the

love. 'Tis confessed that guilt is as natural to sin as
the shadow is to the body. No man can sin at any
time, in any thing, and yet be innocent. But meritorious guilt is one thing, and redounding guilt is another thing. If the dominion of sin is broken off
(that a man loves not sin, but hates it; yields not up
himself unto it, but resists it; is not in league, but in
conflict with it) then the estate of guilt is taken off
so that it shall not effectually redound to the condemnation of the person. Where God powerfully
subdues the sinful nature, there He will mercifully
pardon and discharge the unwillingly sinning and
offending person. If sin is not your lord, then hell
shall not be your portion. He who is become an enemy to his sins, grace rules in his heart now, and
glory shall crown his soul hereafter.

OBJECTION. But will some troubled and, therefore, unably discerning soul reply, "We doubt it not,
but that it is a most singular mercy, a rich grace,
worthy of greatest acceptance and heartiest thanks,
where the dominion of sin is broken off. But, alas,
we fear it is not so with us. We have heavy cause to
suspect that we are captives yet under sin's dominion, so that, though others can happily observe the
yoke broken off, and therefore can be cheerfully
thankful, we find it yet strong, Oh, very strong, and
therefore more reason have we of grief and sorrow."
    Beloved, it is granted that, if a man finds himself
indeed under the dominion of any sin, assuredly he
has peculiar cause of great humblings, speediest re-
formings, vehement beggings at the throne of grace
for mercy, and for the mighty power of Jesus Christ

to release and deliver his soul. But then let us carefully observe whether this of which a man complains is sin in dominion or not. Perhaps it may be something else, and then the soul must be advised and directed in a more especial way.

"Why, I find such strong and manifold inclinations of sin within me, daring forth into so many imaginations, and working down to draw my affections. Woe is me! What is the dominion of sin but this? And who but a slave of sin is hurried with such motions of sin? It cannot be that my heart should be good while inclinations are so manifoldly bad."

To this, let me shape a few answers.

First, I demand how the heart stands affected toward these manifold inclinations? Do you approve them or disallow them? Do you love them or do you hate them? Verily (says the soul) I dislike them and hate them; they are the burden of my soul. And why so? Because God is dishonored by them, and they are contrary to His holy will, and they are evil and filthy. Oh, I would rather be in any miserable estate than in this sinful and vile estate!

Now then observe, sin does not have dominion in you for, where sin has dominion, sin is not formally and purely hated.

The dominion of sin does not consist in the multiplicity of motions. A man may have many enemies to assault him, and yet love and serve none. So a man may have many sins inclining and tempting, and yet be a servant to none of them; for it is not the temptation of sin which infallibly argues dominion, but the willing resignation of the heart. The subjection of the heart to those motions and temptations of sin is required to make dominion. But now your heart does not do so. It does not resign up itself, it does not yield subjection; forasmuch as it hates, resists, and bewails sin even in temptation.

Of all the signs of a good heart (of a heart that is delivered from sin's dominion), this is one of the best and surest. It hates, resists, and bewails sin, even when it is only in temptation. When a man has committed a sin, then the conscience (being made guilty) may alone break and afflict, and this may befall even a wicked man. There is now some other thing besides sin in the filthiness of it to work trouble and grief, which is the guilt and accusation of it; but when sin is resisted and bewailed in the temptation before it has got out into actual commission, now the peculiar reason of trouble is the formal vileness of sin because it is so base, and so opposite to God.

Second, I demand, what do you do against these sinful inclinations? Every man has some weapons or other and, in case of anguish, he is apt to draw them. What weapons do you have in your hand? And to what end do you manage them? Do not many and strong temptations of sin occasion many and strong supplications? The more that sin inclines, the more does your heart incline to God by prayer for more grace to resist, for more strength to subdue.

Do you not, by reading and inquiry, labor to find out the manifold helps and victories of a tempted and an assaulted soul? Do you not keep the precepts of God in your heart, and the threatenings of God in your heart, so that you may fear to offend Him, and the promises of God which yet hearten you to withstand? What does all this demonstrate, but that sin is not in dominion? It is, I confess, your troublesome enemy, but it is not your ruling lord. It is that which molests you, it is not that which reigns in you; it is that which would have dominion, but it is not that which has dominion. It is that which assaults your affection, but it is not that which has your heart. You are but in a greater war. Nevertheless, you are not so much as in captivity, though in a strong conflict.

QUESTION. Yea, but yet I feel one thing perhaps worse than all this. Sin works in me after a more peculiar manner; there is a particular sinful inclination in me, and so has it been all my days. If I were to give you the sum of my life, I could lay out that particular inclination above all the rest like a thread which goes through the whole piece, such a sin, which I have seen long since and felt it, and (I thought) bewailed it, and resisted it a long time, and yet here it lives still, works still. Can it be that sin should not have dominion where some one special corruption yet lives?

I must be warily tender to resolve this question, forasmuch as:

Particular subjection is enough to set up dominion.

Hypocrites are under the reign of special lusts and particular sins, which I touched heretofore, but to the question I will give four answers.

ANSWER 1. When God converts the soul, no one sinful inclination is totally removed, though every one is in some measure changed. The corrupt nature yet remains, and all its principles, or particular inclinations to particular sins; for grace does not change us by a present annihilation of sin, but by a powerful alienation of our hearts from it.

ANSWER 2. Note that sin may work (even in a man rescued out of its dominion) in a more singular or particular way. My meaning is this, there may be in him yet a more particular twang, and more apt inclination and propension, to some one sin rather than another. Sin (yet abiding) may take the advantage of the same complexion still remaining, and of the same condition and calling yet continuing; and, without all doubt, most men living, whether good or whether bad, find more to do with some one sinful inclination than with another.

ANSWER 3. Consider that, usually, that particular inclination which was in dominion before conversion is most frequent in inclination after our calling. And I will give you some probable reasons thereof.

One is because that was the spring of the sin of our custom which sent out and fed the issue, by which the soul was so beaten in the path and way of sinning, so that the old and accustomed nature cannot easily or presently forget its ancient and wonted bents. A custom will hardly or never go off without some after inclinations or dispositions that way.

Another is because the new resistances of a converted heart, and its cares and studies, are most against the particular sin of its special inclinations. There it deals most, opposes most, humbles most. Now sin usually stickles and stir most where it is most pursued. That particular sin, whose death you lay at most, will strive to assail and perplex and entangle you most. The more humble you labor to be, the more shall you find proud thoughts to assault, though not to conquer you. The more meek you labor to be, the more ado shall you have with your passions, forasmuch as no sin will be executed quietly, and every nature stirs busily in its own defense. We are weakest there, and God draws our greatest watch and strength thither. A man sooner falls under lesser conflicts. When a sin has been beaten upon by much temptation and conflict, the heart grows thereby more ready and resolute. And you shall find that, after frequent and long exercise with a particular corruption, it shall not easily get within the soul, but upon a pause and cessation.

ANSWER 4. Observe that there is a difference between the life of motion and the life of affection. It is true, your special inclination lives in you still by way of motion, but does it live in you still by way of affection? It inclined heretofore, and you loved it; it inclines now and you hate it. The inclination is the same for the matter, but your heart is not the same for the disposition toward it. When the iron is hot, you may bring a figure and put it on, and the iron will take the stamp and impression. Bring the same figure and seal to it when it is cold, and it will not receive it. The seal, and the figure of the seal is the same, but the temper and the disposition of the iron is not the same. Ambrose relates the story of the young traveller who went out an unclean person but returned a chaste person; and his old strumpet met with him after his return, and began her wanton salutes unto him, which he angrily turned aside, neglecting her. "Why," said she, "it is I!"

"Yes, but," said he, "I am not me!" I am not; so is it here in this case. The inclination is the same to the same sin, yea, but the affection is not now to that inclination as it has been. But where sin has dominion, affections concur with the special inclination.

Take all that I shall say to this in a few words:

It is certain that in an evil man there is a frequency in a particular inclination, and so there may be in a good man, but they differ as follows.

In an evil man, the frequent inclination is the frequent progress of a king; in a good man, it is the fervent egress or attempt of an enemy.

In an evil man, the frequency of inclination is to maintain possession; in a good man, it is but a malicious endeavor by force (if it were possible) to regain an entrance.

This is some comfort that, though the assault is frequent, yet the resistance is constant, and that concludes against sin's dominion.

Not the frequency of inclination, but the ardency of subjection evidences sin's dominion; not who quarrels with me most, but he who effectually commands me is my lord. Not he who makes the most motions, but he on whom the woman casts her heart is the husband. It is the love and service which infallibly concludes dominion.

OBJECTION. But yet the soul sticks, "I am sold under sin and taken captive. Sin has inclined and prevailed, what surer argument of dominion can there be than victory?"

There are three things which I would say to this

question:

ANSWER 1. It is a very sad question. Any particular victory of any great sin (for to that I intend the case) makes a wonderful change.

ANSWER 2. Comfort cannot be applied, neither will the conscience receive it, till repentance is renewed.

ANSWER 3. Yet there is a difference between a particular victory, and the dominion of sin. There may be a surprisal where yet a kingdom is not established.

For the first of these, all particular victories are sad things. I do not now speak of victories in respect of inward motion, or of passion or distemper through dullness and melancholy, but of victory in respect of action; and that not by mere omission, not by imperfection in best services, but by gross commissions. Suppose it in David's case or Noah's case; the one for uncleanness, the other for drunkenness. These acted wickednesses are sore evils, very abominable to the Lord, very inglorious to religion, very wounding to conscience, extremely quenching of the spirit of grace.

Forasmuch as the more gross any sin is, the worse is it in the commission, every acting of sin receiving some intention and aggravation, from the immediate kind and quality of the sin.

Again, the better the man is, the worse is a lewd kind of sinning in him, the quality of the person ever contributing more exceedingness to the sin; for he sins against more light, against more mercy, against more help and strength, against more active corrections of conscience, with more advantage to the corruption of other men, with more disadvantage to the beauty and credit of holiness. Yea, besides these former vilenesses, Oh, what strange effects break in upon the soul, what horror, what fear, what misgivings, what despair often times with the fruits thereof!

For the second, comfort will never be applied to a person in this condition until repentance is renewed.

Beloved, there is a difference of persons, a difference of actions, a difference of times, and a difference of applications.

Do I find an evil man brought to the sight of his sins, to saddest humbling for them, to sincere desire to come off from them, to pantings after grace and mercy? I now come in with the blood of Christ, with the tender and gracious promises refreshing such a soul with assurance of freest and fullest mercy. Do I find a good man, weak in duty, strong in affection, hearty against all sin, yet troubled with the insolent motions of many corruptions; one who would not do evil, and yet is not rid of it; one who would do good, but then finds evil is present with him? I labor to raise and hold up such a heart to look on God through Christ for acceptance, to lay hold on Christ for strength, for life, for power, for victory.

Do I find a good man weakening himself, bowing under the actual power of some viler lust? O beloved, comfort is not his medicine, but repentance! Comfort is not his first help, but godly sorrow. Sorrow is the work which belongs to a sinner, and comfort that which belongs to a penitent sinner. Until you thoroughly humble your soul, till you

bewail mightily your wickedness, till your heart is
turned into extreme loathing of your sin, and yourself for so sinning, you shall not get a good look
from God, a good word from conscience, any favorable encouragement from the ordinance. Yea, well it
is if, after many years, that ever you see God in that
way of graciousness and free communion as you formerly found him. However, be sure of it, without repentance you shall not at all meet with any solid
comfort.

Third, nevertheless, there may be some differences between particular victories and dominion.
Though dominion is a victory, yet every victory does
not conclude dominion. They may be thus distinguished in respect of their subjects, namely, good
men in whom sin has sometimes a victory, and evil
men in whom sin has at all times a dominion.

Five Differences Between
Dominion and Victory

1. Particular victory depends upon inequality of
actual strength, but dominion depends upon the
fulness of a corrupt nature.

There is in all holy men a habitual strength,
which is seated in the new nature of grace or holiness, by which they are inclined to all good, and
their hearts made averse to all evil. It is the natural
temper of true grace thus to work, and then there is
an actual strength by which, when any particular
good is proposed, they incline unto the obedience
of it. And when any particular evil is objected, they

strive against it and resist. Now it may fall out that, when a temptation presents itself and inward corruption works with that temptation, it may so fall out that the strength of grace may be insufficient. It may not actually equal or exceed that vehement and actual strength of inclination and temptation; though it does resist (as a weak man may a strong enemy), yet it may not be able to conquer but is surprised and led captive. And here the fall depends, not on the disposition of the will or heart, but upon the impotency of resistance. The person does not fall down, but is beaten down. The sin is acted not through choice, but through weakness; not because the person loves it, but because he is not able to conquer the temptation. But, where sin has dominion, there the sinning comes from the heart as a stream from the fountain. It is natural and not violent. It is acted, not because a man is not able to make sufficient resistance, but because the heart is wholly set that way with fullest complacence.

2. Particular victory is a sudden act, but dominion is a more sober work. In the one the soul is surprised; it is hurried, it is precipitated, it is in a flame on a moment. A man does not have space to weigh, to judge, to consider; but sin has, with marvelous quickness, seized on the understanding, wrought upon the memory, struck into the affections, and is driven on in a rash and passionate way. In the other, the work is more sober, not only actively devised, but affectionately adhered unto. A natural strength of corrupt and living affection makes the one; and inadvertency and rashness may be sufficient to cause the other. That arises for lack of watchfulness (as a

camp may be so surprised by an enemy); this arises out of a sworn obedience, as the soldier follows his captain.

3. Where the sinning owes itself not to dominion, but to particular victory or tyranny; there the person, when he comes to himself, feels the yoke and would shake it off. It is true that, while the heat of corruption remains, and the force of temptation yet disables the heart to recollect itself, it is most difficult for any person to distinguish. Neither is he then come to scruple and question. But when things grow clearer in the judgment, and more calm in the affections, when the hurry and tempest is off, then a man beholds his own face, ways, and actions in a right glass again. Now it will quickly appear whether it is tyranny or dominion. If it is but a tyrannical victory? Ah! How the soul loathes itself; how it abominates the sinner, like a man captivated and rowing as a forced slave in the galley, he would cut the throat of the master; or like a man in prison, he would make his escape with the death of him, who was too strong to keep him. But if it is dominion, then a man will not only serve his master, but plead for him. He desires not to escape; he loves his master, and would dwell with him for ever.

4. Therefore, if it is but victory, the person is not only troubled at his fall, not only loathing of the actions, but he is actively working. He is using his victorious weapons to raise up himself, to free himself again. He is grieved at the bondage, desires liberty, and will fight hard for it.

Oh, the humblings, prayings, workings, and applications of the soul to the sword of the spirit; the

declination of the helps of sin, the contentions with
the motions of lust, the watchings, the meditations.
These things such a heart will use, but where it is
dominion the sin is committed with joy, and the
sinner would continue in it with peace.

It is granted that there may be sometimes some
distemper in such a heart, both before the sinning
and after the sinning, but that before the sinning is
raised only upon carnal grounds because of subsequent shame, loss, prejudice; and that after the sinning is only judicial, just throes of an accusing conscience, of which when the vile slave of sin hath got
free, when the cry of the world is off, and when the
cry of his conscience is down, he prepares his heart
again for the sin is sad and heavy until he returns to
his vomit and mire. The work goes on again as
freely and as heartily as ever.

5. Last, if it is but particular victory, the soul will
rise again and it will not rise without revenge.
Though the enemy has got the battle, yet he shall
lose the battle before the vanquished soul has done.
It will not only rise, but fight. A naked combat shall
not suffice, but assault and pursuit; it will work with
the art of holy strength to the more deadly offense
of that particular corruption.

OBJECTION. Yet there is a more difficult case
than any which has been already proposed, and that
is renewed actings of the same sin. The person falls
into the same sin again and again, and this repetition of sinful actings seems to be a sin in custom,
and sin in custom is sin in dominion; thus is it with
me, or has it been with me (does some troubled

soul) reply, and therefore my case is miserable.

SOLUTION. To which case divers things must be said.

1. Repetition or renewing of the same sinful act-ings is (without all doubt), a very fearful and abom-inable thing. What is it else but a further and stronger wedging in of the corruption? Frequent actings of sin ever strengthen the sinful nature. Every soul, being made more apt to sin by more sin-nings, what is it else but a widening of sin? The sin grows bigger in the bulk and higher in the guilt by a continued rather than by a single commission.

Now a man sins against that which his own con-science has condemned as well as the pure word of God. Now a man adventures into troubles against all his former trouble. He has felt the sin to be bitter, and knows that it must cost him either hell (into which God may presently cast him) or great sorrow and repentance (which God may judicially deny him). Now a man sins against all the workings of grace, so that God may bring forth all the former acts of the soul and set them against the thus sin-ning person:

"Look, here are the wounds which you made heretofore, and yet you strike into the same again. Here are the tears which you shed for this sinning heretofore, and yet you will provoke Me again. Here are the sighs which your heart broke out; here are the fears which distressed and perplexed your soul. Here are the prayers which you made for your tender mercies; here are the covenants wherewith you bound your soul. Here are the chapters which you read to support yourself; here is the place where you

poured forth your anguished heart in fasting and
crying. Here is that goodness and gracious love of
Mine, whereby I accepted you upon your humbling
tears into favor again. Here is that peace which I
thereupon created, and commanded into your conscience; here is that word which you said should
guide and rule you for the time to come. Here is that
spirit which I sent to raise you again.

"And yet, after all this, you are at the same sin
again. I might have cast you off at first, I might have
shut up My mercies, denied you recovery, avenged
Myself on you for your foul transgression, yet I
spared you. Though you offended Me, yet I recovered
you; though you provoked Me when you did very evil,
even so you admired the wickedness of yourself; yet I
did you good, showed you kindness, would not
presently forsake you, who so foully forsook Me. My
free and great grace then melted you, then moved
you, then excited and stirred you to great sorrow, to
much care and love. And now, after all, you have returned not in inclination, but in action, into not a
little or small transgression, but into a gross and
foul iniquity. Yea, and when multitudes of withdraw-
ing arguments strove against it, when the conception of that sin, being with so much secret trouble
and fear, could not but presage the great dishonor
which would redound unto Me, and the fearful terror which would befall you upon the active commission thereof." So that, beloved, without any question,
a doubling of sin is in itself a more formal intention
thereof in its corrupt nature, and a more fruitful aggravation of it in guilt and miserable consequence.

2. Consider that it is such a way of sinning as may

justly stagger the heart about its condition.

First, in regard of the eminent propriety which it has in persons who thus sin generally (though not absolutely and simply). Three sorts of persons run on in the frequent and manifold actings of great sins, namely, such as are notoriously profane, such as are closely hypocritical, and such as are despitefully opposing the Spirit of grace. These are they who grow from evil to worse, add sin to sin, and make and fill up the measures of their particular iniquities which must needs stagger any soul, though perhaps not yet run on so far as they, if yet repeating steps in the same paths which the vilest of sinners have trod in before it.

Second, in regard of that dark and rare exemplarity of such kinds of sinning by any, in Scripture characterized for saints or godly persons. It is easily admitted that you may spy upon some of the best, something of the worst, and perhaps thickly heaped upon the same sudden passion and temptation; but you shall rarely find any one of them often at the same foul transgression. I say, you shall rarely find it.

And believe me, it will be a staggering case to any sinning heart where its ways are such as to see multitudes of the worst, and scarce any one of good note, so pacing and walking.

Nay, third, until the soul thus sinning bestows infinite labor, strong care, continued humblings, incessant cries, to raise itself again, in respect of any other evidence, it shall hardly or never distinguish the yet secretly remaining, the miserably defaced frame of goodness within it. A soul in this temper is not so much to dispute and question as to rise and work. The case of frequenting or renewing the same sinful acts will never be answered in your conscience, but by fullest humblings, sound judgings, speedy repentings, careful watchings and declinings, wonderful strengthenings of the contrary grace and acts, diligent fear, fervent communion with God, and more upright walking.

Yet fourth, though it is a rare case, this doubling or renewing of some great sinful act (very few good men do it, and that too, very seldom, perhaps as Job spake, so they may do, "Once have I spoken, yea, twice, but I will proceed no further," Job 40:5. I say, though it is rare, yet it is a possible case that sin may have more than one particular victory where yet it does not have dominion.

I do not speak this to hearten any man to sin, for this would argue sin indeed to have dominion, but to recover a man who has sinned, whose soul is extremely bruised with his second fall, and whose second wound bleeds with such sad and bitter dejection of spirit for his renewed folly that this is an argument, that he is not a cheerful and willing servant to sin, but only an enemy, not able enough to bear off a second shock or assault.

OBJECTION. Yet this does not satisfy, for the most still object is custom, and custom cannot be without dominion.

I answer three things:

ANSWER 1. First, suppose the worst, that it was custom and dominion. What is the course to be taken? Would you think it best to hold on? Would

you live thus still? God has pardoned, and He has
changed many a soul which has been customary in
sin, and in whom sin has had dominion. Nay, not
any before conversion, but sin had dominion in
him, and some sin or other was his customary path.
Your safest and wisest course would not be to stick at
the custom and dominion, but to come unto God
and to beseech Him to show you mercy, and to give
you grace to subdue the dominion, and to break the
custom.

ANSWER 2. I think that a custom of sinning is a
direct symptom of sin in dominion. No man can
trade in a sin, but you may easily say, who is his master? His servants we are whom we obey.

ANSWER 3. But then I would have you to remember that as all continuing inclinations do not argue
dominion, so some continued or repeated acts of
sin do not always argue custom. Though custom
necessarily includes, either in good or bad things, a
repetition of acts, a going over of the same part or
lesson again and again, it being a path often walked
over, yet every gemination of acts is not presently a
custom. I think we may thus distinguish between
sinful acts multiplied by custom (which is rooted in
dominion), and those which fall out by accident, as
it were, and rooted only in tyranny.

There are three differences between acts gemi-
nated and custom:

1.) Where the renewed acts of sin owe themselves to custom, there the possession is both strong
and quiet; for (if I mistake not) it is not merely how
often or how long I have been at or have dwelt in the
house which makes custom, and sees me the lord of

that house, but what right, and what peaceable possession. One stronger than I may hold my land from
me, and dwell in my house a long time, yet if I make
my exceptions, and hold a suit against him, his long
dwelling is but an usurping. Neither is it a legal custom, though perhaps of long continuance. Though
sin still dwells in a good soul and continues there in
despite of him and the person oftentimes (through
the captivating force of it) does many sinful acts,
and perhaps the same ones, yet it is not custom unless the possession be quiet and peaceable. If he
bowed, like Issachar, under the burden and yield up
the writings and keys, if he quietly resigned his
heart up to sin, and so went on from sin to sin, this
would be custom and concluded dominion. But as
long as that soul puts in exceptions, prefers a bill of
tears, complaints, supplications to Christ to conquer
this usurping tyrant, to give grace to recover its
hold, and strength to withstand and subdue it,
though the acts are many, and to be bewailed, yet
they are not come to a custom which sets up dominion.

2.) Where the renewed acts are acts of custom,
there the acting is natural and easy. Custom, we
know, is another nature, and every nature easily lets
go its acts. How easy is it for the eye to see, and the
ear to hear, or the water to moisten, or the earth to
descend. Let nature alone, she has no impediment
from herself to her acts; and it is her perfection to
act and, therefore, her acts are easy. It is thus with
sinful acts flowing out of custom; they come from
the heart as waters from a spring and rise from it as
sparks from the fire.

Oh, how nimble, dextrous, and quick is the sinner to sin! You need not tempt him, he can tempt himself; you need not use arguments to persuade and entice him. The accustomed drunkard knows the way, alone, to the cuphouse, and the covetous heart to unlawful methods of gain. Balaam can quickly get on horseback, for money's sake, to curse Israel; and Judas needs no messenger. He can go himself to the high priest. But when the renewed acts depend rather on tyranny than custom, there they come off more hardly with more difficulty; the sin is marred (many times before it is done). The person sees it is vile and resists it, then the pleasure and profit tempt him to which he begins to hearken, but presently his heart misgives him. It is not right, and it will end in bitterness. He prays and yet is tempted, fights and yet is tempted, resists, and yet is vanquished.

3.) Where the renewed acts owe themselves to custom, there a man is not easily broke off. 'Tis by custom, said the man, I cannot help it, and I will not leave it I assure you. Where sinful acts rise to custom, there is no argument, but either a present fear of hell to hold them in, or a mighty presence of grace to put them off. Words will not prevail with men accustomed to sin. But where the renewed acts owe themselves to tyranny; though many words brought into the sin, yet a few words will serve to break off the sin. One whisper of conscience, "Ah, what have you done?"; one word of Nathan's to David, "Thou art the man;" one look of Christ to Peter made him remember and go out and weep bitterly.

SECTION VI

Now I proceed to a third use, which shall be the last that I will make of this subject; and that shall be for direction how to get off the dominion of sin.

You remember that I distinguished heretofore of a two-fold dominion of sin. One was natural, under which every man is held before his conversion; another was actual, which consisted in a particular prevalency, even upon a man converted and changed. According to either, there must be distinct directions.

For this we must consider two things:

First, what keeps and strengthens that dominion.

Second, what may demolish and subdue it, and accordingly apply ourselves.

QUESTION 1. For the first let us enquire what keeps up and strengthens the natural dominion of sin, and accordingly work against it.

SOLUTION. There are four things which do it.

1. One is ignorance. The blindness of the understanding is a principal guard of reigning sin. You read that they, in Ephesians 4:19, "gave themselves over unto lasciviousness to work all uncleanness with greediness." Like a soldier who gives himself up and takes pay, or like a servant who passes away himself to service, so these resigned up their hearts and lives to all uncleanness. It was their delight, it was their work (this showed the dominion of sin), but what was the cause of this? See verse 18, "Their understandings were darkened, through the igno-

rance that was in them, because of the blindness of their hearts." The ignorance of sin kept up their earnestness and practice of sinning.

If ignorance rules the mind, then sin will easily rule the heart. All sinful dominion is enabled by ignorance. The devil is a prince of darkness and takes special care to keep men blind. Antichrist is a son of darkness and, therefore, above all. He sets up his kingdom by ignorance. So is it with sin itself. Its dominion is maintained by blindness in the mind and, therefore, sin in unconverted men makes the mighty opposition against the Word and the means of knowledge. It knows well that no man turns from sin who does not discern it nor hates it, who knows it not. The prisoner is sure enough under a lock, and in the dungeon.

Now then, if ever you would get over this natural dominion of sin, you must get knowledge, a double knowledge in the mind.

One is direct, and that is a distinct and true apprehension of sin just as the Lord reveals it to be, both for its proper nature and genuine effects.

Another is reflexive, that is sinfulness (which God has revealed to be so vile, so abominable, so fearful). It is in you and it is working in you. You are under the powers of darkness; you must come to yourselves; you must fetch your souls unto your souls. If you will not get a sensibleness of sin (and that is begun by knowledge), you will live and die in your sins.

2. A second thing which keeps up the natural dominion of sin is a violent love of sin. Love is the sinew of the heart, yea, it is the chair of state.

Whatever sin sits in it, is the king of the soul, whether grace or sin, for love bestows the heart. What our love is, that our heart is; it makes all to stoop and yield. There is no talk of parting while love remains; I will not go free (said the Hebrew servant), for I love my master. Why? The soul and sin are in a sworn covenant (like David and Jonathan). If the soul loves sin, until you take off the love, you shall never be able to take down the dominion.

Therefore, this shall be another direction: break down the love of sin.

OBJECTION. But how should that be done?

SOLUTION. First, convince the heart that sin is no lovely thing. There are three things which should not fall under our love.

That which is the object of God's hatred. No man may love that which God hates.

That which is the object of God's curse. That cannot be good which He curses and, therefore, is not lovely.

That which is the cause of man's damnation and misery, for no man is to love the cause of his undoing. Now sin is the only thing which God hates, and which God curses, and which will damn a man.

Second, give to your soul a solid and full object of love; find out something which you should love. Is there not a God, a Christ, a Holy Spirit, His Word, heaven? There is no loveliness in sin, and all loveliness in these things.

3. Another thing which keeps up the dominion of sin is error and deceit. There is a lie in every sin, and the judgment is deceived where the sin is retained. Either a man thinks he sins not, but is es-

caped out of the hands of lust, or that his condition is sound and good; or if it be bad, yet not so bad as others; or if very bad, yet he can at pleasure release himself. And thus, through a vain fancy, he continues under the bondage of his corruptions. And so, for the actions of sin, he deceives his soul. He does not behold them in a comparison to the rule; he does not judge them by the Word, but with a reference to his own corrupt desires and delights, which swallow down infinite sins, sugared over by pleasure and profit.

Now if ever you would get free from sin, get your judgments to be cured. A sound judgment may be a good means to breed a sound heart. You will never be persuaded to be good until the erroneous confidence that you are not bad is removed. Convince your mind of these truths against all errors, that indeed you are sinful, and that no sin is little in its merit; and it is not he who is least wicked, but he who is really good, shall be saved. Do not judge of acceptance or disacceptance by sensible pleasures or profits; but beyond these, look what that is which is so colored and disguised. It is even a snare for your life, and that which hunts for the precious soul.

4. A fourth thing which keeps up dominion is custom. The heart, by customary sinning, grows strong in sin and resolute, and is by frequent committings made more naturally sinful, and more apt for further sinful actions.

Now observe a little, give some checks to the ordinary course of sin. "Why," you will say, "it is impossible." Nay, but it is not. Though it is impossible for a man alone to change his sinful heart, yet it is not to check an outward sinful act. A man may choose whether he will go and be drunk, whether he will speak and swear, etc.

OBJECTION. But if it were done, this would be vain and fruitless, for the dominion of sin subsists in the nature, though manifested in the acts.

SOLUTION. I grant it, yet, first, if the heart is brought to set against the sinful acts, it may be brought to set against the sinful nature. Second, the abating of the acts may virtually conduce to the abating of that sinful nature.

QUESTION. What may demolish and break down the natural dominion of sin?

SOLUTION. I will tell you a few things for this, and I pray you to remember them.

1. That which does this must have a greater power than sin, for natural dominion goes not off but by a stronger hand. Satan is not dispossessed but by one stronger than Satan, and we are not translated from the powers of darkness, but by a hand of omnipotency.

2. That which does this must be a contrary nature unto sin, for no kingdom can subsist by division. Let something come into the soul which makes a division and sin will quickly lose its dominion.

3. Again, it must be something which may gain the affections. It must be able to win the heart, to dispose of love and hatred, for dominion is made or marred by one of them.

4. Again, it must be something which may breed a stiff and courageous resolution, that the heart will not serve sin, but will go free. And hereupon,

against all inward and outward opposition, the heart breaks forth into the use of victorious means.

Directions to Break the Dominion of Sin

Now, then, the directions are these:

1. If ever you would get down the dominion of sin, you must look up to God and Christ. They are able to disannul the covenant with sin, and to subdue iniquities. Romans 8:2, "The law of the spirit of life in Christ Jesus hath made me free from the law of sin and death." Look, as it must be a rich mercy which pardons, so it must be a mighty power which conquers sin. Why? But what is it to the Lord to command your heart home to Himself, to cast down the high imaginations and strong holds? As Jehosaphat spoke against those strong armies, "We know not what to do, yet our eyes are upon thee"; so it is in the sense of your natural vileness and sinful dominion. "O Lord, I am bound, I am in bondage, I am dead in sins. Lord, I am unable to escape, but Thou art able to deliver. O deliver my soul for Thy mercies' sake, subdue mine iniquities, and show forth Thy power." "Who shall deliver me, I thank God through Jesus Christ," Romans 7:24-25.

2. Because mere power does not do it, but power in a quality, working through some quality. Therefore, beg God that He would give you the grace of His Spirit. It is true that naked power takes not off the sinful dominion, nor does the quality alone do it; but both can do it. If God gives a man grace, and mightily assists and works by and through that grace, this now will beat down the dominion of sin.

The light, though it is but a little at first, yet assisted by a mighty principle of light, shall conquer darkness. Pride will have dominion till humility comes in.

Now then, beg of God for grace, for His Holy Spirit, for another heart, for a new heart and a new spirit.

3. Labor earnestly for faith. If two things were done, sin could not possibly contine in dominon: if Christ ruled in the soul and if your love were drawn off from sin.

But faith sets up the sceptre of Christ. It will know no Lord but Christ. "My Lord and my God," said believing Thomas. And faith turns the love to Christ, makes Christ the center of the heart. Oh, it represents such goodness, such excellency, such propriety, such bounty, such love in Christ, as enflames the heart and knits it with love to Christ again. Nay, to add to all this, faith bestows the life on Christ too; He died for me, said faith. I judge it, therefore, most reasonable that I should live to him. Now, where Christ comes to rule, and has love and life, there sin, without all doubt, loses its dominion.

4. Last, take a courageous resolution. We are held many times by our lusts through a faintness of spirit. Why, we shall never get down these sins, and what will people say? And we know not what to do! So let us address that question.

OBJECTION. We do not know what to do!
SOLUTION. Why, up and be doing; for what is past, the Lord will mercifully pardon all of it if now the yoke is broken. And be confident of this, if you

are setting against your sins, you do that which God likes very well, for He has commanded it as a duty and has set out means and promised His help and His blessing. Therefore, stand not hovering and halting. "Was I best? Shall I? Shall I yet?" Oh, no, your life lies upon this or your death.

Therefore, resolve on it to set against your sins. Say this to yourself, "If I suffer sin to rule thus, I perish forever; if I get off the dominion, I live forever; if I continue in this sinful estate, I must bid God farewell, Christ farewell, heaven, and all the comforts of my poor soul farewell. I confess I may get a little pleasure by my sins, but I am not sure to enjoy them one moment, and why should I venture eternity of misery for one draught of sinful water? If I could get off sin's dominion, Oh, what a God might I look on, plead with, sue unto? What a Savior should I get? What precious joys? What heavenly consolations? What peace here? What hopes for hereafter? Well, come of it what will, though I have been sinful, I will not still continue so. To God will I come, to Christ will I go. I will beseech them to have mercy upon me a sinner, to give me grace and to change my heart. I will not serve my base lusts any longer, I will never leave praying, hearing, reading, studying, inquiring, working, till I am delivered from this bondage and translated into the glorious liberty of the sons of God."

Thus for directions against the natural dominion of sin.

How to Break Actual Dominion

Now I proceed to some helps against actual dominion, which is the particular prevalency of a sin into act.

Let me premise a proposition or two, and then you shall have the special directions themselves.

1. Actual dominion (I speak in respect of gross acts) is usually in respect of some particular lust which works with more strength in the soul than any other lusts. Though it be most true that in every man there is a universal root of sinning, yet you find it in experience that the multitudes of sinful inclinations, thoughts, and temptations run ordinarily in some peculiar way, with most frequency and violence.

2. Actual dominion is ordinarily by such a sin which has the advantage of a natural complexion and outward condition, occasions, and affections. Upon these does sin set the temptation, as an engineer places his battery upon such a piece of ground which best advantages and furthers his shot against a city.

A man's natural temper and complexion mightily facilitates his acts, and a man's calling or condition of life may (accidentally) be a forcible persuasion to him to much infidelity, impatience, and indirectness. And occasions in conversing, actively or passively, have infinite baits in them; and when our affections may run in some lawful measure and manner, there sin takes occasion to tempt and prevail with ease. If we do not look to it, he may quickly be cast down by a sinful temptation who is already prepared thereunto by a sinful affection.

Therefore, if ever you would keep off the prevalency of a particular sin, observe distinctly and work wisely against all the things which may advantage it in its temptations.

3. Consider that many things may keep back (for a while) the explicit actings of a particular sin which yet are not able to weaken the natural power of the sinful inclination.

There are two sorts of principles (as it were) which have an influence upon a man. Some are violent and forcible, which work by a strong hand, thus far (sometimes) prevailing to hold back so that a man dares not do such an evil (as shame, love of a man's credit, quiet, profit and safety); and some are powerful, too, but yet inwardly weakening the very nature and disposition, as all sorts of graces. Now then, if ever you would be thoroughly kept from the actual dominion of sin, do not content yourselves with merely forcible restraints, forasmuch as these may often times fail you, and then your hearts will deceive you. You will venture to foul iniquities, having nothing now within you of a contrary virtue; but, above all, be striving for grace, which is contrary not only to the sinful acts, but to the sinful nature, which is the fountain inclining the soul unto them. Get chastity into the heart, and meekness into the heart, and humility, and soberness into the heart, and heavenliness, and faith.

4. Improve that strength which God has given unto you every way.

Though this is true, that a man by his natural strength can never change his sinful nature, yet assuredly he may do much against sinful acts if he would bestir himself. Why, is not a man able to deny his eye a look, or his tongue a word, and his feet a walk? You know this, that sin is set on fire by occasions, and by many things which lie directly under our power, and it may be much stayed by the doing of many things which we are able to do. If a man will let his eyes still roll upon vain objects, whereas (if he would) he might check their motion, no marvel if his heart is still set on fire by lust; and if he will associate himself with persons provoking him to filthiness and drunkenness (whereas, if he would, he might decline that society), who can think it strange that such sins should have actual dominion over him? If you will, you may read, hear, and apply yourself to all the means by which grace may be wrought and sin subdued; and if you did so, who can tell what God may do for your soul?

Nay, let me tell you more, that if a man who has received grace (and therefore more power than a natural man) will not improve his strength, he shall hardly keep off the actual dominion of some one sin or other. If he will not decline that which he should and may, and if he will not do that which he should and can, it is not his naked praying that will keep him up. Prayer (without all question, as you shall hear by and by) is of singular force and use against the prevalency of all corruptions; but we must not rest only upon the prayer, but pray and work, pray and forbear, pray and deny ourselves, pray and shun occasions, pray and follow our help, etc.

FOUR SPECIAL DIRECTIONS AGAINST THE ACTUAL DOMINION OF A PARTICULAR LUST

Now I come unto some special directions against the actual dominion of a particular lust.

1. *Preserve in your soul a constant and humble fear, and that will keep off the actual dominion of your sin.* Remember Solomon's advice, "Blessed is the man that feareth always," Proverbs 28:14. And God's promise, "I will put My fear within them, and they shall not depart from Me," Jeremiah 32. Without this, you are gone; you will quickly lose your standing if you lose your fear.

There are some graces which are, as it were, the guard of other graces. Look, as faith is a grace which feeds all the rest, so fear is a grace which keeps all the rest. This holy and humble fear has these properties (all which strengthen the soul against actual dominion of sin). It has God still in eye; it sets a man, his ways, and acts in the presence of a holy and glorious God. Joseph said, "How can I do this great evil and sin against God?" Genesis 39.

Again, it prefers God's pleasure and God's frown above all encouraging or discouraging temptations. Yea, but I must do this, for God requires it and delights in it; yea, but I may not do this, for God hates it and will be provoked by it. I prefer His favor above all false honor and pleasure, and I account His frowns worse than death itself. Now if I should thus sin, why, I provoke His wrath, and provoke the Lord to jealousy. I cause Him to rise in displeasure against me. Why, how would the Lord take it if I should thus sin?

2. *Get a sound and uncorrupt judgment.* There are
three cases in which a man is apt to fall under the
actual dominion of sin, and corruption of judgment is a main cause of them.

One is when he thinks or says that the sin is little.

Another is when he says that his own strength is
great.

A third is when he assures himself of easy pardon
and recovery. Sin is usually a cloud and then a
shower, a corruption in the judgment before a victory in the affections. A man will quickly tremble
under the guilt of some great commission who has
dallied with little sins, or with the opinion that they
are so. And he who ventures far unto any occasions,
upon his own strength, bids fair for some foul fact,
under which he shortly falls if God shows him not
the vanity of his self-confidence. And so is he ready,
very ready for a gross transgression, who has secured
his soul already for his pardon. What sin will he
stick at who has persuaded himself that the pardon
is already granted, although he presumes to sin?

Now, cleanse the judgment of these corrupt principles and believe it that no sin is little. That must
be great which provokes a great God and endangers
a precious soul. He who is brought to such a holy
tenderness that he sees greatness of guilt in little-
ness of sinning shall, by God's grace, be kept from
the dominion of any sin. Every sin (even the least) is
a foul spot and is the object of divine hatred and
curse. It may prove like a little spark to consume a
house, or like a little leak sufficient to drown a ship,
or like a little thrust into the heart, enough for a

man to lose his life.

Believe that your own strength is not sufficient. Even the strongest ship, left to itself, cannot venture far, but it is upon rocks or sands. Anything may prove too strong for him who conceives himself too strong for anything.

He who will venture upon sinful provocations and occasions disarms his soul and lays his very heart naked to a conquest. A Christian may do very much in good ways, with God's warrant to lead him and God's promise to keep him, but, if he alone will be presuming, as the Israelites, who would go up to fight upon their own humour, fell and lost, so shall a man presently learn his own weakness by the strength of sin's surprisal.

Many a man has been spiritually wounded, not because he had no grace but because he would adventure upon the strength of it without any security from God.

Believe that pardon is not so easily obtained, nor the soul so quickly recovered, after particular dominions.

It is an easy thing to slip into sin; it is difficult to get out of it. A little thing will serve to distemper our health, and yet much medicine is required to set the humours straight again. All entrances to sin are with the greater facility; for then temptations and carnal affections blind our judgments, but the recoveries are the harder; for now the vileness and heinousness of the sinning appears more distinctly, and the conscience works more sharply and vehemently, and our very graces are the more disabled.

Assuredly, if you will venture to sin, you lose a

friend of God, encouragement in conscience, and strength in your souls. This very conceit, that you should easily make your peace with God and find mercy (though you sinned), I say, this very conceit will mightily afflict your soul and aggravate your transgression when you behold your soul in blood for sinnings. Mercy is the most singular ground of repentance; and nothing stings us more for sinning than this, that we abused mercies to invite us. Therefore, when sin tempts you, resist it, do not yield to it. Say this, "Who would adventure the sweet mercies of a gracious God to satisfy the lusts of a damnable sin, and why should I be so mad? Having health, to make myself sick, to break the bones which yet are whole, to unsettle the peace of my conscience, to weaken my graces, to disjoint my estate. If as now I am, I have much to do. Ah, what folly is it to make more woeful work for my soul! How justly may God leave me, who will forsake Him for that which I know will displease Him? And what if He should righteously deny me grace to repent, who proudly will abuse His grace to sin?"

Beloved! Let the judgment at all times be thus effectually convinced, and it may prove a singular means and help against particular temptations of sin, by which dominion is attained.

3. *Do not be in the ways of dominion.* Great sinnings do not alway prevail at first sight, but they have a train and method to prepare the soul, and then, all of a sudden they violently surprise it.

There are these methods:

First, perhaps naked motions. The vile heart gives up only a show of a particular sin, in an imagination our thought presents the kinds of sinning, and so falls in again.

Then, perhaps, a careless use of our senses, which wandering (without regard) light upon some object which fits the former sinful motions, and strongly enlivens them.

After this, active contemplation of these sinful motions, not to detest and bewail them, but to look upon them in an idle way.

After this, a meditation of them, which is a more deliberate entertainment of them, which now rises to a kind of treaty in the mind where the sinful motion craves entertainment, by arguments of profit, of pleasure, or credit, then a darting down to the affections to harken and delight.

Then, upon the next occasion, an acting of all this sinful imagination and plot.

Brethren, if you love your souls, take off sins in their entrances before they gather head. If a man could keep sin from pleading, he might keep himself from acting. Break the egg and you need not fear the flying of the bird. Crush sin in motion, and it is a clear way to prevent sin in dominion. The match will never be made if all treaties are rejected. Little motions are the principles of great sins, as springs of rivers, and sparks of flames. Therefore, let us do this: resist motions to sin as a man should resist the actings of sin. Do not say, "It is but a thought." Jehu's army came after the scouts. Great sinning may attend little and flattered imaginations. He who slights inward thoughts, and is careless of his outward senses, is in a fair way to become a great sinner.

4. *Sue out your standing by prayer and faith.* I will tell you two things:

First, the strongest grace cannot free us from the fiercest assaults. Even the best heart, and the most eminent Christian, is exposed to the foulest and most violent temptations of sin and Satan.

Second, this resisting strength which keeps sin from dominion is in God and not in himself. We become good from the goodness of God's grace; that we do not prove bad is from the greatness of God's power. No man is able to change his own heart, nor is his heart his own guard.

Therefore, under all temptations, be at prayer and faith. These are the two wings of the soul. Some victories are best had by standing up, but that against sin is surest by kneeling down. Oh, when the heart is much in prayer, it is then most in strength. Prayer engages all heaven against a corruption, and God has promised to subdue iniquities, and that sin shall not have dominion, Romans 6:14. Now, what He has promised, that He is able to perform, and will, if we can pray and believe. We give sin great advantage when we slack our prayers and lay aside our faith.

It is the wisest art of a tempted soul to decline all occasions, to be under prevailing ordinances, and to use prayer and exercise faith according to the nature, kind, and measure of sinful motions and inclinations.

5

"Then shall I be upright, and I shall be innocent
from that great transgression."
Psalm 19:13

You may remember that, heretofore, we have handled David's petition against sin in secrecy, in presumption, and in dominion. Now we proceed to speak something of the conclusion or inference, which that holy and sweet Psalmist draws from all this, "Then shall I be upright and innocent from that great transgression."

To me it seems that David's special aim, that mark which he had in his eye, was to be upright. He knew well that this was what God looked for, which God most of all prized, and which (for his soul) would prove most necessary and comfortable; and withal he well knew that the allowance of secret sins, or the wallowing in great transgressions, was quite contrary thereto. Therefore, he prays earnestly against them so that he might secure and maintain this.

"O Lord, above all things in the world, I desire to be upright, and this I shall never be unless my heart is cleansed of secret sins, and my life of presumptuous and reigning sins! For Thy mercies' sake, cleanse my heart, let me not love and work wickedness there; and, for Thy goodness' sake keep my life. Let me not act transgressions there. O that Thou would do this for me; then, then, should I be that which (above all) I desire to be, then should I be upright!"

I will stand no longer about the words, only they afford unto us this proposition, that it should be the great bent, aim, desire and endeavor of a man to be upright.

Genesis 17:1, "I am the Almighty God; walk before Me and be thou upright." It is as if God were to say, "This is all in all which concerns you, which I esteem, and which you must study." Deuteronomy 10:12, "And now Israel, what doth the Lord thy God require of thee, but to fear the Lord thy God, to walk in all His ways, and to love him, and to serve the Lord thy God with all thy heart, and with all thy soul." It is as if God should say, "I have done you much good, thought on you in your afflictions, brought you out of Egypt, preserved you through the sea, and in the wilderness vanquished all your enemies for you, brought you into a land flowing with milk and honey. Now all that I require, and that you are to look to, is that your hearts be upright, that you bestow your love on none but Me, your service on none but Me, that I have all your heart, and all your soul." Joshua 24:14, "Now therefore fear the Lord, and serve Him in sincerity and truth." This is the thing that concerns you nearly, this is the end of all your mercies, and the utmost of all your returns. If you will be anything, or return anything to God (who has done all for you), then be sincere and true, be upright. 1 Samuel 12:23-24, "I will teach you the good and the right way. Only fear the Lord, and serve him in truth with all your heart."

"You have showed false hearts towards your God in that you would put off His government, and you may perceive by the thunder and rain how He takes this at your hands; but repent, and forsake Him no more, but get upright hearts to walk with Him, and cleave unto Him. Philippians 1:9-10, "This I pray...that you may approve things that are excellent, that you may be sincere."

I need not quote more places from the Scripture, which abundantly delivers this truth unto us. Only, for the further explication of it, I shall enquire into these four particulars:

1. What it is to be upright.

2. Why we should so studiously aim at and labor for uprightness.

3. What useful applications in all kinds of this to ourselves.

4. Then the resolutions of some cases of conscience for the stay of those who suspect their own uprightness.

SECTION I

QUESTION 1. What is it to be upright?

ANSWER. The logicians pursue a double inquiry, what is the name and what is the reality? I will briefly, therefore, open the several words and phrases which are used in the Scriptures to import uprightness, and then I shall, with more ease and better satisfaction, couch out unto you the lively nature of it.

1. For the first of these (what is the name?) know that uprightness is sometimes applied to God, Psalm 25:8, "Good and upright is the Lord." Psalm 92:15, "To show that the Lord is upright." Isaiah 26:7, "Thou most

upright dost weigh the path of the just."

In this respect, it notes that just and equal nature of God which is as an answering rule, righteously disposing of all His acts and dealings.

Sometimes, uprightness is applied to man, and thus it may be applied both to good men and bad men; for uprightness may be considered either as arising out of a renewal disposition, as appearing in the course of a renewed conversation (in which respects it is proper to good men only), or as manifesting itself in a particular fact. And so Abimelech might say, "In the uprightness of mine heart I have done this," Genesis 20:5. Now uprightness, or to be upright, as applied to good men, is delivered unto us both in the Old and in the New Testament by sundry words and phrases. Sometimes it is called sincerity, as in Joshua 24:14, "Serve the Lord in sincerity." Something is said to be sincere when it is without mixture, a metaphor from honey which is then reputed pure and right when it has none of the wax mixed with it. The heart is upright when it is sincere, and then it is sincere when it is unmingled. Beloved, there is a difference between adherence and mixture.

To the purest wool there may adhere some thread or uncomely spot but, in mixture, the qualities or substances are in a sort mutually confounded. Sin adheres or cleaves to the nature of the most upright person, but yet it does not mingle. It is a thing which the renewed heart is thrusting off; it would be rid of it. The new nature, like a spring, is working it off, so that a man may be said to be upright whose heart will not suffer any sin to incorporate or settle in itself. "Search me," said David, "see whether there be any way of wickedness in me," Psalm 139:23-24.

If a man has a heart upon which sinful ways not only fall, but with which they close, if his heart knows it, allows it, and will walk in it, that man's heart is not upright in him. Sometime it is called oneness, or singleness, so in Jeremiah 32:39, "I will give them one heart and one way, that they may fear me forever." Acts 2:46, "They did eat their bread with gladness, and singleness of heart."

There are two sorts of persons, hypocrites and upright persons, and the Scripture opens them by their hearts.

Hypocrites are said to have "a heart and a heart." Psalm 12:2, "With a double heart do they speak." In the original it is, with "a heart and a heart." So it is in Hosea 10:2, "Their heart is divided, now shall they be found fault;" and, therefore, in James 1:8, they are called "men of two minds," double-minded men. They are in some things for God and in most things for themselves, now for His service and later for their lusts. Look, as hypocrisy mingles sin and the affection together, so it mingles God, sin, and the world together. It does not look on God for God's sake, but for profit's sake, or pleasure's sake, or honor's sake. On the contrary, upright persons are persons of one heart, or of a single heart, as the Zebulonites are said not to be of a double heart, 1 Chronicles 12:33, which is expounded, verse 38, by a perfect heart. A man's heart is upright when God alone, His ways alone, and His truth alone satisfy, order, and bound it; when a man can say in truth, as they in the matter of choice, "Nay, but the Lord is our God, Him will we serve." "I have chosen the Lord to be my God, and His truths to be my guide, and His precepts to be my paths, and His glory to be my end; and hereto only will I stick;" when the soul does not halt between two, or divide itself in a service of any side or way, but keeps only to God.

Sometimes it is called perfection, and the upright are called perfect, as in Genesis 17:1, "Walk before Me and be thou perfect." Deuteronomy 18:13, "Thou shalt be perfect with the Lord thy God." Psalm 37:37, "Mark the perfect man, and behold the upright."

There is a double perfection:

One is absolute, in respect of degrees, which no man can now attain unto in this life, no not the most upright, for "in many things we offend all."

The other is evangelical, which consists in the evenness of desire an endeavor; when a man sets up and exalts the Word of God, and strives to square his heart and his life in all things thereby.

As Paul, exercising himself to have a conscience void of offense, and willing to live honestly in all things. When a man (as it were) measures his paths as by a line, he sets them by the compass of a divine rule or warrant, not willingly straggling on the right hand, or bending toward the left; not willingly omitting the least duty, and committing the least sin. He is an upright person when the heart is as large as the precept, and the whole will of God is complied with, in will, desire, and endeavor.

Sometimes it is called a spirit without guile, so in Psalm 32:2, "Blessed is the man in whose spirit there is no guile," and, as Christ said of Nathaniel in John 1:47, "Behold an Israelite indeed, in whom is no guile." A hypocritical heart is a cunning heart; it has many devices, shufflings, windings, and turnings. This heart is not plain and sound, therefore hypocrites are said to have corrupt thoughts, to flatter with their tongues, and to have crooked ways. They do not, indeed, hate the sin which they pretend, nor love the holiness which often times they praise and sometimes act. Some ends they have of religion for their belly, and for their own advantage, but they do not heartily hate sin nor truly love holiness.

Now, on the contrary, a upright heart is without guile. It is even plain and down-right; therefore it is in the parable called an honest heart, and, says Paul, "we speak the truth in Christ." And upright walking is called a walking in truth, and serving God in truth and in spirit. The meaning is that the upright man is indeed that which he professes. His life and profession is not a painting which owes itself to an artificer, but a natural color which owes itself to the soundness of temper. He is one who has truth in the inward parts, as David speaks, Psalm 51:6. He does, without base ends, directly love God and from his very heart hate sin. Though he cannot express himself in that flourish of formality, yet for Christ he can plainly say, as did Peter, "Lord, Thou knowest all things, Thou knowest that I love Thee;" and touching sins, as David said of God's enemies, "I hate them with a perfect hatred." Thus he is in good earnest.

Sometimes it is called the "allness or wholeness of heart." So Deuteronomy 4:29, "If thou seek Him with all thine heart." Deuteronomy 26:16, "Thou shalt keep and do them with all thine heart, and with all thy soul." Psalm 119:10, "With my whole heart have I sought Thee." When the heart is upright, the whole man comes in unto God, and the soul, and all the body. None shall dispose of them but God, and God shall dispose of him in every precept. The very bent of a man is to please God in all things, and the whole soul, in the understanding, will, memory, and affections, bears a respect to all His commandments. There are other phrases to set out this business of uprightness, but I must pass them over and pitch upon the description.

2. Now to the second inquiry (what is the reality?), I conjecture that uprightness may be thus described. Uprightness is a sound and heavenly frame or temper of a gracious heart or spirit, given by God, by which graces are acted, sins are opposed, duties are performed affectionately, directly and plainly in reference to God and not for by-respects.

What Uprightness Is

I will briefly open this description in its particulars:

First, it is the temper or frame of the heart. The seat of uprightness is the heart or spirit; hence is it called uprightness of heart. 1 Kings 3:6, "Thou hast showed unto Thy servant David my father great mercies, according as he walked before Thee in truth, in righteousness, and in uprightness of heart." It is called singleness of heart, Acts 2:46, truth in the inward parts, Psalm 51:6, and a service in spirit, Romans 1:9, "God is my witness, whom I serve with my spirit in the Gospel of His Son."

Hypocrisy is a color but skin-deep; a painting which lies only upon the superfices or surface of the wall, upon the visibles or outwards of profession or action. But uprightness, like health, is an inward crisis or temperature. As the conversation renders itself to the eye of man, so the inward disposition strives to render it-self to the eye of God's approbation. If a man is up-right, it is with him as with Solomon's Temple. Though the outward parts are comely, and uniform, yet the in-side was covered with the most precious gold, and had the sweetest incense.

All counterfeit things are best in their show and worst in their substance and virtue; but uprightness is best where least it can be seen. The actions are nothing to the inward affections and desires.

We only, as the Queen of Sheba, hear half of the goodness of an upright man by what he does. If you would but look into his heart and converse with him there a while, you should find the heart, the disposi-tion, the desire of his soul, infinitely to exceed all that he does, Psalm 119, "O how I love Thy law, O that my ways were so direct!"

The heart oftentimes mourns when the eyes can shed no tears, and the heart believes when the tongue cannot speak much faith. And the inward man (the heart) would do that and much more than what is done or performed.

Second, it is a temper or frame of the heart, a com-position, as it were, in which, I think, two things may be observed:

One is that uprightness is not a single or transient act or motion. I think that even a hypocrite, whose heart is rotten, corrupt, false, abominable, may yet step out into actions materially good, and so may feel mo-tions within him both against what is evil and unto what is good. He may, either through the force and power of evidence and conviction in his judgment, or through the irresistible actions of his enlightened and

stirred conscience, or through the great desire of a
glorious blessedness, have many fits and inward humours of being good and doing good.

But all this is passion and not temper. The philoso-
pher, in his rhetorics, accurately distinguishes between
the ruddiness which springs out of a natural complexion, and that which arises out of a violent anger and
passion which soon fades; not rooted in nature, but in
distemper. So is it with the hypocrite. But uprightness
is a temper and frame, like an instrument well-tuned;
like a complexion which is a uniform (if not principled
yet) instrument of actions. It is like that leaven of
which Christ spake which invades the whole lump; it
sweetly seasons and disposes the whole man for God as
the bent of the stone is to the centre, and of the fire to
ascend.

Another is that uprightness is rather a general influence, in the graces, than any distinct grace. I will not
make this point a controversy, only so far as I yet apprehend that uprightness is rather the temper of a
grace than the grace itself. It is not fear, but fear
rightly tempered and ordered; it is not love, but love
rightly set. It is not desire, but this orderly carried.

Third, it is a sound, incorrupt, and heavenly frame
of heart.

A thing may be termed sound or solid, either when
it is real (not light, slight, or superficial), or when it
can abide trial; as true gold is really so, and not in
color only. And, if you reduce it to the touchstone, you
shall find it so, if you cast it into the fire. Thus it is with
the heart that is upright, and it not only a form of godliness but the power; and not only a name that it lives
but the life itself. It is (indeed) holy, humble, meek,

believing, loving of God and His servants, desirous to walk with God, Psalm 116:16, "O Lord, truly I am thy servant. I am so indeed." This is not a compliment, a garb, or a pretence, but a reality; so is it with the man indeed. "An Israelite indeed," said Christ of Nathaniel, John 1:47. Yea, so real that, if you bring the heart either to the examination of the Word (which being truth can find out all truth), or to God Himself who can search the heart and reins, or to conscience that bears witness, 2 Corinthians 1:12, or to afflictions, yet even there, uprightness can find approbation and testimony so that the person loves, serves, and fears Him. Job 1:8, "The Lord said unto Satan, hast thou not considered My servant Job, that there is none like him in the earth, a perfect and an upright man, one that feareth God and escheweth evil?"

Fourth, it is an incorrupt frame. Though the extreme parts may sometimes be faulty, yet if the vitals are sound, if the heart, if the lungs, if the liver are so, we say that man is a sound man. In morals it holds that, if the heart is void of all obliquity, the person is upright. Many infirmities in action may consist with uprightness but not in affection; the very bent of the heart is set against sin, without distinction of great or less, advantageous or incommodious, honorable or dishonorable. If it is not so, then the heart is corrupt. It mingles, it is not sincere and upright; but of this more later.

It is given by God. So the prophet says in Jeremiah 32:39, "I will give them one heart and one way." Every man naturally is a hypocrite, would seem to be that which he is not, and so misdirects all his actions to a wrong end. God has set a certain beauty in goodness and left a notion of vileness upon sin, so that most men, though they hate goodness, yet would be thought good (they think it a more creditable title) and, though they love and act sin, yet would not be thought or reputed to be evil.

Besides this, if we but seriously observed and confessed how it is in our own spirits, we should find in all our pious pretenses (take us in our naturals) we are all of us most formal and artificial hypocrites. We draw near to God with our lips, but our hearts are far from Him. We come to church when we mind neither prayer nor sermon, and listen oftentimes, and (God knows) not to obey but to censure, or but to get matter to talk of and the like. And when we have got ability to speak of any good, the Lord be merciful unto us, we do it, not minding God's glory, but our own vain applause and estimation. So, then, the hypocritical heart is from ourselves, but the upright heart is from God. "Every good and perfect gift is from above," James 1:17. The perfect heart is from the perfect God, the true heart from the God of truth. It is He who teaches truth, makes us upright, and writes His law in the inward parts.

The fifth thing which I would observe in uprightness is its office of administration. It is such a thing as deals: 1.) about graces; 2.) about sins; and 3.) about duties.

1.) For our graces. Uprightness looks to them so that they are rightly acted. Beloved, uprightness does not give grace, but orders and directs the acts and operations thereof.

Two things I grant, that all the habits of grace are, in themselves, intrinsically considered, really true; and though imperfection may be in them, yet no moral falsity or counterfeitness; and that the action of all those holy habits, considered entirely as streaming from them (only as so) are, likewise, truly holy and good.

But then, these acts or actions of gracious habits, as working in a subject which has some falseness and byeness yet remaining, may, by reason of that corruption, be misdirected and misguided.

For hypocrisy not only consists in the putting of a good shape upon an evil action (as a fair color upon a rotten thread), but also in the ill intention or application even of an act (in itself) truly good. Charity (without all doubt) is a gracious quality, yet if uprightness attends not some of its acts, they may be referred to a private and vain-glorious end. The like may be said of some other graces, as of the love of God and the fear of God.

2.) For sins. Here also uprightness comes in to act itself. Holiness (which is nothing else but the newness of nature) makes opposition to sin, but uprightness is an evenness or impartiality of opposition.

To oppose a little sin and yet to close with a great sin, to oppose many sins and yet to hold a known and a willing confederacy with any one, to oppose sin in others and yet to act it ourselves, to oppose sin as open to the eye of man and yet to fall to it in secret, where it is naked to the eye of God; to oppose a sin to which constitution and age deny concurrence of delight or strength and yet to wallow in others agreeable to our complexions, conditions, and years; to oppose the unprofitable sin, which brings nothing in but pain, and yet to admit of gainful sins which come with rewards of divination in their hands; to oppose any sin only because it is painful and not because it is sinful; to oppose sin in our straits, and not in our liberties, in sickness, and not in health, when only we fear death and not at all under life and strength; I say all these are but hypocrisies. There is an unevenness of the heart as was in Saul, who spared the choicest and mortified the coarsest of the cattle; or as in Balaam, who would be happy in his death, though a curser of God's people (in respect of his own intention) in his life.

I confess this to be true, that uprightness is not the utter annihilation of sin. No, that effect appertains to glory, and perfection above, but it is the even and impartial opposition of sin, of secret and presumptuous sins (as David says here in this Psalm), of great and small. In a word, it is a conjunctive opposition of sin, that is, it carries the heart against all sin. Psalm 119:1, "Blessed are the undefiled in the way", and verse 3, "they do no iniquity"; that is, their hearts are for no sin. And the prime reason of all this opposition, I say, the prime and immediate reason, is direct and not reflexive. It is because sin is so opposite to God, and not primarily because it is so painful in the event to the person.

3.) For duties. Here uprightness expresses itself both for matter, wherein it does not shuffle and cut, pick and choose, take the lighter (like the hypocritical Pharisees) and leave the heaviest to others, but it makes a man to have (with David, Psalm 119:6) a respect to all God's commands.

For the manner: Any performance will not serve where the heart is upright. David danced before the Lord with all his might, and Paul served God in his spirit. That which came next to hand will serve Cain, but Abel must present the best of the cattle, not the lame and the blind, but the best. God shall have the best manner of service. If I hear, that does not suffice unless it is with reverence and faith. If I pray, that does not suffice unless it is joined with brokenness of heart, humbleness of spirit, fervent affections, and faith in Christ. A mere tale of brick will serve for Pharaoh, though the Israelites reputed the service a bondage, but when we bring offerings to the temple, they must be willing, and of the best, too.

Sixth, the last thing which I would observe in up-rightness is its end and scope.

Beloved, I pray you to remember that uprightness causes a threefold reference of our services. One is to God's precept; that's the square and rule and compass of upright motions. Another is to God's glory; that's the spring which turns the wheels, the wind which blows the sails. It is for Christ's sake, said Paul; and "whatsoever ye do, do all to the glory of God," said he again. A third is to God's acceptance and approbation, so that God will accept and approve. 2 Corinthians 5:9, "We labor that, whether present or absent, we may be accepted of Him." 2 Corinthians 10:18, "Not he that commendeth himself is approved, but whom the Lord commendeth."

More plain and punctual is that of the same apostle in Romans 2:29, "He is a Jew which is one inwardly, and circumcision is that of the heart in the spirit, and not in the letter, whose praise is not of men but of God."

The schoolmen's observation is sound and true, that a particular deficiency is sufficient to mar a good, morally considered, but a universal concurrence of circumstances is required to make the action good. Look, as in reading of Hebrew, leave out but one tittle, one point, and you mar the sense; or as in a dose of medicine, leave out one ingredient, and you spoil all. So our actions, if one circumstance is left out, if the right and genuine end is not eyed, it is enough to blanch them with hypocrisy, though for substance they may be commended. To pray and to give alms, no man will question that these duties, substantially considered, are good and such which the upright person performs. But then, if a man prays or gives alms to be seen of men, Christ tells him that he plays the hypocrite. If, in the performance of any piously external duty, we set ourselves as the end, if all these things are done, and with very much fervency and assiduity, yet only to play the merchants for ourselves, to make a bridge over to our own estimation, to blow up our own names, this is but hypocrisy and, I fear, a kind of idolatry. We fall down and worship ourselves, like the men of Shechem who would admit of circumcision, "shall not their cattle and all that they have be ours?" The same indifferentness may be found in men forward for outward duties; shall not profit be ours, preachers' good opinion ours, the glory and credit ours? This is gross hypocrisy.

Now uprightness consists in this, to devolve all the honor of holy services on God, like the faithful servant who works painfully and speaks considerately, and all this for his master; or like the shadow which in the dial moves from point to point, and all this points upward to the sun in its motions. The humble heart knows no fountain but God's grace, and the upright heart knows no end but God's glory.

They distinguish of a double end.

One is the end of the work, and that shall be our glory hereafter, as the Apostle spoke of faith, "the end of your faith, even the salvation of your souls," 1 Peter 1:9.

Another is the end of the workman, and that (if the heart is upright) is God's glory, "for of Him, and through Him, and to Him, are all things, to whom be glory for ever," Romans 11.

Yet, by your favor, this I must suggest by the way (and perhaps shall handle it more copiously shortly), that in a way of subordination, an upright heart may do God service and His glory no wrong if, with all in its fit place, order, and measure, it casts an eye also on its own reward. "Moses had an eye to it," Hebrews 11.

SECTION II

QUESTION 2. Now I proceed to a second question. Why should we strive, aim at (as David here did), and endeavor to be upright?

ANSWER. There are abundant reasons thereof, I will deliver a few unto you.

1. *This uprightness is the great thing which God looks for.* John 4:23, "The true worshippers shall worship the Father in spirit and in truth, for the Father seeketh such to worship Him." God's seeking notes either His grace, which prevents us, or His pleasure, which enjoins us. The Father seeks such to worship Him (that is; the Lord, by all means, would have men, in His service to come with spirit and truth, to be upright. Proverbs 23:26, "My son, give me thy heart." It is as if God should say, "Though the body is made by Me, and ev-

ery part thereof, and though that whole frame is made for Me, as well as by Me, and you are to glorify Me in your body, yet that which I principally enjoin you in My services is to bring them with your heart, with affections, entirely and not pretensively."

2. *Nay, this is it which the Lord looks at.* See Jeremiah 5:3, "Are not thine eyes upon the truth?" Why, it is not your words which God so much regards, nor is it your looks, nor your tears, nor your cries. That which the Lord sets His eye on is the truth of the heart, in and under all these, uprightness there. Excellent is that place in 1 Chronicles 29:17, "I know also my God (said David) that Thou triest the heart, and hast pleasure in uprightness. As for me, in the uprightness of my heart I have willingly offered all these things." In that place you find David contributing toward the building of the temple and stirring up others to that work. And David, for his part, gave like a king thereto, even three thousand talents of gold, of gold of Ophir, verse 4, and seven thousand talents of refined silver; and the chief of the fathers and the princes gave also five thousand talents of gold, ten thousand drams, of silver ten thousand talents, of brass eighteen thousand talents, and one hundred thousand talents of iron besides precious stones, verses 6-8. Now what a goodly gift was all this, but David presently subjoins, "I know my God that Thou triest the heart, and hast pleasure in uprightness." It is as if David had said, "O Lord, all this is nothing. Thou will not accept it, Thou will not look upon it, if uprightness be wanting; O, that is it which Thou regardest. The heart, the heart Thou triest and, if uprightness is found there, that is it which Thou regardest."

You read that the Jews made many prayers, but God would not hear them. They brought many oblations, but they were vain; that is, of no account, Isaiah 50:11, 12, and 15. They remember the solemn feasts, but prevailed not with God. He shut his eyes; nay, they were at their solemn fasts too, but God took no knowledge, Isaiah 58:3. He gives the reason in both places, in Isaiah 1:15, "your hands are full of blood;" verse 16, "wash ye," etc., and Isaiah 58:4, "Behold, ye fast for strife and debate, to smite with the fist of wickedness;" verse 6, "Is not this the fast which I have chosen to loose the bands of wickedness." God is saying, "Away, you hypocrites, do you commit and allow cruelties, villainies, oppressions, and whoredoms, and then bring multitudes of sacrifices and oblations, and cryings, and think that I am taken with these? Go and cleanse your hearts, mend your lives, leave your sins, be plain and upright with me, that is it which I look at more than any thing; that is it which pleases Me."

Hence it is that oftentimes in Scripture, the Hebrew word (*Jashar*) which signifies right, is many times translated pleasing, as in Numbers 23:27, perhaps it will seem right in the eyes of the Lord, we translate it, "peradventure it will please God." So true is that of Solomon, Proverbs 11:20, "Such as are upright in their way are His delight;" yea, and so that phrase of walking with God (which is nothing else but the path of the just or upright) is rendered by the Septuagint, pleasing of God; as in Genesis 5:22,24, holy Enoch walking with God. The Septuagint renders it, "he pleased God."

3. *This seems to be the only thing that God expects*, 1 Samuel 12:24, "Only fear the Lord, and serve Him in

truth with all your heart." Deuteronomy 10:12, "And now, Israel, what doth the Lord thy God require of thee, but to fear the Lord thy God, and to walk in all His ways, and to love Him, and to serve the Lord thy God with all thy heart, and with all thy soul." When the Lord entered into the covenant with Abraham, Genesis 17, and promised to be an all-sufficient God unto him, what did He require of Abraham but this? "Be thou upright." When He advanced Solomon to the kingdom, and enriched him with honor, wealth, and wisdom above all who ever sat on the throne, what did He require of him? 1 Kings 3:14, "Walk in My ways, keep My statutes, as David thy father did." How was that? Look back to verse 6, "David thy father walked before Me in truth and righteousness: and in uprightness of heart." When Paul had commended many singular things of knowledge and duty to the Corinthians, he closed up all with "finally, my brethren, be perfect," 2 Corinthians 13:11. It is as if he had said, "Will you have me to give you all in word? Why then, be perfect; be upright."

4. *Uprightness brings the whole man unto God.* It is that which commands all and carries all with it. It carries the thoughts, these inward and sweet breathings of the mind. "Let the meditations of my heart be always acceptable in Thy sight, O Lord, my strength and my Redeemer," said upright David in Psalm 19:14. The words, "Let the words of my mouth be acceptable"; so he also says, "The mouth of the righteous speaketh wisdom, and his talk is of judgment," Psalm 37:30. It carries the heart; the law of his God is in his heart. Psalm 57:7, "My heart is fixed," said David. Again, it carries the conversation, so that is ordered aright,

Psalm 50. Has a man any gifts, many gifts? Why, uprightness brings in their use and strength to God. Has he any graces? Why, uprightness brings in their service to God; it keeps us in with God, makes us one with God, and will not suffer us to deal falsely with God.

5. *God judges a man by his uprightness.* You are, in His judgment, good or bad, according to the presence or absence of uprightness. This is that which distinguishes between the precious and the vile, between the faithful and the unsound. In outward appearances, and in the color of visible services, the good and the bad may go hand and hand. Both may hear; both may read; both may pray; both may preach; both may receive the sacraments; both may give alms; but God judges not as man judges, by outward appearance. He is a spirit, and truth itself, and therefore judges actions by the spirit and as done in truth. He searches the heart and reins and, notwithstanding all the outward appearances of the strict and pompous Pharisees, yet He reputes them as hypocrites, and so condemns them, Matthew 23:28.

Metals (you know) are not judged and valued to be gold, by the gilt put upon them, but by that power and excellent substance which is in them. And the natural gold, though it look sometimes pale, if yet it has the true nature of gold, is judged and reckoned above all counterfeit and gilted pieces; so even pompous services, which seem fair and glorious to the eyes of men, may be rejected of God. And the pretenders severely censured, because their hearts, under these, are false and rotten, like a dead man clothed with a fair robe, or a sepulchre garnished outwardly, yet within filled with dead and loathsome carcasses. And the upright

Christian, whose works are not so specious to the sight, whose prayers may be sparing in words, who is yet filled up with sighs and groans, whose services may be interrupted with many distractions (by him resisted and bewailed), may be graciously accepted and rewarded because his sincerity is observed by God's eye. The poor widow could cast in but a mite, a very small coin; yet of great account was it, it was more, in Christ's exposition, than the treasure cast in by others. Why? Because she did it in uprightness; her heart laid down the mite and only their hands put in their gifts. Her gift was to succor the poor. The end of their bounty was to flame their own praise. The church of Philadelphia had more praise than all the other churches, and yet we read she had but a little strength, Revelation 3:8. A little strength, yea, but it was upright, for she held fast the truth, and God judged her by that.

Thus for the explication of the proposition. Now I proceed to the application of it to ourselves, which I shall reduce to these heads: 1.) Of trial and examination; 2.) Of consolation; 3.) Of caution; and 4.) Of exhortation.

SECTION III

The first use shall be to reflect upon our own hearts and feel their temper. Beloved, this is it which God looks on, and which gives unto us our denomination. It is not naked actions which make us or mar us, our affections are (in a sort) all in all. God complains many times of the Israelites, that they brought him no incense, no sacrifice, no service. Why? Was there none of these at all? Perhaps sometimes many of these, yet God accounts them none. It is not what we do, but with what heart, which makes God to reckon of our services. They are but as cyphers (which make no number), without uprightness. God you know is truly good, infinitely wise and searching, and spiritually holy; that must be brought to Him which is like to Him or else it is not approved. Would you be paid with counterfeit gold? Does the show please you without the substance? Will the compliments of men satisfy you without a real friendship? Will a gaudy, rotten house content you which has no solidity and goodness? Would you take the words of your servants and their legs as sufficient, while their hearts are false in their callings? Nay, would you be content that God should make a show only, a pretense that He would pardon you, and help, comfort, save you, and yet deny you real love, real mercy, real comfort, real help and salvation? Then, think how God should take shows from you without uprightness of heart!

Therefore, I pray you, take some pains with your hearts. Bring them to the balance of the sanctuary; weigh them there, reduce them to the rule, try them there to see whether they are upright or not.

Let me premise a few particulars which may prepare and quicken you to this trial for uprightness of heart.

EIGHT TRIALS OF UPRIGHTNESS

1. *First, there is no deceit or error in the world of more dangerous consequence than for a man to deceive himself and*

to err about the right temper of his soul. A man may mistake himself in the depth of his riches, or the altitude of worldly friendship, or latitude of his intellectual qualifications and abilities; he may think himself rich, favored, and learned, when perhaps he is not so. But these mistakes are about *nostra,* not about *nos; ours,* but not ourselves, and the danger may be only a tempest, but not a shipwreck. But, for a man to deceive himself about his heart, about his soul, why, what more does he have? What does he have like them? They are fundamental errors. If a man lays a rotten foundation instead of a sound one, all his building, at length, sinks to the ground. If a man sets forth in a fair ship, whose bottom is unsound and leaking, he loses himself in the voyage. Why? Upon the right and solid frame of the soul depends the eternity of our happiness, and, therefore, the error here is great and irrecoverable. When a man has passed over many years in a form of godliness, in an ingenuity of a civil carriage, in a courting of God by some external and naked performances, and comes to die, then his conscience rises up and opens the secrets of his heart and life, and makes him to know and feel that, notwithstanding all his pretenses and conceits, his heart has continually harbored many known lusts, and he did not mind God, but himself basely in all that he did. What a fearful day will this be? How it will make the soul to tremble when it has no more time now but to see, and eternally bewail, its own errors and deceits. "O Lord," said that oppressed man, "I have deceived my own soul. I thought myself thus and thus; but my heart has deceived and beguiled me."

2. *Yet consider that hypocrisy, which is apt to beguile and*

deceive us, is a very natural and common thing.

There are three sorts of persons in the world:

1.) Openly profane, who fail in the matter and in the manner. They are neither really good, nor seem so to be; they are really wicked, and declare themselves so to be. The plague of their heart breaks out into carbuncles and blotches.

2.) Closely hypocritical, who fail not so much in the matter as in the manner; who are wicked, but seem good; who act some good, but love more wickedness.

3.) Truly upright, who are so in the matter and manner of God's worship.

Now I say that hypocrisy is very natural; it has been, and is, a very common sin. Job 15:34 speaks of a congregation of hypocrites, as if there were whole assemblies of them, or at least some of them in every congregation. Isaiah 9:17 complains that every one is a hypocrite; scarce a man but did dissemble with God. So Isaiah 29:13 says, "With their lips they do honor Me." David tells us often of the Israelites flattering God Himself with their mouths, giving Him in their distress mournful, yielding, and promising language. Oh, what would they be, and what would they do, if God would deliver them! And yet their heart was not right in them. Jeremiah accuses those of his time for this very thing too. Many of them, nay, most of them, cried, "The Temple of the Lord, the Temple of the Lord", and yet committed adultery and lies. When Christ was in the world, His greatest contestation was with Scribes, Pharisees, Hypocrites; Paul bitterly dealt against those who took on them the form of godliness, but denied the power thereof, and, in 1 Timothy 4:2, he foretells of much lying hypocrisy which would befall in the latter times and, verily, we need not go far for the proof of it.

How many among us, with the foolish virgins, carry lamps without oil, or, with the fig tree, bear leaves without fruit? We are like the crow who took the feathers of another fowl, but kept his own nature; or like the ass, which took the lion's skin, but not his body. It was Machiavel's rule that the show of virtue was easy and profitable and, therefore, he advises men to put that on; but the study and habit of virtue were difficult and, therefore, he advises to let that alone. How abundantly this satisfies many. If they can look like good men, though they will not take pains to be so; if they can speak like good Christians, though they will not live so.

A tradesman, many times, when he gets a minister to supper, will speak of heaven and such things, as if he were upon his deathbed, and yet that man does nothing in the world but scrape for the world, and tires out his own soul and body and his servants in a drudgery for earth. Yea, rather than not be rich, he will cast himself upon most indirect means. How ordinary is it for us to frequent the church, perhaps to listen a while (if we cannot sleep quietly), and then to bestow a little holy water upon the minister, a word or two, that he spoke well, and go home. And yet we do not strive to put any one holy counsel into the love of our hearts, or obedience of our lives.

Nay, to let these things pass, take the general tenor of our best ways. The good God is merciful to us. What a distance is there, many times (when we pretend to serve God), between our tongues and our hearts, between our eyes and our hearts, between our ears and our hearts, between our bodies and our hearts? Our tongues are praying, our mouths singing, our eyes looking on the minister, and our ears as if hearing; and, at the same moments, our hearts are plotting, projecting, ordering our own domestical affairs or, which is worse, basely contemplating, and acting of some abominable lust within us. Now, do you call this uprightness? If this is not hypocrisy, I know not what is!

Nay, yet a little more, take our most complete performances, when we bring our thoughts and intentions, and some affections, some workings, to our work; yet tell me, seriously, whether in it you are not looking beside God. When you many times pray long, and with many affections in company (though when you are alone, a little shall serve the turn), do you not, like the chameleon, live upon the air? Is not Jehu's pang in you? "Come and see my zeal." Is not the Pharisees' humour of vainglory highly acting? "To be seen of men", and is not this hypocrisy? Directly and intentionally to jostle God aside, to serve our own praise is a pretence of serving Him that others may admire and speak well of us.

Nay, I could add one thing more which, perhaps, may make some of our hearts to tremble. Are there not those who, explicitly and deliberately, with much studious art, snatch unto themselves a robe, a look, a discourse, a garb of holiness, for no other end in the world but to provoke to sin, and to blind their secret actings of sinning from the eyes of the world? The soldiers in the field cast up a transverse line to cover their digging enterprises from the enemy's observations. This is a most execrable kind and method of hypocrisy yet, as Gehazi used his master's name to gratify his covetous desire, so many abuse the name of religion, only to satisfy their beastly and damnable lust.

3. *A hypocrite may go very far and, therefore, is all the more reason we have to see that our hearts are upright.*

In general, I conceive that there is not any one external part of religion or duty into which the hypocrite may not only step, but perhaps (for show) exceed the sincerest and most upright Christian. What Paul spoke in another case of himself("Are they Hebrews? so am I; are they Israelites? so am I; are they the seed of Abraham? so am I," 2 Corinthians 1:22), that may the hypocrite say for his part in this case about the actions and parts of duty. "Does the true Christian hear? So do I. Does he pray? So do I. Does he shed tears? So do I. Does he fast? So do I. Does he give alms? So do I. Does he show respect to the minister by salutes and invites? So do I. Is he forward? I am zealous. Does he reprove? I thunder. Does he speak some words in prayer? I speak many. Does he do any good? I do more, in hearings more, in fastings more, in discoursings more, in outward actions, every way more."

Cast and order duties every way for object, for place, for time, still the hypocrite keeps up for duties to God (I mean the external parts of His worship), in praying privately or publicly, hearing, reading, preaching, yea, and all these with some transient affections of joy. All this may be in him.

For duties to man? Why, a hypocrite may be as civil, as just, as fair, ingenuous, affable, bountiful, compassionate, as any one that I know. The Pharisees (whom Christ condemned for very hypocrites; yea, even those self-same Pharisees) were yet the punctilioes of the times. No persons living were more exact, they tithed the very mint and cummin, as if they would have observed the whole law to a hair.

Yea, and for privative piety, which consists in exceptions from gross sins. hear one of them for all the rest, blessing and commending himself, "I am no extortioner, no adulterer, nor like this publican, etc. I fast twice in the week, I give alms of all that I possess."

4. *His heart is rotten, and his grounds are rotten, notwithstanding all this.*

Though man cannot discern him, yet God can, and has limned him out for unsoundness in His Word. There is some secret lust which consists and stands, notwithstanding all this, either Herod's sin, or Demas's sin, filthiness, or worldliness. The Pharisees were wondrously covetous.

And his ends are base. The pirate may rig, trim, steer, and order his ship as artificially and exquisitely as any pilot who is the King's most faithful servant; only their hearts and their ends are different. One is disloyal, the other is true; one goes out to catch a prey and a booty, a prize for himself, the other sails for his master's honor and service. The upright heart falls upon duty with fear, yet with affections. He cannot do as much; yet it is in truth, and what he does, as it is by his master's strength, so it is faithfully intended for his master's glory. But self-love, pride, and vainglory fill the sails of the hypocrite. If you could pare off those accidental and by-causes, he would be no more able to hold on in duties than the bird to fly without her wings, or the ship to run when the wind drives and does not fill not the sails.

"Will the hypocrite pray at all times?" said Job, so

that all which the hypocrite does is with a base heart,
like a slave, and for base ends, like a flatterer.

5. *It is a vain and foolish thing to be hypocritical in our
services.*

This is certain: a man cannot be a hypocrite, but he
must take some pains; he must be very officious in pre-
tences and duties. It must cost him some money to give
alms, and much time to pray and, when all is done,
nothing comes of it.

In respect of God, he has no reward with Him.
There is no reason to give him wages who does not bestow his service on us. The hypocrite served himself
and not God, his own praise and not God's glory and,
therefore, he can expect no reward from Him. He
cannot say, "I prayed for grace that I might honour
Thee, and for abilities that I might glorify Thee."

In respect of man, for if a man is known to be a
hypocrite, then he loses himself on all hands. Evil men
hate him for the very show of goodness and good men
scorn him for his base dissimulation and rottenness.

But suppose he can conceal his hypocrisy. Then all
the reward that he has from men is but an airy applause. Matthew 6:5, "When thou prayest, thou shalt
not be as the hypocrites are, for they love to pray standing in the synagogues, and in the corners of the streets,
that they may be seen of men; verily I say unto you,
they have their reward"; that is, they have what they
look for, the applause of men, and that's all. Let them
not expect any other reward. And, brethren, this is a
sad thing, when a man's reward is only from man,
when all his reward is in this life, and no rewards re-
served for him hereafter.

Nay, and the hypocrite is not so sure of this reward from man, either. He may miss it, and that will vex his heart, like fiddlers who regard ear service, whose whole strain is to please the humors of men. They sometimes get but little and, with that, many reproachful words and blows. So it may fare with a hypocrite, whose actions are set only to the itch of applause and commendation.

6. *Nay, hypocrisy is a most perilous sin.* "You shall receive the greater damnation," said Christ. Damnation! Oh, that is the eternal grave of the soul! It speaks misery enough, everlasting separation from God and everlasting flames of wrath in hell! Yet that is the portion of the hypocrite. Isaiah 33:14, "The sinners in Zion are afraid, fearfulness hath surprised the hypocrites, who among us shall dwell with the devouring fire? Who among us shall dwell with everlasting burnings?"

Greater damnation: an ordinary hell is not all for a hypocrite. It is as if the furnace were heated seven times more hot. The lowest and deepest punishment shall fall on him who presumes to put on the fairest show with the foulest hear. And do not think this strange, for what is hypocrisy but a mocking of God? The hypocrite (as it were) puts tricks upon him, and thinks to deceive omniscience, and basely esteems Him, as if mere shows would satisfy Him. Nay, he jostles God out of His prime place by referring all his services to himself and not to God, and so adores his own name above the name of God. Verily, my brethren, these are sad things; and if our hearts are not made of rock and stone, they may awaken and startle them to

take heed lest we be guilty of this hypocrisy, which is so
diametrically opposite to uprightness.

7. *Again, consider that it is a very difficult thing to be upright.* Though it is that acceptable frame of spirit so
pleasing to God and so comfortable (as we may hear)
to us, yet it is not so easy to be upright, when you consider:

1.) The deceitfulness which is in man's heart.
Jeremiah 17:9, "The heart is deceitful above all things."
In other words, there is not such a cunning thing as it,
not a thing in all the world which can delude us so easily, so often, as our own hearts. Oh, what ado have we
with ourselves many times to speak a little duty? What
disputes oftentimes against it, how many reasonings
must be answered and silenced, before we will yield to
do the very work, so much as to hear, as to pray by ourselves and with others, and to give alms? And then, if
the work is extorted from us, yet what pumping before
any water comes, what collision, and striking before a
few sparks of fire will fly out?

My meaning is, it is much ado to bring our hearts
to our tongues, our affections to our services, without
which they cannot be upright. And, when this is done,
then to set up the right end and scope, and then to settle our intention fast and plain, Oh, how difficult!
Many by-aims and indirect ends often present themselves, so that it is with us as with boys in writing: we
draw many crooked lines; or as with them in archery:
we shoot by hither, or beyond, or beside the mark. It is
not easy to do good because God commands it, or only
because He may be glorified.

2.) That spiritualness which is required in upright motions. I tell you that the very soul must act itself if the heart or way will be upright. Not only his lips, but his spirit, must pray; not only his ear, but his heart must hear; he must not only profess against sin, but his soul must hate and abhor it. And there is no revealed and known duty to which his very heart does not strive to obey, yea, and the ground of all this must be spiritual and not carnal, from God and for God.

Assuredly, these things are impossible to an evil man, and he who is most good shall confess it to be most hard, to be plain with God, and to walk evenly before him.

8. *Lastly, to be upright is a possible thing.* A man may attain to it, nay, every good man does attain unto it. Noah was upright and walked with God, Abraham was upright before Him, David kept himself from his sin, and served the Lord in uprightness of heart. Hezekiah did so likewise, "Remember, Lord, that I have walked before thee in truth, and with an upright heart." Paul served God "in all good conscience, willing to live honestly in all things." Though no man can say that he does all that God's commands require, yet he may say he has respect unto them all; and, though none can say he has nothing in him, or nothing is done by him, which the law of God forbids, yet he may say, "I hate every false way, and search me, O Lord, if there be any way of wickedness within me." And this is uprightness.

MARKS OF AN UPRIGHT MAN

OBJECTION. But, you will say, if the case be so, how may one know that he is indeed upright?

SOLUTION. There are many discoveries of it. I pray you to observe them, and try yourselves by them, let your consciences testify for you before the Lord this day.

1. *If a man is upright, he will mostly strive for an inward reformation of his heart.*

There are two things which the upright person most looks at: his God and his heart. Hypocrites (as our Savior testifies) are for the outside; they wash the platters and the cups, and beautify the tombs. They are like an adulteress whose care is to paint, and set a fair face upon the matter. All their care is to the eye of man, how to be seen and heard, how to be well thought on. Now uprightness is mostly for the heart and spirit; not that an upright person should or does neglect the well-ordering of his life. Oh, no! As to neglect our hearts argues hypocrisy; so to neglect our lives argues profaneness.

But the principal care of uprightness is the reformation of the heart. Though it looks to the cleansing of the hand, yet principally it is of the heart, according to the Apostle, James 4:8. Why, brethren, it well knows that the heart is it which God looks for and looks at. The heart is it which God delights in; if it is right and true, He is pleased. "Thou lovest truth in the inward parts," Psalm 51. "The upright in heart are His delight." David is full in this concerning his heart, Psalm 119:10-11, "With my whole heart have I sought Thee. Thy word have I hid within my heart that I might not sin against Thee. Incline my heart unto Thy testimonies, and not unto covetousness." Romans 1:9, "God is my witness, whom I serve with my spirit." The heart of man is the fountain of life or death, and everything is strongest in the heart and most dangerous. Sin in the heart is worse than in the life, that is, when a man's heart is set upon his sin.

Now, try yourselves in this particular. What care have you of your hearts? What pains do you take with them? You may, at times, have humble looks, yea, but have you not still proud hearts? You have, many times, contented words, yea, but have you not still impatient and discontented hearts? You have, many times, heavenly discourse; yea, but have you not still earthly and worldly hearts? What do you with them? Do you not let your hearts still loose? Do you not give them way to be filled with wicked contemplations, vain imaginations, filthy inclinations, with envy, malice, and unbelief? Or do you mourn under these? Do you strive to cleanse within? Is it not insufficient that your outward actions look well unless your hearts are made better? Oh, if this heart were holy! If this heart were humble! If this heart were heavenly! If this heart were believing! The hypocrite does not care if the thread is rotten as long as the color or gloss is fair; but the upright person is more for substance than show, and has more to do with his heart than anything. He would have the law written, not upon his tongue, but upon his heart; he would have his heart cleansed as well as his life beautified.

2. *If a man is upright, then a little holiness will not serve his turn.* He is not content with some measures, but

strives after perfection. You see this clearly delivered by
the Apostle in Philippians 3:12-15, "Not as though I
had already attained, or were already perfect, but I follow after, if that I may apprehend that forwhich also I
am apprehended of Jesus Christ. I count not myself to
have apprehended, but this one thing I do, forgetting
those things which are behind, and reaching forth
unto those things which are before. I press toward the
mark, for the prize of the high calling of God in Christ
Jesus. Let us therefore as many as be perfect, be thus
minded." In other words, if you are upright, thus will it
be with you; you will not be satisfied with small begin-
nings or with received measures, but you will reach on
for farther conformity to Christ.

There is a difference between desires of holiness
for itself and God, and for ourselves and by-ends. A
hypocrite could be content to have as much holiness as
would serve his turn, his own turn, his own ends; as a
tradesman is willing to be at cost so that his apprentice
learn to write and cypher, so much and so long as he
may be enabled to keep the accounts, but he will not
be at cost to teach him the excellency of writing or
cyphering. But now, the upright person desires grace
and holiness for God that glory may be brought unto
him, out of an intrinsical love of the beauties of holiness, for the farther rooting out of sin, and for the better enabling to holy services. His ends are public and,
therefore, a little serves not.

If a man is upright, then a man will walk by a right
rule. He orders his conversation and ways according to
the Word of God. A right ordering of all our actions,
by a right rule, in a right way, by right persons, out of
right principles, for right ends, this is uprightness.

3. *A person may know whether he is upright or not by the conscionable disposition of his heart about all sins.* David, spoke of such who were undefiled, Psalm 119:1, saying, "And sought the Lord with their whole heart," verse 2. He added, verse 3, "They also do no iniquity." In other words, this is not their work, this is not the thing which they approve or allow, in which they live and walk. Sin is not the upright man's work, it is a strange work, and a stranger work. And David, to manifest his own uprightness, said, Psalm 18:23, "I was also upright before Him, and I kept myself from iniquity." Yea, Psalm 119:101, "I have refrained my feet from every evil way." "Job was an upright man, one that feared God, and eschewed evil," Job 1:1. There was never any hypocrite living but his heart was false; it never condemned all sin in him. Peruse the Scriptures and you shall read of none of them but they had some one way of wickedness or other. Jehu had his calves, notwithstanding all his zeal for God. Herod kept his Herodias, notwithstanding all his forwardness and gladness and reverence to John the Baptist. The Pharisees kept their covetousness, notwithstanding all their formal strictness and rigour. The young man would not sell all, notwithstanding all his profession of former obedience and questionings, "What yet lack I?" So, on the contrary, there was never any person upright but his heart made conscience of all sin. What is that? That is, he would be rid of all, he would not allow himself in any one, he would not keep up the covenant with sin by being dispensed within any one particular.

OBJECTION. "But," you will say, "this may be hard, for who can say my heart is clean? Even the just man sins seven times a day."

SOLUTION. Beloved, you mistake me. I do not say that this is a sign of uprightness, that a man has no sin in him, or that he never acts sin; indeed this would be hard. No man living would be upright by this standard! But I say that the upright person makes conscience of all sin, he sets against all sin, he opposes, he condemns, he disallows all sin, he will not be in covenant with any sin.

OBJECTION. Yet you may object, but how may I know that I make conscience of all sin?

SOLUTION. I shall not insist on all which may be spoken, only take three things which will show your uprightness in a conscience of all sin. If you are upright:

1. You will make conscience of secret as well as open sins. Why, the fear of man, the regard of our own credit, the love of our own advantages, may prevail with an evil man, with a hypocrite, to keep in, to work craftily. Not to sin at noonday, to hold off in public, and yet the love of sin prevails upon him with ease, to work wickedness in the dark, in private, in secret; for, he says, none see me. A hypocrite is a secret sinner, restraints are then taken off. But the upright person hates sin because it is sin and, therefore, he does not act it because it is secret, or decline it because it is open; but he shuns both the one and the other because they are both sinful, Job's heart was not secretly enticed, Job 31:26-27. Is David in his family? There will he walk in an upright heart, Psalm 101:2. Is Joseph alone? Yet he dares not do so great a wickedness and sin against God, Genesis 39. Nay, David hates all vain thoughts, Psalm 119. And Solomon said, that the thoughts of the righteous are right, Proverbs 12:5. The upright person strives against secret inclinations, and

would have even the imaginations cast down, which are seen only by God.

2. You will make conscience of the least sins. We usually divide sin into gross and foul, into little and small; not that any sin is small in a relation to the rule, but that one is not so great and heinous in comparison of one sin with another. Now, where sins are reputed gross, foul, and palpable, even the civil man and the formal hypocrite may be very precise, very conscionable, very tender; but for lesser oaths, for usual omissions, for trifles, for sinful attires, for sinful associating with lewd and vile persons. Alas! These are poor things, small things! Why should we stand upon them? Nay, be not deceived. God is not mocked, the mote must be plucked out, as well as the beam. David's heart smote him for cutting of the lap of Saul's garment as well as it rose against the vile counsel to cut off Saul's life. He that is not faithful in the least will not be faithful in the greatest. And that man who will dispense with himself in small sins, if occasion serves, will likewise give himself a commission for great transgressions. Uprightness knows no such distinction (in respect of approbation and allowance) between great and small. It is probable that Ananias laid down a great part of his estate, yet herein was the falseness of his heart that he kept back some of the estate. Hypocrisy does not consist in this, wallowing in all sins, but in this, that a man will allow himself in some sins. Now, try yourselves in this, conscionableness about small sins; even lesser sins (to upright persons) are objects of great hatred and causes of great trouble.

3. You will make conscience of sins which are, in a sort, more innate. Though every sin, in respect of the

original principle of sin, is natural to man in his corrupt estate, yet there are special sins which have, in respect of their actings and course, more immediate favor and countenance from a sinner—those of particular inclination, those of custom and frequent practice, those of a man's particular condition and calling, and those of present profit and pleasure.

I conjecture that there is scarcely any one man living, unless he has entirely given up himself to Satan, who casts away himself upon the service of every sin whatever; and that there is scarcely a person, who is not haunted with some particular sinful inclination more than another.

Now, where the heart is hypocritical, it will proclaim defiance against many kinds of sinning. As Naaman spake in another case, so does the hypocrite concerning some particular lusts, "Only herein the Lord be merciful unto me." In this I must be spared. Therefore, Zophar spoke of the wicked and the hypocrite, Job 20:5, that "wickedness is sweet in his mouth, he hides it under his tongue," verse 12 and verse 13. He spares and forsakes it not, but keeps it still within his mouth. He is besotted and entangled, and sets himself unto the power of some pleasant and profitable lust or other, and no word of command or threatening, no passage of affliction and trouble, no experience or sense, no inward accusation and rebukes of conscience, will ever be able to draw his heart from it. Though the hypocrite may contend against many sinnings, yet he never stands against the sin of his profit or pleasure. Like a fisher, he may throw away many of the small fishes, but he keeps those which will make a sale and merchandise. But now, if the heart is upright, then a marvelous tenderness and conscience will be found in you, even against those sins which formerly you loved as dearly as your own life.

You will set against that profitable sin of which Demetrius said that "by this craft I get my wealth." And you will set against that sin of which Herod spake, that she pleased him greatly. That sin which formerly was to your affections, as the oil to the lamp, and as Joseph to Jacob. Now, you will strive against it, as the only enemy and betrayer of your soul and salvation. David (if I mistake not, and interpreters deceive me not) made this a testimony of his uprightness in Psalm 18:23, "I was upright before Him, and kept myself from mine iniquity." Iniquity may be called mine, either in respect of approbation and covenant (as a man may say, this wife is mine, this master is mine) or in respect of special inclination. So a man may say, "This is my iniquity; that is, that sin to which, above all other, I find myself most apt and ready and prone." So David said here, "I kept myself from mine iniquity," that is, from the iniquity into which I am naturally so apt and prone, and this he makes as an argument of his uprightness. As he did not hunt after other sins, so when his special corruption did incline and tempt, when those worked upon him, unto which (if he spoke but the least word, and gave the least leave) his natural inclination would have thoroughly and easily kindled and thrust out itself, yet he would not harken, but opposed. He more narrowly and punctually watched, and besieged his heart in these.

Let me add these things about uprightness:

It will endure trial. Psalm 119, "Try me, O Lord, and see if there be any wickedness in me."

It will often try and examine itself lest any sin should settle.

It scares itself and is suspicious. "Master, is it I?" said the disciple. "And Job offered sacrifice, lest his sons have sinned."

It will bless God for being kept from sin, as David did for Abigal's counsels.

It is most severe against our own sins. A hypocrite is a severe judge of others, as the Pharisees against Christ; but an upright person throws the first stone at himself.

It condemns sin in all, in parents, as Jonathan did Saul's prejedice against David; and as Jacob severely judged and condemned sin in Simeon and Levi, and in Rachel; and John the Baptist in Herod, and Christ in the Pharisees at their own table.

It grieves for its own sins, yea, and for the sins of others. David not only waters his couch with his tears for his own sins, but also rivers of tears ran down from his eyes because men did not keep God's Law.

It is more moved for sins against God than injuries done unto ourselves. David cannot bear Goliath's blasphemies and reproaches, yet can bear Shimei's railings.

Abstinence does not suffice without hatred; hatred does not suffice without mortification.

4. *The fourth trial of a man's uprightness may be his disposition and temper about holy duties and services.* Look, as a man's heart is false when it pretends a respect to God, and yet will allow itself in any sin which offends

---

* This follows point 3 from page 265.

God, so is it false when, notwithstanding all semblances of pious observances, it will not be brought upon to be truly and entirely obedient to God.

But I will not digress. I conceive there are five things about our duties and services which may manifest the uprightness of our hearts.

1.) Universality. David took this for a special testimony of his uprightness, that he had respect unto all God's commands, Psalm 119:6. And Paul thought it so, who exercises himself to have always a conscience void of offense towards God and man, Acts 24:16. So in Hebrews 13:18, "We must trust that we have a good conscience in all things, willingly to live honestly." True obedience neither disputes nor divides; it is given unto God upon a bare command, and it does not crave a dispensation in part where God's commands are more easy. There the upright person goes on with cheerfulness and, when they seem strange and more hard, there he goes on with readiness. Abraham is resolved to obey God in all things, though it means to part with his country, yea, with his son. The rule is good and true: he who serves and obeys God for God's sake will equally obey all that God commands him. No one command is unjust or unreasonable to him whose heart is upright in obedience. I do not question but that the hypocrite may go very far in the visible parts of duties and services. You may find him forward and stirring, and not a little boasting with Jehu, "Come and see my zeal"; and yet if Jehosaphat had gone a little farther, he might have seen his calves too, contrary to God's commands.

A hypocrite's obedience cannot be universal, for his ground and motives are particular. This is a truth, that no motion exceeds its motive. According to the strength, amplitude, or restrictiveness of it, is a man set to work.

Now the reasons and inducements of the hypocrite's obedience are partial, and not conjunctive and common. He may come to hear the Word, and he may receive it with singular joy; he may find his affections marvelously raised. Only the question now is, how far, and upon what grounds? Verily, only because, and only so far as, the Word is a pleasing Word, as far as it is clothed and apparelled with a spruce elegance of phrase, or with some unusual notions, or some delicate elocution, all of which fit his humour and claw the itch of his mind. But now he is not equally delighted, this acceptance of the Word is not universal. Let the same Word be delivered as a searching, dividing, and condemning word, then it is otherwise. Now you shall see, that the shaking of the tree will make the rotten fruit (which yet looked red and ripe) to fall to the ground. Let the Word come close, lay hold, and search him to the quick; now you shall see the hypocrite like the wounded or crazy part. Though clothed as fair as the sound parts, yet if strictly handled, the party cannot endure. He cannot abide it, he grows impatient and unquiet. Touch a hypocrite upon the main duty. "Go," said Christ to the young covetous person, "sell all and follow Me." What does he do now who pretended he had done all before? The text says, "He went away very sorrowful." Herod heard John the Baptist gladly and did many things; yea, but "It is not lawful for you to have your brother's wife," said John unto him. How does this doctrine, this duty, go down with him? John lost his liberty, and then his head, for his labor.

2.) Constancy of obedience. The physicians observe a difference between the natural and preternatural heat in men's bodies. The preternatural heat which arises from distemper may be more for the present, but as it exceeds for measure, so it abates for times, because the natural heat is a more equal, moderate, and durable heat. Every part has an equal share; and it is not extreme, and yet it continues. Thus it is with hypocrites and upright persons in the matter of obedience. The hypocrite may (in a kind of preternatural heat), in a fit, in a present heat, fall violently upon duty, upon resolution! Oh, what a man will he become, how shall his family be reformed! And now he will read, hear, and pray; and he will leave his sin. But later he has lost his heat; the cold fit takes him. He restrains prayer, he lays aside his resolutions. "Will the hypocrite pray always?"

There are three times wherein a hypocrite may express great forwardness in duties, in services to God.

One is when straits of conscience are on him and the fear of death is ready to lay hold on him. "In their affliction they poured out a prayer unto me," Isaiah 26:16. Pharaoh and Ahab were much wrought upon in their exigencies, Psalm 78, "When He slew them, then they sought Him."

Another is when obedience and duty are not dangerous, but calm and commodious, as with the Samaritans when the Jews prospered. Therefore, Christ sets out a hypocrite by that ground which was stony, and had not much earth, upon which the seed fell, and forthwith sprang up (with any more ado), Matthew 13:5. "But when the sun was up, it was scorched and withered away," verse 6. He applies it to hypocrites who hear the Word and receive it with joy, verse 20. "And yet this endureth but for a while, for when tribulation, or persecution ariseth because of the word, by and by he is offended," verse 21. If God's service is so hot, if it must cost him his liberty, his estate, his friends, his ease, his life, then farewell to it. When the wind arose, the house built on the sands fell, Matthew 7:27.

A third is when he has some props, or, in the presence of others. Many do duties while Moses is present, or Jehoiadah lives, or the good judges continue; but if Moses is absent, then the Israelites turn idolaters; and, if Jehoiadah dies, then Joash is naught; and if the judges die, then the Israelites do what is right in their own eyes.

But where the person is upright, there the obedience is constant. He does righteousness at all times. Paul serves Christ in fasting and prayer, in bonds and afflictions, and many temptations. And Job, who was an upright person by God's own testimony, chapter 1:1, followed God continually (verse 5), and, although Satan thought that hard exigencies would have turned him off from his obediential course, yet he still cleaved to God after the loss of cattle, estate, and children. You may read of his constancy in chapter 2:3, "The Lord said unto Satan, Hast thou considered My servant Job; that there is none like him in the earth; a perfect and upright man, one that feareth God, and escheweth evil? and still he holds fast his integrity, although thou movedst Me against him?" Yet mistake not the right compass of constancy in obedience, as if there were no act of disobedience; as if a man were not upright unless there were an inviolable succession of obedience in every thing, which he does at every moment. Oh, no! I know no such kind of constant obedience which is exempted from all interruption; but the constancy of his obedience lies in an opposition to fits, starts, and imports throughout the course and bent of his life, which is always to walk with, and to obey, God.

3.) Simplicity of obedience. Austin distinguishes of love to God that one may love God for God and a man may love God for himself. The same holds in service and obedience. A man may serve God for God, and serve God for himself. "Doth Job serve God for nought?" Job 1. That, I confess, may be truly said of a hypocrite who has an eye only to the wages, like the Germans in their wars, who do nothing without pay. The unsound heart will spare out his work acccording to the pay; his eye is much upon this, "How will this make for my profit? How will it advance my pleasure, my credit?"

These things fire and enflame an unsound heart. Come to such a heart and say, "Such or such a thing is to be done, for it is God's expressed will, and it will be made for His glory." These (alone) are cold motives, and weak inducements to a false-hearted person. But come and say, "God will have you to do it and, if you do it, you shall be highly thought of, you will be esteemed for it, you shall have much applause, you may happen to get well by it." Why, now the unsound heart stirs as the ship which has a right wind to drive it and carry it on.

But the upright person is simple in his obedience; a naked command is reason enough for him to obey, and God's glory is a sufficient motive. If a servant is faithful in his factorage, why, it is enough to him in the managing of business if he can set forward his master's

stock. His prosperity is all that he looks on, and thus is
uprightness described in our obedience, when we
mind God above ourselves, when God alone is cause
enough of our obedience unto God.

QUESTION. How may one know that he looks not
at himself but at God's commands?

ANSWER. Either by his cordial blessings and rejoic-
ings at the good done by others, whereby God has
glory though he may not be the instrument, as Paul,
Philippians 1:18; or by his acting for God under disgraces and discouragements, as David and the three
children.

Though our services may lack encouragement from
worldly motives; nay, though they meet with many discouragements and prejudices to us, yet so that by them
God may receive glory, and I may express my obediential respect to him; here is wind enough to fill my sails.
I dare not do it because God forbids. I will do it, because God commands. I will not cease to do it, though
I receive frowns and loss, but will hold on to do it because God receives glory.

This is simplicity of obedience, and this argues the
person to be upright. Paul speaks of this simplicity of
obedience, for his own part, in the exercise of his ministerial function, which he well joins with godly sincerity, 2 Corinthians 1:12, and verily so it was with him,
that the love of Christ was sufficient to constrain him,
2 Corinthians 5:14. And he went through good and
through bad report; yea, and he was not discouraged
by all the bonds which attended him, nor did he count
his life dear for Christ. It was all the same to him so
that Christ might be magnified, whether by life or
whether by death.

4.) Spirituality of obedience. There is a twofold acting of duties.

One is carnal—when we do them as ordinary works, as works of course. The mere material acting of them suffices us so that we say some words, it makes a prayer; so that we give some money, it makes up our charity; so that if we are at church, it makes up our hearing; so that we go over a chapter, it makes up our reading; so that we study and speak a sermon, it makes up our preaching; so that we eat no meat, this makes up fasting. It does not matter what melody and harmony we make as long as we touch the strings.

Another is spiritual—when duties are performed in obedience to God because He commands them, and also the very heart and soul, the spirit and the affections act themselves, they cooperate with our services. The desire of our souls is to the remembrance of Thee, or as David, "with my whole heart have I sought Thee." When a man can say, as Paul, "whom I serve with my spirit", Romans 1:9, or as David, "My soul, praise thou the Lord, and all that is within me, praise His holy name," Psalm 103, or with Mary, "My soul doth magnify the Lord, and my spirit doth rejoice in God my Saviour," Luke 2, or as the Apostle said, 1 Corinthians 14:15, "I will pray with the spirit, and with the understanding also; I will sing with the spirit, and I will sing with the understanding also"; or as Christ said, "Thou shalt love the Lord thy God with all thy heart, and with all thy soul, and with all thy might."

A hypocrite may do so much about duties as to manifest the excellency of his gifts, but he does not that regarding duties that will argue the efficacy of grace. He may be high and admirable in the visible

parts, in the very works. He may hit upon as ample and
pertinent phrases in preaching, and sweet expressions
in praying as another. His lips may draw near, but yet
his heart is far off. It can suffice him to do service to
the eye of man.

But in an upright person, there is fire and incense
in his sacrifices. He must present living and reasonable
services. Why? If he hears, and not with attention, not
with reverence, not with fear, not with faith, he is
greatly troubled. He knows that God must be served
with godly reverence, and fear; for preaching, "let him
speak as the oracles of God," 1 Peter 4:11. "If I do this
willingly, I have a reward," 1 Corinthians 9:17. See 1
Thessalonians 2:4. If he prays and his mind is drawn
aside by distractions, and his affections do not work
with sorrow, hope, with earnest desire and some confidence, he accounts that the work is not done. He has
said something, but he thinks he has not prayed. It is
true (and he confesses so much) that the cause of acceptance of all services is in Christ, yea, but he must
serve and strive to serve the Lord with all his heart. He
looks to the manner of service on his part, "In singleness of heart, as unto Christ, not with eye-service,"
Ephesians 6:5-6. See Romans 12:8 and 3 John 5.
Whatever you do, you do faithfully.

5.) Humility of obedience. Why, this argues the
uprightness of a person. There is no person more
proud of his work than a hypocrite. Christ tells us that
he cannot give alms, but the trumpet is immediately at
his mouth.

There are two things which may befall a man upon
the performance of any holy duties.

One is rejoicing, and this is lawful when God has

enlarged my heart in prayer; when He has quickened me in His service, raised my affections, animated my faith, assisted me more than ordinarily against my dullness, distractions, unbelief, temptations. I may rejoice that my heart should be raised to bless the Lord and (in some cases) to speak of this His goodness, to His glory.

Another is boasting, when a man (like the cock) claps the wing upon his own body; when he sets out himself the more, deals with others more to admire him, to extol him, when he blesses himself and bestows the honor of all his performances upon himself. Now this is base, and argues that the heart is not upright; but the upright heart does all the holy performances by its Master's strength and for its Master's glory. When it is to do duty, it begs for God's grace; when it has done duty, it gives God the glory. 1 Chronicles 29:13-14, "Now therefore, O Lord our God, we thank Thee, and praise Thy glorious name. But who am I, and what is my people, that we should be able to offer so willingly after this sort? For all things come of Thee, and of Thine own have we given Thee."

Like a faithful servant who craves direction how to sell and trade and, when that is done, the money which he takes, he puts into his master's coffer, nay, more than all this, the upright heart fears itself greatly lest, by any means, it should finger any part of God's glory by well-doing, lest any praise from man come near. "O!" said the upright person, "what have I which I have not received? Not I, but the grace of God in me; it is but duty, and that not done so much or so well as is required, so that God will pardon my failings and accept me in Christ. It is enough."

OBJECTION. It is true that, upon some extraordinary actings, even an upright heart may feel some secret thoughts of self-applause and ostentation.

SOLUTION. But these are felt as temptations, as snares, and resisted; yea, and such secret flies cause many tears to be cast after singular performances. But the hypocrite seeks praise and acceptance of it; he loves the praise of men and knows how to cry up himself. Epaminondas went weeping because of the vainglory of yesterday's victory and triumph. The hypocrite is proud even of his humility.

5. *A fifth trial as to whether a man is upright or not is if the bent and purpose of his heart be unto God.* Mere particular actions do not conclude (either way) the estate of the soul. A hypocrite may do some good act, and an upright person may do some sinful act; but that which, even in such cases, may testify unto a man his uprightness is the true bent and purpose of the heart. Look, which way the heart is set and purposed, in the habitual temper of it, convinces either of hypocrisy or of uprightness.

By the heart of man, I mean the soul in its principal faculties, the mind or understanding, and the will with the affections. If God has these, then assuredly the man is upright; when a man can say in respect of his mind with Paul, Romans 7:12, "The law is holy, and the commandment holy, just and good." Verse 16, "I consent unto the law that it is good"; or with David, Psalm 119:128, "I esteem all Thy precepts concerning all things to be upright;" when he can say in respect of his

---

* This follows number 4 from page 270.

will and affections, with Paul, "willing to live honestly in all things," Hebrews 13, with him again; Romans 7:18, "To will is present with me." Verse 19, "The good that I would do." Verse 22, "I delight in the law of the Lord after the inward man;" or with David, "I delight to do Thy will, O my God, yea, Thy law is within my heart," Psalm 40:8. "And Thou art my God; I have determined to keep Thy Word," Psalm 119. This in Scripture is sometimes called a preparing of the heart to seek God, as Jehoshaphat, 1 Chronicles 19:3, and a cleaving to God with purpose of heart, Acts 11:23, all which intimated uprightness.

OBJECTION. "But," you may reply, "if uprightness may be truly discovered by the bent of the heart, then the vilest person may be upright, for they confidently affirm that they mean no harm. Their desires are good, they would know more, they would believe and repent, and leave their sins; yea, they strive to enter in at the straight gate."

ANSWER. To this I answer, first, if any man who has been wicked now finds the purpose and bent of his heart set for God, so that the desires of his soul are unfeignedly to please God, I should not doubt but God had changed this man, and his heart had now been made upright.

But, second, I conjecture that no wicked man does, or can, have this bent and purpose of heart to please God, to obey God in all things; for it imports these things:

An inward desire joined with love, Psalm 119, "O that my ways were so directed, that I might keep Thy statutes." But, then, afterward, "Thy law is my delight."

A habitual inclination, not a pang of the soul, not a

mood, not a fit of ague, not a flash of lightning, not as the morning dew, "But my soul breaketh for the longing that it hath unto Thy judgments at all times," Psalm 119:20.

Third, an active purpose, "Herein I do exercise myself" (said Paul), Acts 24:16. Though the purpose in an upright man exceeds his actions, yet there is some active and working ability with his purpose, he will be doing service to God. It is with evil men in their purposes, as with Pilate. He was purposed to let Christ go, but yet he gave sentence. So they pretend a purpose to please God, but still live in their sins, and do not stir up themselves at all to all the means by which they may get grace and strength.

6. *There are many other trials with I shall but mention unto you.*

The upright person will not balk at the greatest duty, nor the least sins.

He will serve God, though alone, Joshua 24:15.

His care is to order his conversation by the Word, that is his rule.

His motives which set him to work, are direct; not the breath of the people, praise of man, love of himself. It is a great matter to observe what sets the soul on work.

His dearest communions are secret.

SECTION IV

A second use of this point is for comfort to such as are upright. There are many sweet comforts which may greatly revive and cheer up such as are upright. I will touch some of them at this time.

1. *One comfort is that there is a gracious acceptance of their weak services.* The king of Persia lovingly accepted the poor man's handful of water, put it into a golden vessel, and gave him that vessel of gold.

To set this on, consider, first, that all our holy services are the tithes (as it were) of our graces, the rents of our helps, a certain homage which we bring in to God. They are such expressions or actions by which we strive to bring God glory, and to please him.

Consider, second, that the best services are imperfect. As no man does as well as he should, so the best Christian does not do as well as he should. Look, as the highest grace is still in defect, so the most solemn duties are still in default. It is with the best man in duty as it is with the moon, though it is full and shines most clearly, yet even then it has its spots. So, when the heart is most enlarged with intentions and heavenly affections, there is yet some contrary twang, or some shortness, some blemishableness notwithstanding.

Therefore, Aaron was not only to bear the iniquities of the people, but he was also to bear the iniquity of the holy offerings, Exodus 28:38.

For it is with us as it was with Jacob after his earnest struggling with the angel. He arose with a lame and halting thigh; so is it with all of us, both in and after our most affectionate performances. We are weak in our feet. That is not good which is done by a good man; and, though he does much which God rewards, yet he does nothing so completely but God needs, in something or other of it, to pardon and cover. Not only our sins can accuse us, but some sinfulness in our best actions. No man prays, hears, or acts any service of piety or charity, in that full and ample eminency or integrity of degrees, but that he may, with the elders in the Revelations, cast these crowns down to the ground.

Consider, third, by reason of these imperfections in duties, there is more reason (in a strict way of justice) that God should refect all, than that He should accept of anything.

Beloved, it is granted that God does not reject the services of His servants. Nay, as He requires them, so He will accept them and reward them; but this is not for the dignity of the servant, but from the graciousness of the Master. For if God should answer any imperfect service (yea, that which has but a very little and particular imperfection, suppose them to be some contrary transient thoughts, or some thinner indispositions hanging about us in our duties), I say, if God should answer them from the court of pure justice, you should find that the mixture of a little sin would easily cry down the acceptance of much good. The most good which I bring in my services is but duty; and the least evil which I bring is besides the duty, and the evil duty. Though it is not able to make that part which is good to be bad, yet it is able to shut out the service from acceptance, because, by reason of that evil, the service is not as good as God may and does require, if He should stand with us upon terms of strict justice.

But then, consider, fourth, though there are many imperfections cleaving to the services of men, yet if they are upright, God will, notwithstanding, graciously accept their services. Though I pray (and with many distractions) and hear (and with many interruptions) yet, if I am upright in the performances of these, that is, if my heart is for God (indeed), under these that I bring in the truth, and present the strength of my spirit, with all humble respect to God's commands, and unfeigned integrity of aiming at God's glory, the services are graciously accepted with God.

Yea, though I cannot always use so many words in prayer, though expressions are not so many at this time as at another; nay, though I do not find that liveliness and cheerfulness now as heretofore, yet if the heart is upright, the service is done and accepted.

There are two things which may assure a good man that his services are accepted.

One is faith, when he presents his services in the name of Christ. Look, as every sinner needs a Mediator of redemption, so every good man still needs the same Christ as a Mediator of intercession for his services. And, though services (as done by us) can find no favor, yet, as presented by Christ, they are always a sweet savor before the Lord. He is that Angel who has a "golden Censer, and hath much incense, which he offers with the prayers of all saints before the throne," Revelation 8:3. Though our services are but weak testimonies, yet Christ's intercession is a strong and mighty ingratiating, both of our persons and actions.

Another is uprightness, when the heart is true and plain in what it does. Beloved, remember this, as God does not respect the strongest parts which are passive and idle, so He does not reject the meanest abilities, if uprightly employed. No, the day of small things is not despised by Him; if the flax is smoking, though it flames not, He will not quench it. That is, He will not only not slight it, but cherish and accept it, 2 Corinthians 8:12. The widow's mite, the cup of cold water was accepted.

If a man can truly say, "Lord, I would believe more steadfastly if I could, and I strive to believe, and I would pray better if I could; yet, as well as I can, I now present my supplications before Thee. I would serve Thee more fully, more entirely, that is the desire of my soul, and my endeavor. If I had wherewithal, Thou should have a better heart, more lively affections, more ample and cheerful duties; all should be better, if I had better power."

I say that, notwithstanding the many imperfections, yet this uprightness, this holy frame of a complete and active will (wherein all the powers of the soul are bent to services according to the present power of the measure of grace received) is a most sweet smelling sacrifice, and mounts into the most gracious acceptance of God in Christ. I pray you, remember that saying of David, "Like as a father pitieth his children, so the Lord pitieth them that fear Him," Psalm 103:13; and that of the Prophet, "I will spare them as a man spareth his son that serveth him," Malachi 3:17. The father commands his child to lift up the weight, and the child readily addresses to obedience. He lifts, and essays, and still he gives another try, but perhaps he cannot get it quite up. Why? The father likes his child for this, and though, perhaps, the weight is where it was, yet he calls this act of his child true obedience. Why? Because, though that is not done which the father imposed, yet it would have been done if the child had more strength, and he endeavored with all his strength to do it. Or thus, the father wills the child to shoot an arrow. The child draws the arrow perhaps but half way and, though his eye was upon the mark, yet his arrow falls short many bows' length. Why, the father will yet commend all this for, though he sees that the arrow is short, yet he observes that the bow was drawn and, although the mark is not hit with the arrow, yet it was aimed at with the eye of the child. So it is with God our Father, who commands such and such duties to which, if we address ourselves with uprightness, He will wink and pass by the weakness in action, while He both observes and accepts the integrity of intention and affection.

Comforts to an Upright Person

OBJECTION. Oh! says an upright person, I find such infinite heaps of other thoughts, such dullness and deadness of spirit, such untowardness, so many weaknesses every way, all which are the grief of my soul, and it troubles me much that I cannot do the good that I would. How will the Lord take such broken services from me?

SOLUTION. I answer by giving you some comforts.

1. The first comfort is if your heart is upright in these interrupted services, God has mercy to pardon the weaknesses, He has wisdom to find out the uprightness, and He has graciousness to accept the dutifulness.

A goldsmith will not cast away those lesser rays of gold, though mingled, and (to an inexpert person) confounded with various heaps of dross and dust. Now, he has an art to find out the little gold and put aside the dross. Though, with all our holy actions, there is much corruption and weakness mixed, yet there is such a wise art in God's gracious mercy as to find out uprightness, and holiness of desire and endeavor in a service performed with many infirmities, 2 Chronicles 30:8, "The Lord pardon every one." Verse 19, "that prepareth his heart to seek the Lord God of his fathers, though he be not cleansed according to the purification of the sanctuary." Verse 20, "And the Lord hearkened to Hezekiah, and healed the people."

2. A second comfort is that if a man is upright, he shall not only find acceptance for services, but also indulgence for offenses.

You must ever distinguish between the cause and the subject. The cause of all-pardoning indulgence is the free grace of God in the blood of Christ; but the subject of indulgence is the person to whom God is pleased to give His pardon and release.

None comes in under the wings of the mercy-seat so as the upright person. Uprightness in Scripture has (in a well understood sense) seemed to cover all. You read of King Asa, and of many passages which greatly blurred him both as a king, and as a good man. He did not break down the high places; he sought to the physicians, not to the Lord. He joined himself to the king of Syria, he cast the prophet into prison who reproved him for it, yet (2 Chronicles 15:17) "the heart of Asa is said to be perfect all his days." How? All his days; and yet such sinnings sometimes. Yes, all his days, for sins stand upon the account, and seems to be reckoned, not so much when they are done as when they are done with a sinful heart.

And they lose upon this account, they are struck off. God passes over them when the bent of the heart is against them. See that place and passage of David in Psalm 32:1-2, "Blessed is he whose trangression is forgiven, and whose sin is covered. Blessed is the man to whom the Lord imputeth no iniquity." Verily, brethren, that man's estate is blessed whose sins are pardoned: Oh! If the Lord is reconciled to a man, if the Lord covers his sin, that is, will not look upon them in a judicial way so as to account and reckon with the sinner for them; if the Lord will not impute iniquity to him, that is, though he has iniquity, yet the Lord will forgive it, it shall not redound unto him in punishment but it shall be blotted out and be as if it had never been. Tell me, seriously, is not this a blessed thing? Tell me now, you whose hearts are ready to break asunder with the sense of guilt, whether pardoning mercy is not a most blessed and desirable thing. You will freely confess it is, but then the question is, who is that man that is so blessed? What is his temper? How is he qualified?

See on in verse 2, "He is one in whose spirit is no guile." What's that? That is, he is the upright person whose spirit is really and plainly for God, who in truth desires to please Him, who in truth hates all sin. This is that blessed man, and in this is a great part of his blessedness, that the Lord will not imput his iniquities unto him, but will forgive and cover them. That is, He will so forgive them that they shall not rise upon the account any more. Paul, upon this, concluded, by way of testimony to himself, and for others, that there was no condemnation unto them, Romans 8:1. Why? What was Paul? What was his temper? Verily it was upright.

OBJECTION. Upright? Why, he complains of sin, that he was sold under it. He complains of the law of his members warring against the law of his mind. He complains that he was brought into captivity; he complains that when he would do good, yet evil was present with him. How, then, can he say that there was no condemnation for him? How was he upright?

SOLUTION. Thus, his being upright did not consist in the fact that he had no sin in him; nor in this, that he did not sin; nor in this, that he did all the good which he saw should be done; but in this, that he hated the sin which dwelled in him, that he resisted the evil working in him; that his inward man approved the good and condemned the evil; that his inward man hated the evil and was delighted in the law of God. This was his uprightness and, upon this, he concludes that there was no condemnation; that is, his sins should not sink his soul to hell. They should not separate him from the love of God in Christ; they should not be imputed to him, but Christ would take them away.

3. A third comfort to an upright person is that the Lord is his God in covenant. You are not ignorant of the covenant which God stipulated with Abraham, Genesis 17:1, "I am the Almighty (all-sufficient), walk before Me, and be thou perfect." What is the meaning of that? In a covenant, you know, there are two parties, and they mutually undertake and agree. So, here is God on the one part, and here is Abraham on the other part, and God promises and Abraham promises. God promises to be all-sufficient unto him, and engages Himself in an everlasting covenant to be his God. In verse 7, Abraham promises to walk uprightly before the Lord, and this is all that the Lord agrees with him for, "Walk before me and be upright," and then "I am your God, and I will be your all-sufficiency."

OBJECTION. "Why," you will say, "this is granted. It

is clear that God covenants to be a God to an upright person, but what is so great a comfort in that?"

SOLUTION. Nay, then, I have done. If yet you do not understand, if yet you think it so poor, so mean a thing for God to be your God in covenant, I tell you brethren, when God becomes your God in covenant, when He says to a person, "I will be a God unto you", it is infinitely more than if the Lord should say to a man, "I will give unto you all the world."

Oh, for God to be my God! What is it but this? "I am yours, and all that I am, or have, or can do, shall be yours and for you. I am a holy God and that shall be to make you holy; I am a merciful God and that shall be to pardon your sins. I am a powerful God and that shall be to help you, to deliver you, to conquer for you. I am a faithful God, and that shall be to make every promise good which I have made unto you. I am a wise God, and that shall be to bring in your comforts, your deliverances, your helps in the most desirable season. When sins trouble you I will pardon them; when they are too strong for you, I will subdue them. When your heart is sorrowful, I will comfort it; when your graces are weak, I will strengthen them. When men disgrace you, I will honor you; when dangers arise, I will preserve you. What you need, that I will give you; what you have, that I will bless to you."

All this, and far more than this, it what it is for God to be our God in covenant. Nay, and all this is ours by covenant, that is, it is not a fair and empty pretext; it is not a glorious and vain compliment, but really so, and firmly so. The Lord, if He is our God in covenant, binds Himself to be all this unto us by the fidelity of His nature, by the truth of all His promises, by the seal of the blood of the Lord Jesus Christ.

Now what do you think? Do you now not think the people are happy who are in such a case, whose God is the Lord, Psalm 144:15? I tell you, we are not able to imagine the height and depth and breadth of this one comfort, that God is our God in covenant and yet, whatever you apprehend of it, whatever you feel of it, whatever it is, it is the portion of the upright person, "Thou art my portion, O Lord, for ever," said upright David, Psalm 119.

4. A fourth comfort is that uprightness entitles the person to all blessings of heaven and earth. As David spoke of Jerusalem I may say of the upright person, "all my springs are in Thee;" or what Jacob said of Joseph, that he was a fruitful branch or bough. Uprightness is like Aaron's rod full of blossoms. You know that place, Psalm 84, "The Lord God is a sun and shield: the Lord will give grace and glory: no good thing will he withhold from them that walk uprightly." What is the sun but the great and inexhausted fountain of light, of heat, of influence, of comfort? That is what God will be to them that walk uprightly. What is a shield but the defense and safeguard of a person against shots and blows? That also is what God will be to those who walk uprightly.

Will grace do their hearts good? Will glory do their souls good? Is there any good which respects the militant condition? Is there any good which respects the triumphant condition? Neither grace nor glory nor any good shall be withheld from them who walk uprightly. Noah was upright and had an ark. Ebedmelech had his life given him for a prey, Jeremiah 39:18. "Munitions of rocks for the upright," Isaiah 33:15-16.

What shall I say, brethren? All the promises which you know are the treasures of heaven, the cabinets of our comfort, the storehouse of our want, the hand which holds and delivers out all our supplies, why, all of them (as it were) beset and encompass the upright person. Are you an upright person, and do you look upon your family? Proverbs 14:11, "The tabernacle of the upright shall flourish." Are you an upright person, and do you cast an eye upon your posterity? Why, Psalm 112:2, "The generation of the upright shall be blessed." Are you an upright person, and do you desire such or such a necessary outward comfort? Why, Psalm 37:4, "Delight thyself in the Lord, and He shall give thee the desires of thine heart." Are you an upright person, and do you suspect the continuation of your outward estate? Why, Psalm 37:18, "The days of the upright and their inheritance shall be forever." Are you an upright person, and do your comforts seem, for awhile to be clouded, and does it seem that you can not spy any one hopeful crevice of future joy? Why, Psalm 112:4, "Unto the upright there ariseth light in the darkness;" and Psalm 97:11, "Light is sown for the righteous, and joy for the upright in heart." Are you an upright person, and do you not know how to break through the manifold fortifications and strength of envy and power? Why, "The Lord will bring forth thy righteousness as the light," Psalm 37:6. What can keep down the rising of the sun? And "the eyes of the Lord run to and fro through the whole earth, to show Himself strong in the behalf of them whose heart is perfect towards Him," 2 Chronicles 16:9.

5. A fifth comfort is that it will comfortably season all our conditions. You know, this life of ours is capable

of many changes (the weather does not change as often as our temporary conditions do), calms and tempests, light and darkness, comforts and discomforts, friendship and then malicious opposition; health, and then a painful fit of sickness; riches, and then a sinking poverty; liberty, and then some hard restraint or exile. One day gain comes in, another day it is dashed out by the greatness of loss; this day full of joy, the next day all is forgotten by the abundance of sad tears, over the death of a parent, of a yoke-fellow, of a child, of a friend.

Nay, and the soul has its changes too. Sad conflicts, bitter assaults, strong accusations from Satan and the like. What now is a choicer ark to bear us up in all these waves? What harbor is like this one of uprightness? Why, said David in Psalm 73:1, "Yet (or however) God is good to Israel, even to the upright in heart;" and Paul, 2 Corinthians 1:12, "Our rejoicing is this, the testimony of our conscience, that in simplicity and godly sincerity, we have had our conversation in the world."

Oh, brethren! Nothing brings on affliction, a loss, a scandal, an accusation, as close as a false and base heart. When a man's heart can smite him for a hypocrite, for a lover of sin, hypocrisy sinks the conscience under these burdens. But uprightness can look an accusation in the face and bear up the spirit in a storm and, though uprightness may be exposed to many crosses, yet it can comfort a man in the saddest day, for it always has a good friend abroad in God, and within of conscience.

6. Here is another comfort, uprightness will be a good friend in death. Psalm 37:37, "Mark the upright

man, and behold the perfect, for the end of that man is peace." The upright person has most conflicts (ordinarily) in life, and most quiet (ordinarily) in death.

Oh! When death shall approach the dwellings of the profane and hypocritical, and shall say, "I have a message unto you from God. He has commanded me to arrest your soul, and to present it before His judgment seat." How does the heart of a profane wretch gather into fear and horror! Yea, and how does fearfulness and confusion fly up in the breast and countenance of the hypocrite! His conscience delivers up his morsels from which he would not part, and shames and strikes him for his abominable collusions and closings in the service of God. It reports unto him that he must presently stand before a God who is spirit and truth, and who never could abide unsoundness, but will be avenged of hypocrisy. Good Lord! How the heart of this man trembles and sighs; he would thrust out the thoughts of dying, but cannot. He would stay a while longer here below, but may not. O! Now he is gasping, trembling, sighing, dying, and gives out life and all with heart-breaking despair. But now, if the person is upright, even the message of death may be welcome. If the Lord calls for me, I may answer, "Here am I, O Lord, look upon me and accept me in Christ;" and "Remember now, O Lord, I beseech Thee, how I have walked before Thee, in truth and with a perfect heart; and have done that which is good in Thy sight; I have fought a good fight, I have kept the faith, I have finished my course," 2 Timothy 4:6-7.

More comforts might be added:

7. Uprightness begets confidence towards God. The

upright has boldness, he may freely make his prayer, and be sure to be heard, 1 John 3:21-22.

8. It will hold out in evil times, Luke 8:15. The fourth ground held out even in times of persecution because the Word was received into an honest heart.

9. The upright person is sure of salvation. Psalm 15:1, "Lord, who shall dwell in Thy holy hill?" Verse 2, "he that walketh uprightly." Matthew 5:8, "Blessed are the pure in heart, for they shall see God."

OBJECTION. But all this will not strike into some hearts. While we suspect our estate, we always deny our comfort. "O!" says a person, "I fear I am not upright; therefore, all this goodly portion of sweet comfort does not pertain to me."

I answer to this a word or two in general.

1. A man may be upright or hypocritical in a double respect, either, first, really, or, second, in opinion and fancy. If a man is really a hypocrite, though in his proud opinion and fancy he will think himself to be upright, I say, to such a man that no one portion of that comfort before delivered belongs unto him. Sound comfort was never (by God) laid up for a false heart.

Again, a man may really be upright, and yet have a false opinion of himself that he is a hypocrite. It is thus with the best that they, oftentimes, both suspect and falsely charge the true estate of their souls. A child in a distemper may question the inheritance which is entailed on him; yet, if the heart is truly upright, all comfort is your portion. As our distrustful fears do not prejudice the reality of the estate of grace, so our frequent suspicions do not cut us off from the title and right of promised comforts.

2. All prevalent disputes about our personal uprightness hold off the application and taste of comforts, though they do not disannul the title and right. Even the good man will walk uncomfortably, as long as he concludes and strongly fears that his estate is sinful; for sensible comfort rises or falls, comes on or goes off, according to the strength of our judgment and present apprehensions. It is not what indeed our estate is, but what we judge it to be, which breeds in us sensible comfort or discomfort. A false heart may even break with a tympany of foolish joy upon an erring persuasion of his estate; and so may a sound heart be very heavy and disconsolate upon an unsound misconstruction and judging of its true condition.

3. There are some times which are very unapt for an upright person to sit upon his estate and to pass sentence. The best soul has divers changes and straits; sometimes it is clear, free, and able to see things as they are. Other times it may be boisterous and perplexed and, then, it is apt to judge itself by feelings and new representations, not according to secret truth and substance. Remember one thing, times of conflict and afflictions and temptation are best for praying and worst for judging. If a man will, at such times, pass sentence on himself or estate as a judge, he will judge unrighteous judgment; for then the soul is not itself, and is apt to take Satan's works for its own proper accounts; yea, and then, usually, it will see nothing but what makes against itself. In passions and temptations we neither see God nor ourselves rightly.

4. We must never stand to that judgment which we pass upon our inward frame which is irrational or with-

out sufficient ground. Look, as we may appeal from the sentence of our judgment, which acts itself in time of passion as he did from Alexander to Alexander, so neither must we vainly vex our hearts, and dash out our uprightness, when this sentence is rather of imagination than of reason; when a man thinks, and thinks that he is not upright, though all the evidences of uprightness appear in him; and when he cannot produce any one inherently distinguishing ground of a hypocrite in himself. Why, this is but an imaginary judgment, and utterly unreasonable. This is to con-demn the innocent without cause.

That soul will never be settled with comfort which gives way to its own imaginations; and has a conceit that every sinful thought, violent temptation, more durable conflict with an inward corruption, or frequent distractions in holy duties, cannot stand with uprightness. Where a man has either no grounds at all, or those that he has are false, he should never settle so on them, and yield and entertain them, as to question his estate for them, or for them to shut him out from comfort.

5. If ever we would decide our uprightness, and so take our parts in promised comforts, we must follow the voice of the Word and subscribe to the sentence of conscience following that Word.

Be sure of this, if the Word will allow and warrant your inward frame, if it approves of it as sound, assuredly it is so; for that rule cannot err, nor is divine judgment (which is contained in the Word) capable of falsehood or deceit, actively or passively. If God says that your heart is right with Him, maintain it against all disputes whatsoever.

Yea, and if your conscience, enlightened, rectified and quickened by the Word, acquits you as being upright, so that now, standing before the presence of the eternal God and all knowing Judge, it can say this much for you, that though, heretofore, you loved and allowed yourself in sins, yet now you hate all sin, and there is no known way of wickedness; and that, though heretofore you shuffled and cut, dealt falsely in covenant, would not obey in all things, but now you have respect to all God's commands, and all out of a respect to God's glory; I say, you are an upright person, though your misgiving fancy or judgment may give up to the contrary.

QUESTION. "But," some troubled and misgiving heart may reply, "nay, it is not thus and thus with us. We are sure that we are not upright, and the grounds which make us thus to conclude are not imaginary, but real. It is true, we labor to abstain from sin, but this is out of a fear of God's judgments; and, we confess that we perform some or many duties, but these are done out of a fear of hell. Now, none of this can consist with uprightness, forasmuch as uprightness does all duty out of a pure love to God, and not out of a base fear, which may befall the vilest person. What do you think? Can the man be upright whose services depend on fear?"

CASE 1. This is a notable case and craves a solemn resolution, towards which observe two things:

Some things that must be granted.

All abstinence from sin is not an infallible testimony of uprightness, forasmuch as there may be many arguments which may be sufficient to hold us in from the acting of sin, yet which are not effectual to strike off the love of sin. Shame of men, love of estimation, fear of death, the accusation of a stinging conscience, defect of occasions, denial of opportunities, may be cords to bind the hand and yet not be plaisters to heal the heart. A man may deeply love that which he seldom acts. If his abstinence from sin is grounded only on private respects, and not on a divine command and new nature, such an abstinence may befall a man whose heart is so far from uprightness that it may be either grossly profane or basely hypocritical. Not so much the naked abstinence, as the grounds and immediate causes thereof, demonstrate uprightness or hypocrisy.

This also must be granted, that all doing of duty is not a convincing or immediate argument of uprightness. Uprightness is not so punctually decided by matter as by manner. The quality of the mind designed them more than the bounty of the hand. That may be safely affirmed of all duties, that not so much what is done but how it is done, argues our uprightness. Let never so much be done out of base and sordid motives and ends, or by vain glorious respects, or merely servile reasons, without a voluntary and dutiful affection. All the work, though much, though great, though frequent, yet it does not infallibly assure and conclude uprightness.

We must be informed of three things.

First, all abstaining from sin out of fear, or performing duties from it, does not necessarily conclude that a man is not upright. Nay, a man who is upright may abstain from the one and perform the other without any check or prejudice to his uprightness, which I shall clear by these arguments:

If a man may be upright who in duties has an eye to the reward, then, by the same argument, he may be upright who in them has an eye to the punishment; for both these are intrinsical motives, and alike conclude a respect to a man's self. But a man may be upright who yet in his duties has an eye to the reward. Moses was faithful in all the house of God, Hebrews 3:2, that is, very upright. He had yet in his obedience a respect to the recompence of reward, Hebrews 11:26.

If persons, reputed in Scripture to be upright, have yet abstained from sin, and performed duty out of fear (and these acts of theirs have been approved), then services done out of fear may consist with uprightness. I confess that all which has been done by upright persons does not presently testify uprightness, but that which has been done by them, and is rewarded by a way of approbation, does not prejudice uprightness.

But upright persons in Scripture have abstained from sin and have performed obedience out of fear, and this hath been approved of, ergo,

Job was an upright person by God's own testimony, chapter 1:1. The man was perfect and upright, yet the fear of God's wrath kept Job from sin. See Job 31:1, "I made a covenant with mine eyes, why then should I think upon a maid?" He dared not give way to wanton looks nor unclean thoughts. Why? What withheld him? See verse 3, "Is not destruction to the wicked, and a strange punishment to the workers of iniquity?" In other words, this was the way to wrath and plagues, to judgment and to hell. So, in verse 21, "He durst not lift up his hand against the fatherless," that is, wrong, oppress, or defraud them. Why? Verse 23, "For destruction from God was a terror to me, and by reason of His highness I could not endure."

You will think that Paul was an upright person who exercised himself to have a conscience void of offence towards God and man; who had the testimony of his conscience, that in simplicity and godly sincerity, he had his conversation; yet he was the more diligent and the more conscionable in his ministerial discharges out of fear. See 2 Corinthians 5:11, "Knowing therefore the terror of the Lord, we persuade men; that is, we know that we must all appear before the judgment-seat of Christ, and every one must receive according to that he hath done, whether it be good or bad." And it will be a terrible day to us if we are found careless and negligent; and we, knowing this terror, therefore persuade men.

Nay, a man cannot be upright in duties or services if he does them not out of fear. The fear of God is the inward principle of them; it is that which God requires with uprightness. "What doth the Lord thy God require of thee, but to fear Him and to serve Him with all thy heart, and with all thy soul?" Deuteronomy 10:12. Why, what is that fear of God but an awful regard to God, as when Joseph forbare to sin against God out of a regard to his greatness, Genesis 39:9.

Last, let me add one thing more. Jesus Christ requires nothing of us which will prejudice uprightness, but He has willed us to "fear Him, who hath power to cast into hell," Luke 12:5. Yea, I say unto you, fear Him.

For my part, I know no more reason why service done through fear should prejudice uprightness than the services which are done through love; for the motive of my service in both is God immediately.

But then, in the second place, observe that there is a double abstaining from sin and doing of duty out of fear.

One is single and absolute, when fear is all the reason or motive; as, were there not wrath, were there not punishment, were there not a hell, I would not abstain from sin. I would not do any one duty or act of obedience unto God. I would be like an unwilling slave who would break away, or would not put forth himself in acts of service, were it not the mere fear of the lash or the whip that forced and awed him.

Another is mixed and compounded; when, though a man abstains and acts out of fear, yet not only or principally out of fear, but also out of love mixed with that fear. A child, though he forbears many things out of a respect to his father's power and displeasure, will yet cease from them out of a love to his father's goodness and kind affection. Thus may it be with a person who is upright; he may forbear sin out of a fear of God's power, justice, and displeasure, and yet also out of a love to a holy and gracious God and Father, for both of these may have their work in him without prejudice one to another, or either to the temper of uprightness, Hosea 3:5, "They shall fear the Lord, and his goodness."

The love of an upright man is so pitched on God's goodness that it gives way to fear to apprehend His greatness; and yet the fear of his God is not so awed by greatness. But love may come in to enflame the soul to make it either abstain or act out of a respect to God's goodness. Therefore Paul, though he persuaded men because he knew the terror of the Lord, was yet also exceedingly industrious, because the love of Christ constrained him, 2 Corinthians 5:11, 14. Both had an influence upon the Apostle, terror and love, judgment and mercy, as we read of the women who departed from the sepulchre, that it was with fear and joy, with the one and with the other, so may our services come out, and our sins be held off, both out of love and out of fear. For these two are not opposite one to another, as grace and sin, but may mingle together as several ingredients in the same medicine.

Yet one word more must be added by way of distinction; that there is a twofold fear.

One is servile, which depends entirely on compelling arguments, without any natural inclination or disposition of the person. The acts here are drawn out, not from any aptness of the will or private approbation of the judgment, nay these, absolutely considered, sway and incline a man quite a contrary way, contrary to the acts of abstaining or acting. If a man (who works only with servile fear) might do what he liked, and might choose his own way and service, he would rather a thousand times be at his sins and lay aside his work of duty.

Now I said, if a man abstains from sin, or acts out his duty, merely out of a servile fear, he is not upright. Why? Because in uprightness, the heart is carried against sin and the will is inclined to duty, both which are wanting where fear is only servile.

Another fear is ingenuous and filial, which is an enlarging fear, such a fear as is not only not against the holy bent and inclination of the heart, but is likewise a furtherance and help. It is, as it were, a further strength imprinted into the bowl which is rightly framed to run and draw with a true bias. This fear consists with uprightness, and is necessary to every good Christian, who ought to set up all the arguments which God is pleased to propound to the soul, either to keep it off from sin, or to draw it to duty, yet so as love acts its part, too.

OBJECTION. But now there will fall in one scruple with all this: How may I know whether my abstaining from sin or actings of duty springs out of naked fear, or else out of a fear mixed with love, and out of love rather than fear?

SOLUTION. To resolve you in this (and let me tell you this conduces much to the discovery of uprightness), consider:

1. That where they proceed out of naked and mere fear, two things:

There is a contrary and full regretting of the heart against them. The bent of the heart is otherwise set, for all acts of mere fear (I speak of moral acts) are reputed violent and involuntary; they arise from a constraint, and all constraints urge out acts which the nature (if it were itself) would not incline to. Nay, the nature draws against what it does, if it does anything, out of mere fear.

Acts depending upon naked and mere fear cease when the motives or causes of that fear cease and are still. As the fable has it of the frogs, though naturally they are inclined to croak, yet when Jupiter threw down the tree amongst them, they hushed and were silent, yet at length seeing no harm to ensue, they set up their ugly note again; so evil men, whose hearts are bent to sin, may yet in the time of fear, draw in and hold off from sinning. The beastly drunkard will not call for a cup to carouse, nor the filthy wanton for his harlot to embrace on his death-bed, for he fears the flames of hell instantly to clasp him; but let the motives of fear cease and he is as adverse to that reformation he professed, and he is as facile and forward to that evil which he seemed to defy, as the water is to fly out and run in its course which has been, for a while, violently barred up and stopped. It is as it was with the Israelites who came off from sinning and into obedience upon the mere call of the stroke either of the sword or the plague; "they did start aside like a broken bow," Psalm 78:57. They served under the rod but, when that was off, they returned to the accustomed bent of sinning presently.

2. Where they proceed out of fear mixed with love rather than out of love alone, four things:

1.) If love is mixed with fear in obedience, there a man has an eye to divine glory, as much if not more, than to his own safety. Where mere fear prevails to the work, there it satisfies the man if he may, after all, sleep in a whole skin; if he may be preserved, and be secure. He does not care what glory God may have, nor does he mind it directly. But now, if service springs out of love to God, here my safety does not satisfy me. I aim at God's glory for I love Him and love His praise. On the contrary, where a man abstains from sin out of mere fear, he does not abstain because that would dishonor God. Dishonor to God is not that which prevails, but his own quiet and personal exemption from pain, wrath, and infamy; these only sway with him.

2.) Where love and fear concur to set out the obedient acts, there acceptance is propounded by the soul as well as recompense. It will not suffice that I shall have my pay, but it more affects me that God will be pleased to accept me. This is a truth, that nothing but love will satisfy love. The love of acceptance exceedingly answers all the acts which come from the love of obedience: that I shall decline vengeance by such duties; alas, that is not all; nay, but I bend and strive to find acceptance with my God and Father.

3.) Love is not only mixed with fear, but is a more predominant cause in abstaining from sin; where the contrariety of the act to God sways and works more upon the soul than the contrariety of the punishment to the man. That is, the offense, by the vileness of sinning, is far more grievous to my soul than the sense of punishment for sinning. Nay, when the soul (in a free and able estate to judge) can utter from a sound conscience that, were it to make its choice, it would rather a thousand times submit to the punishment of sin than to the acting of sin. Verily, if such a person abstains from sin, the abstaining is not out of mere fear, but out of love joined with fear; nay, rather out of love than fear.

4.) Last, much may be guessed by the strong and habitual actings of the soul in times of security and in times of perplexity; when a man dares not yet to break out to sin, when all is quiet and full of peace, but desires to keep everlasting friendship with his God and communion with his God. When a man will not fail in duty though God fails in courtesy, that is, seems to deal hardly and harshly with him, yet he will serve Him, this argues a predominance of love in our obedience, as in that case in Psalm 44:18-19.

CASE 2. A second case in which a man may fear

that he is not upright may be this: his particular sin-nings. The case goes thus: uprightness is an even car-riage of the heart and life, and every sin is an uneven-ness in motion (it is a wryness, a crookedness, a devia-tion form the right rule and path), yet this is my condi-tion, says a person, and therefore just cause have I to question whether I am upright or not, for the upright do no iniquity, Psalm 119:2. He walks according to the rule; he departs from sin. Though the line may be straight which hath many blurs, yet the line cannot be straight which has many or any windings and turnings.

I will speak something to this case; and it is worth the while to open unto you whether, and in what re-spects, any sinnings may consist with or else contradict the frame of uprightness. For the absolving of this, ob-serve the propositions.

1. That particular sinnings are compatible with a gracious frame. Though none are with a glorious con-dition, though no darkness, no clouds can be mixed with the sun in the heaven, yet both may be in the air which is enlightened below. Our best estate on earth is mixed and not absolute. Glory annihilates all sinful principles, but grace only weakens them. An upright man is an imperfect good man, and has reason daily to bewail his failings as well as cause to bless God for his performances. You never read of any upright person in Scrpture but you will find some scars on his ways; like Jacob halting one time or other; David, very good, yet not upright in the matter of Uriah; Noah, one that walked with God, yet overtaken with excess of wine, etc. Such twinklings do, and will, accompany the high-est and fairest stars. He who dances best may be found sometimes all alone, so the most even Christian may be

surprised with many unevennesses.

2. There are some kinds of sinning which do contradict uprightness. Give me leave briefly to distinguish.

There is a double uprightness:

One is habitual, which is the constant frame of the heart and the general course of the life, bent, and inclination to God in duty, and for God against all sin.

Another is actual, which is the even carriage of the heart or life, in respect of this or that particular act or motion.

There are two sorts of sinning:

Some are particular and by way of fact; when this or that fact is inconsonant to the rule and by it condemned.

Others are general and by way of course; when the frame and tenor of the life is either notoriously vile or, in some private path of wickedness, constantly drawn out and followed.

Out of these distinctions, observe these particular conclusions:

Particular sinnings, or sinnings in respect of particular fact, though they cannot stand with actual uprightness, yet they may consist with habitual uprightness. Look, as tripping or falling may be the opposite of standing or moving on in the partiuclar, yet they are not so opposite to the course of motion in a journey that a man, by reason of them, should be said not to be going on in his journey. Or look, as every particular stain does not blemish the universal fineness of the cloth, so neither does this or that particular fact disprove and deny the general bent of the heart. Particulars may not decide the estate either way.

It is true that a man, by a particular sinning, is denominated guilty, but by no one particular can a man's estate be challenged either for good or bad. Asa, in some particulars, was very faulty (as you heard heretofore), yet the Scripture says he was perfect all his days. And David, though some grievous sins fell from him which did not stand with actual uprightness (hence that clause, "except in the matter of Uriah"), yet his epitaph is written by God Himself from the general bent of his heart and course, "that he walked before Him with an upright heart."

Courses of sin, known and allowed courses, directly contradict uprightness. You must distinguish between frequent temptations, daily inclinations, and courses of sin. Even the most upright heart may be frequently assaulted by Satan, and daily molested with inward corruption, tempting and enticing; but all this may be with resistance, detestation, sorrow and grief so that the heart may be very upright, notwithstanding all these disquietments. But if the heart has a way of wickedness, if it has a path of sinning in which it will walk assuredly, such kinds infallibly testify that the heart is false and not upright.

He who knows sin and yet will sin, he who sins and allows himself in sinning, whether the kind of sinning is single or multiplied, one or many (as the prophet spoke of the proud man Habakkuk 2), I say of this man that, his heart is not upright in him.

There are two things which show great rottenness of heart. One is when any sin has our warrant sealed with secret allowance. Another is when we drive on the sin with a customary trade and continuance. It may befall the most upright heart as it does the best metal blade; it may be made to bow and bend, yet there it does not stay there, it returns to its straightness again. So even an upright person may step into an uneven path, but he does not walk, he quickly returns to the King's highway, into the ways of obedience and righteousness. But it is with a base heart as it is with base metal; it will easily bow and steadfastly keep its crooked figure. The bias draws that way; the heart is set on sin, and regards it. It sins and allows it; it will sin and loves it. Now this is an infallible sign of a false and hypocritical heart, that it regards any known iniquity, as David spoke, Psalm 66:18, or that it has a wickedness, as he spoke in Psalm 139:24.

CASE 3. A third case in which a man may fear his uprightness may be some inequalities about holy services. It goes thus: Sometimes a man finds his heart much enlarged in duties, yet other times, much contracted and straitened. Sometimes he is full of life and quick affections, yet other times he feels no active or lively disposition. He can find no mind or heart almost, insomuch that either he can do little or nothing and, what is done by him is but done. All cheerfulness and quickness seems to fall off like the green leaves from the tree, so that nothing but a mere naked carcass of duty is acted by him.

Now the case is whether a man may be reputed upright who many times finds himself thus in his services.

This is a case which ordinarily perplexes many a good heart. How cunning is Satan still to vex the soul, if he can prevail with us to omit duty. Why, then you are plainly wicked, if the soul is less free and compliant in the duty. Why, then it is secretly hypocritical. Thus he ensnares us; but to the resolution of the case thus:

First, all inequalities in holy services do not conclude that a man is not upright. Look, as the natural life has many spaces and, as it were, degrees of latitude. A man may be able to run and yet, sometimes, be scarcely able to go. These motions (you will say) are unequal; nevertheless the man lives both under the one and under the other. So may it be with the spiritual life, for it also has its different and unequal spaces. Sometimes a man may do his services all in joy, other times all in tears. Sometimes his will is great and performances answerable; other times his will is disposed, but he cannot act in any proportion, yet his heart lives uprightly in either.

Nevertheless we must distinguish inequalities in holy services. There are two sorts of them:

Some arise from weakness of strength.

Others arise from falseness of heart.

You see a man sometimes able to move a weight of a hundred pounds, yet at another time he is scarcely able to lift a walking staff. Why? Because his strength is failed, and then it is no wonder that his actions vary. So it may be with an upright man. God is pleased, sometimes, to afford unto him a strong degree of heavenly assistance. He clears his judgment, enables his faith to apprehend and discern, quickens his affections, restrains Satan, and puts down the force of the inward contrarieties. Why? At such a time the soul is mightily active in the power of received and conferred strength. At another time the wind slacks, and then it is no wonder that the ship does not post as fast. The Spirit blows when and where and how He will; there is not always such a communication of actual strength, and then our

desires may be great, but our performances will be unequal. And this observe, by the way, that if the inequality depends only on weakness of strength, the heart still
keeps its bent. Nay, the heart is most inwardly stirring
in desires and propensions, though it be not able to do
the good that it would.

But there are also inequalities which arise from
falseness of heart. When a man has a disease which in-
fects his humour or spirits, or both, he has one good
day and another bad day. Or it may be as it is with a
land-flood, this hour posting in with such a high speed
as if it would domineer over all the country, and yet, by
and by, it spends away itself. There is no more of it to
be seen. So it may be with a man whose heart is false to
God. It may be with him thus: he may have his moods,
his starts, one time like those accompanying Christ,
and magnifying him with a "Hosannah in the highest";
another time quite turned and crying out, "Crucify
Him, crucify Him." Here one day, or one week; who
but God, and what but duty; not a sermon missed, not
a prayer neglected; yet, all of a sudden slow to hear,
careless to pray, indifferent to any holy performance.

Now, if the inequality arises from the falseness of
heart (and I pray you to observe this), it is ordinarily in
three cases.

1. When the performance was attempted merely to
compass some outward good; a hypocrite may take
great pains for his own ends of honor, profit, pleasure.

2. When the performance was attempted merely to
remove some inward or outward evil, as pangs of conscience within or shame and censure without.

3. When the old lust is returned to new strength,
the bitterness of death is off. And now, the heart re-

turns to its former haunt and natural bent, to the love and practice of such or such a sin, which will easily beget and declare an inequality in duties; for love and practice of sin will either make all duty to cease, or any method of duty to stagger and change.

Observe that there are two sorts of inequalities about holy services. Some respect the will, and, as the schoolmen speak, the first springings of it, its secret inclingings and motions.

Others respect the exercise or fact. From these I infer two conclusions.

Inequalities of holy services, in respect of the exercise or fact, may consist with uprightness. A man one day may be able to find words more readily and abundantly in prayer, and liveliness in his affections, than at another time, and yet be truly upright. Look, as a preacher may be able to study and to preach one day better than another; and the tradesman to follow his particular calling; yet both the one and the other are truly upright in their particular calling. So I say of the expressed and external acts with respect the course of our general callings.

Intrinsic inequalities, those in the will and purposes thereof, argue defect of uprightness. When a man's will is one while strongly purposed for duty, and by and by it is totally bent and set for sin, here the inequality depends upon the division of the heart, which is hypocrisy and falseness.

Cheerfulness or uncheerfulness in the performance of duties are not infallible symptoms either way. By cheerfulness, I mean the liberty or freedom of the spirits; and, by uncheerfulness, the sadness, heaviness, or dullness of them. As it may be a day though the sun does not shine (the sun keeps on its natural course and motion under the ecliptic line whether you see the cheerful body of it or not), so a person may pass on from duty to duty with all affectionate uprightness, though there is a habitual cloud of sad spirits still seemingly wrapping up all his performances.

I think that we do not distinguish always rightly and, therefore, perplex our hearts. There is a difference between affection in duties, and cheerfulness in duties; as much difference as between life and liveliness, between burning and flaming. A brand may be red hot and burn to purpose, and yet not flame at all. So a man may bring living affections to his services; he may present and offer them out of the dearest love to God, and truest respect to His honor, who yet does not feel any such sparkling and flaming enlargements of his spirits in the times of discharge of such services. Defect of affections is one thing; liveliness and cheerfulness is another thing.

If I serve God without any degree of affection, then I am not upright; but I may and do oftentimes serve Him without cheerfulness, with much dullness and heaviness resting upon my spirits, and yet I may be upright. For uncheerfulness does not necessarily, absolutely, and only arise from a lack of grace; it may entirely depend upon natural cause. A man's natural temper may be sad and melancholy; his body may be sickly, and faint, and crazy. Now, as a musician may play over his ditty singularly well, though he makes every note to reel and tremble with infinite quivers; so the Christian may do his services with truest uprightness, though not with that lively cheerfulness as another perhaps may do.

Though cheerfulness does not always accompany our duties, yet uprightness may be evidenced by these things:

By being humbled that we cannot serve with that liveliness as we desire.

By maintaining the services even out of a respect to God. I will yet serve Him. Though I find reasons to humble me, yet I will not allow those to keep me from duties. Though I lack spirit, yet I find a heart to pray and to read. If I cannot serve God with smiles, yet I will with tears. If my body will not carry my soul to duty, yet my soul shall hale my body unto it.

By bringing in the present measure of strength. As much as I can do, Lord, I do now unto Thee; if I were able to utter more, or better, or longer, why, Thou should have it.

When I am humbled that I can do no better and, when I strive to exceed myself, when I will serve God for God's sake, and do not willingly withhold my strength, and yet present all in the name of Christ for acceptance, this is uprightness, though the looks and spirits may be heavy and clouded.

QUESTION. Does all self-love contradict uprightness? Suppose a person acts his duties out of a regard to himself, whereas uprightness seems rather to set up all work with a single respect to God's glory.

SOLUTION. I will not insist much on this, only observe a few particulars:

1. Self-love (naturally considered) is an inbred quality, by which a man affects his own good and benefit. This God has implanted in every man to desire and work for his own safety. The first care and respect

should be for God, the next for ourselves, and the rest for others.

2. Self-love, as it is natural, so (absolutely considered) it is very lawful. He that said, "Thou shalt love the Lord thy God with all thy heart," said also, "Thou shalt love thy neighbour as thy self." If we are to love them as ourselves, then is it lawful to love ourselves. Yea, and the Apostle said, "No man ever yet hated his own flesh", and advises every man to love his wife even as himself, Ephesians 5:29, 33.

3. Duties may lawfully be discharged out of a self-love. A man may (in their discharge) have a lawful respect unto himself. That is, he may regard his own comfort, peace, mercy, and happiness. For example, I may lawfully apply myself to the hearing of the Word, to reading, to praying, to a very careful walking with God, because I would preserve the peace of my conscience, because I would keep up my comfortable interviews of God's loving kindness, because I would be saved and eternally blessed. A man may lawfully aim at comfort and salvation in his duties, and this, in no way, contradicts or disannuls uprightness. God propounds these things in His Word (which is our rule of doing and working) as motives to set us on to our labor. "Be abounding in the work of the Lord (said the Apostle) forasmuch as ye know that your labour is not in vain in the Lord," 1 Corinthians 15. "Blessed are the pure in heart, for they shall see God," Matthew 5:8. "Blessed are you when men speak all manner of evil of you," verse 11. "For great is your reward in heaven," verse 12. "He that continues to the end, shall be saved. Repent, that your sins may be blotted out," Acts 3:19. "And will render to every man according to his works, to them

who, by patient continuance in welldoing, seek for
glory and honour, and immortality, eternal life,"
Romans 2:6-7. Whatsoever God propounds as a motive
to duty, and whatsoever God promises as an encouragement or reward, on that the soul may most lawfully
fix the eye. Why does the Apostle press the Philippians
to mutual love and accord? By the consolations of
Christ and the comfort of the Spirit, Philippians 3.
Why does he press the Romans to the service of righteousness? By the assurance of eternal life, Romans 6.
It cannot be that to cast an eye on these was unlawful,
or that a man could not be upright who did so.

Nay, verily not only that, which God has propounded, and that which God has promised, but that
which I may pray for, on that I may cast an eye. Now,
may not the upright person pray for peace and quiet of
conscience? May he not pray for the joy and comfort of
God's Spirit? May he not pray for the salvation of his
soul? Nay, that which another good man may pray for
to me, may I not pray for that myself? Now, said Paul,
"My heart's desire to God for Israel, is that they may be
saved."

Why, it is granted by us all, and it is practiced by us
all, that we desire heaven; and what is it to desire
heaven, but to desire salvation; and what is it to desire
salvation, but to desire a real, glorious, blessed, and
eternal union with God? And what greater good can a
man desire to, or for himself, than this?

4. But then, in the last place, there is a twofold self-
love:

One of subordination, wherein my aim is first and
most to God's glory. To myself, indeed, there is a respect, but not first of all, not most of all, not only to

myself. Such a self-love, in the discharge of duties, is very lawful, and the upright have it.

Another of competition, wherein I regard not the glory of God. I mind it not, or else I respect myself more than it, so that all may be hushed up, so that I might have joy, heaven, and escape hell. I care not for the glory of God, I would not do duty, but to preserve myself. Such a self-love as this is opposite to uprightness; for, though God gives us leave to mind and respect ourselves, yet He commands us first, and most, to respect and aim at His glory.

QUESTION. Is all self-applause and vain glory incompatible with uprightness?

SOLUTION. I shall briefly absolve this inquiry.

1. Self-applause is the magnifying of ourselves for duties happily performed. It is a kind of adoration and admiration of ourselves by higher opinions of ourselves, or thoughts also, than others will highly imagine of us, and admire the eminency of our parts, gifts, quick abilities, and enlarged affections.

Now this I say, though a man may be lawfully enlarged with joy and thankfulness to God, who has graciously assisted and enlarged him in the performance of duties, and his spirit thereupon may be the more cheered, yet self-applause is naught and opposite to uprightness. It is nothing else but a forgetfulness of our God, of His strength, and of His grace by which we did His service. It does not spring from humble uprightness, but from a proud conceitedness. It is the afterclap of Satan and our sinful hearts, which kick down and undo that work which otherwise had been very well done.

2. Again, vainglory is the setting forth of ourselves
in duty; it is the using of our master's coin for the servant's benefit. When a man hears, or preaches, or
prays, or gives alms, only or principally to be seen, to
be esteemed, to be spoken of, his own credit is the end
of his work. This is a manifest fruit of hypocrisy; Christ
has delivered it fully in Matthew 6. Look, as he plays
the hypocrite, who does some good but yet will not do
all duty, and who does much duty but loves some sin,
so likewise he plays the hypocrite who does all duty
merely to advance and trumpet out his own name, estimation, and glory. Self-applause is a subsequent hypocrisy which follows the work; vainglory is an antecedent hypocrisy which moves us to the work.

3. Nevertheless, you must distinguish between vainglory and self-applause. They are either:

Naked acts or motions.

Habitual qualities or dispositions.

Even the most upright person may find them in respect of motion, but the hypocrite has them in respect
of disposition. In the one, they arise up as temptation,
for it is a most difficult thing totally to be rid of ourselves, either before, or in, or after duties. In the other,
they rise up as natural affections; the one feeds on
them as on meat; the other is troubled with them as
with poison. They break the heart of the one with
pride, of the other with sorrow and humblings. In the
one, they are approbations; in the other, they are vexa-
tions. In a hypocrite, they are like the wind which fills
the sails; in an upright person they are like the wind
which troubles the stomach. The duties done by a hypocrite are like glasses made and blown up only by
breath; the applause of men breathes strongly upon his

affections to set out his services. But it is with an upright person in this case as with a leaf on a tree: a little breathing of the air makes it to tremble. An upright person is afraid of his own high opinion or the commendation of others. He can be highly glad when the honor is cast on God; and, if any after-risings begin to grow for former duties, he is not well till he has cast them down by after-humblings. The upright person is much with God before duty, and all for God after it. He takes all the strength of action out of God's hand and, therefore, would not finger the least scruple of praise. He looks on inward applause as a cross and an oblique as a danger; in the one I hate myself, in the other I fear myself.

OBJECTION. It is lawful (I confess) to know what God has given us, and to acknowledge the good which He has done in us, or by us. How else can we be thankful?

SOLUTION. But then, it is necessary to make Him the end, whom we acknowledge to be the cause; to give unto God the glory, who has given to us the strength.

No more to this case, but His; beg for much grace to do duty and, when you have done it, beg for much strength to give God the glory of it. A hypocrite is made up of himself and men; but the upright person is made only by God, and for Him.

SECTION V

A third use of the doctrine shall be to stir us to get uprightness, and to keep it. There are two things which here offer themselves.

Motives to persuade us.

Means to direct and help us.

For the first of these, what shall I say? How shall I persuade? If all the arguments of heaven or earth might be available, I have them at hand to present them unto you, to excite your hearts to this labor. If there is any regard of a God, of a Christ, of your souls, of your comforts here, of your happiness hereafter, then think of uprightness; do not content yourselves till you have it. Why?

1. *God does not regard you if you are not upright.* His eyes are upon the truth, and He will be worshipped in spirit and in truth. Thousands of rams, and rivers of oil, daily oblations, solemn humblings, cryings and callings will not do it. He hides his face from them if the heart under these be false and doubting.

The Word of God condemns you if you are not upright; it will not acquit you. If you have lamps without oil, a form of godliness without the power thereof, though you make many prayers, though long prayers, though you give many alms, if your hearts are not upright in these, the Word will condemn you as hypocrites, and will give you your portion with them who shall have the greater damnation.

Your conscience will secretly reproach and vex you, in the day of your calamity. When any judgment hangs over your head, or any affliction comes near unto you, then will your conscience rise up and gall and wound you for your close unevennesses and hypocritical practices of sin against your better profession of holy walking. What the prophet spoke of the unjust gainer, "He getteth riches, and not be right; he shall leave them in the midst of his days, and at the end he shall be a fool," that say I of the hypocrite. He heaps up duty upon duty, works upon works, but the day of trial comes and then he shall appear to be a fool. Ah, vain man! To think there is not a day for the discovery of secrets, or that there is not a God who searches the hearts and reins; who greedily hunts after the applause and credit of men and declines the approbation of the great judge.

Oh, when your accounts are to be presented and given up before the tribunal seat of the holy, true, and terrible God; and you shalt then say, "O Lord, all the outward good I did, I did it only to get myself a name; all the services of religion, I labored in them only that men might think well of me. Some of Thy precepts I liked, but others I did not care for because they thwarted my ends. Much good I did, but it was only to cloak and cover the much secret evil which I loved, and in which I walked. So many years I lived, and kept company with Christians against whose powerful practice of holiness my heart did rise. Many a time did their heavenly discourses find out and condemn my private lust, yet I bleared their eyes, I yet wrestled with my conscience. I would not yet leave all my sins, and now woe is me! Thou dost love truth in the inward parts, this I knew, yet I played the hypocrite."

Nay, if more may be added, then take this, the Lord God, after death, will shut the door against such foolish persons who content themselves with lamps without oil, and who cry, "Lord, Lord, have we not preached and heard Thee in our streets, and yet were workers of iniquity!" Look, as the Lord takes notice of a man's hypocrisy now, so "this people draws near unto Me

with their lips while their hearts are far from Me," so
He will take notice of the hypocrite hereafter, not only
to shut heaven against him, but to cast him into everlasting burnings, Isaiah 33:14. So then, here are motives enough to stir us up to be upright because, otherwise, the Lord regards us not, neither persons nor
works; yea, His Word condemns us and our consciences condemn us. We walk under a sentence and
shall die under a curse, and God will be against us too
in judgment. He will not know us, but abominate us
from His presence.

2. *But then, consider on the other side, how acceptable a
thing uprightness is to God, what delight He takes in such
persons, how His covenant is with them, and what infinite
promises are their treasuries, how God will hear their prayers,
accept their persons, pass over their weaknesses, increase their
blessings, establish their comforts.* What defenses, and
secret, strong, and comfortable acquittances uprightness breeds in the conscience! What confidence it gives
in our accesses to God, what solace under all our
crosses! What peace, quietness, and strength, notwithstanding all contrary suggestions! What boldness in
death, what grounds to plead with God! What a
certainty of acceptance now, and truest glory hereafter!
Oh, how might these things work upon our hearts, to
labor to be upright!

OBJECTION. "But," you will say now, "what may we
do to get uprightness, and to maintain it?"

SOLUTION. Now we come to the means of uprightness, for which take these particulars into consideration: directions for getting it, directions for preserving it, and some other considerations and meditations. For the first, I commend these things unto you.

Directions for Getting Uprightness

1. If ever you would have upright hearts, you must then go to God for them. Hypocrisy is a natural weed; we need not go beyond ourselves to find a cause of it. Even a child is able to frame actions to the eye of others, but uprightness is a flower of heaven. Only that God who can make new is able to made the heart upright. I pray you to consider that all the holy qualities and tempers of the New Covenant come from no other spring than God's grace. None can bestow them but God, and He can do it. Now the upright heart is a spring of the covenant, Jeremiah 32:39, "I will give them one heart, and one way, that they may fear me for ever." Is there here a person this day who is sensible of the guile of his spirit, of the hypocrisy in his heart, that he cannot be so for God as he should, that he is uneven, and oft times crooked in his walkings? Why, go to God! Pray with David, Psalm 51:1, "O create in me a clean heart, O Lord, and renew a right spirit within me."

QUESTION. "But," you will say, "may a hypocrite come to God? Will God regard him though he calls upon Him? Will He not shut out his prayers? Will He hear the prayer of him who regards sin in his heart?"

ANSWER. I answer, first, it matters not how much hypocrisy has been hatched within you, and acted by you heretofore. If now you come to be sensible of your hypocrisy and to condemn it, and to bewail it, and to abhor it; if former hypocrisy is now come to hearty conflict, though it is giving out into many thoughts of self and base ends, yet do not be dismayed. Go to God. He can subdue it, He can take out that guile of your spirit, and He can fashion a straightness and rightness of heavenly frame within you. He is able to make good whatsoever He has promised.

2. If you would find uprightness in you, then get an exceeding and predominate love of God, and His ways. Love is of great force and influence to a man's ways and actions; it is like the rudder which masters the ship in the motion. It can turn and wind it any way; so love prevails with the soul. It has a command over it about a man's ways and actions. If a man had a strong love to God, if he heartily, and with great affections, inclined and strove for God, for His glory, for His truth, this would prevail with him to be upright, Deuteronomy 10:12. The love of God is put in as a means to walk in all His ways and to serve Him with all our hearts.

The lack of uprightness comes from the lack of love; as the falseness of a woman to her husband, grows upon want of conjugal love. It is the love of the world which draws a man so often aside, which makes him off and on, and it is the love of sin which makes a man so hypocritical.

If a man could love God above all, he would delight to walk with Him, he would be careful to please Him, fearful to offend Him, ready to obey Him, would be kept in for God. He would not make so many strayings; he would mind God's glory more.

3. Get a hatred for sin. A secret love of sin (after all restraints and pauses) will draw the soul aside; it will (like a covered disease) break out again.

There are three things in hatred which contribute to uprightness.

It is an inward aversion. The very heart is drawn off from an object, and the heart is filled with a loathing and detestation of the evil; not the tongue and looks only, but the very inclination of the will is turned aside.

It is universal, for hatred is of the kind. The evil, in the whole latitude of it, is the object of hatred, "I hate every false way," said David, Psalm 119.

It is permanent and durable. Passion is a storm which will quickly off, but hatred is a settled quality, arguments allay it not, nor does time remove it. "What have I to do any more with idols?" said Ephraim, Hosea 14:8. "They shall defile their coverings, and say unto them, Get thee hence," Isaiah 30:22. So that if a man could get the hatred of sin, he should quickly find an even uprightness.

A man is not even in his walking from one of three reasons. First, his heart is not bent against sin but gives a delightful way unto it; it does not resist and loathe it but harbors and favors it.

Second, some one particular lust wins and gains upon the soul. Though some are unacted, yet one special lust is retained which has power to command and rule the life.

Third, he is carried against sin upon mutable and decaying grounds which, being removed, the heart then returns to its proper and natural bent.

But now, if spiritual hatred of sin were implanted, then the combat between sin and the person would be inward, the very heart would loathe the nature and inclinations of it, and it would be universal and constant so that here would arise a general evenness in a man's conversation. Unevenness, though it appears without, yet it begins within. The heart is the main wheel of a man's course and, therefore, if love gets the heart for God, and hatred rules the heart against sin, you may

very well believe that these two will yield out a very upright endeavor and course of holiness. In spirituals,
that which keeps the fountain, keeps the stream, and
that which betters the heart, likewise well orders the
life.

Directions for Preserving Uprightness

For the second, which respects the preserving
means, take these directions:

First, if you would preserve uprightness, you must
preserve a holy fear of God. You know the promise, "I
will put My fear into their hearts, and they shall not
depart from Me," Jeremiah 32.

Sinning is the only departing from God. He never
leaves us but for sin. Our departing is our unevenness,
and we never leave Him but by sin, and our "un-up-
right" walkings; but that which now which keeps us
from departing is fear. "The fear of the Lord is a fountain of life, to depart from the snares of death,"
Proverbs 14:27. If a man could always keep an aweful
and powerful regard to God so that he stood in awe of
His attributes and His Word, he would keep plain with
God. He would not transgress for a morsel, nor think
that it may be safe for him to sin.

A holy fear of God has these two properties.

It puts the soul and actions in God's presence. One
said that God is all eye to see everything and all ear to
hear everything. So holy fear represents God as One
who is now beholding all that I do and as One who
understands my thoughts afar off, from whom no not
the whisperings of the mind, nor the imaginations of
my heart, nor the closest and most secret actings can

be concealed.

It stands in awe of this all-discovering God. "How can I do this great wickedness and sin against God?" said Joseph, when there were none but he and his mistress and his God together, Genesis 39:9. I fear His justice, that it will break out upon me if I should dare to sin; and I fear His mercy, that it will draw off if I presume to offend. Psalm 4:4, "Stand in awe and sin not." Psalm 119:161, "Princes also have persecuted me without a cause." Why, this might stir up strange qualities in David. Oh, no, but "my heart standeth in awe of Thy Word." In other words, I dare not break out to sin for all that. Thy Word which I feared kept me in.

Faith breeds and preserves uprightness and evenness. I remember the Apostle's caution, Hebrews 3:12, "Take heed, brethren, lest there be in any of you an evil heart of unbelief, in departing from the living God." Unbelief is the root of all hypocrisy and apostasy. That men are but half in duties, is because they do not indeed believe the extent of obedience to God; and that they keep some private lust is because they do not indeed believe the truth of God's justice, power, and wrath.

But faith causes evenness, for:

1.) It sets up prevailing arguments. The soul never doubts in the way but, by the strength of false arguments, either false pleasure or false profit is forcible with the heart, and ensnares it. We step aside always by the cunning of error. But faith not only discovers false inducements, it also brings better and stronger motives; it knows and teaches where the soul will be at a loss, and holds it off by the goodness, kindness, and loving favor of God. Who would venture his comfort-

able aspect of God and sweet communion with Christ
for a morsel of stolen bread, or for one draught of unlawful pleasure?

2.) It constrains the heart to singular love of
God and Christ. The more faith, the more love. All
true faith is enflaming, for it sees and feels much love
and, therefore, kindles much. Now much love raises
much evenness in walking. While the love is kept up
close to God, the heart and life ordinarily are kept in
an upright motion, for all true love is tender, careful,
and pleasing.

3.) It purifies the heart. Faith is like fire, which
has one quality to ascend and another to burn. So faith
negotiates for us at heaven and, likewise, it breeds
more intrinsical renovation of the heart by holiness.
Faith is the best friend to our graces, the surest help to
our affections, the strongest prop to our duties, and
the sorest enemy to our sins. No grace does so much
for the heart as faith; our assistance for good and our
resistance of evil depends most on it. We find, experi-
mentally, that many sins break out when we lose the
sight of God. As long as we can eye God, the soul is
safe. See God in His promises, see God in His precepts,
and see Him in His threatenings, and then we hold up
and go on; but if once we lose Him in the sight of His
promises, then impatience, murmuring, discontents,
and unlawful projects and ways appear in the heart and
life. So it is also, if we lose Him in the sight of His precepts, which guide and bind. Now looseness, careless-
ness, and indifference appears. Lose Him in the sight
of His threatenings, and now pride, presumption, and
other bold adventurings appear. But if we could, by
faith, see Him who is invisible, if we could see the

goodness, fidelity, and immutability of His promises for all kind of good supplies, and if we could see the power, authority, and equity of all His precepts, respecting our actions and ways, and if one could behold the justice and terror of the Lord, by faith, in all His threatenings, Oh, how might the soul be bounded and kept like a river between its banks, in a constant and sweet course of even and upright walking!

3. If you would preserve uprightness, then you must get and preserve humbleness of spirit. Remember this, the humble Christian receives most good and lives best. The slow hand writes the fairest copy; and the low valley, of all the parts of the earth, is most yearly fruitful. Highness of spirit and much unevenness ordinarily keep company.

There are three properties in humbleness which show that it greatly conduces to uprightness:

One that it is much with God; hence we read of the cries of the humble and the desires of the heart. The humble soul is like the weak ivy which clings about the strong oak. So it is with a mighty God. You shall seldom find the humble person without a tear in his eye, a complaint in his tongue, and a prayer in his heart. Either you will find him upon his feet, standing to hear what God will say, or upon his knee, craving what God will give.

Another is that it has much from God. There are high mountains which are above all clouds; the proud heart is most empty because most lofty, but God gives grace unto the humble, James 4. The poor beggar gets the alms, and the low valley gets the showers; and the humble heart gets the grace of God, and both preventing grace which makes good, and assisting grace, which holds on in good, "Thou hast heard the desire of the humble."

A third is that it does all for God. There are two things which the humble person most eyes.

One is God's rule, another is God's glory. A good servant takes commands from his master's mouth, and lays out himself for his master's advantage. All is from him, and by him, and therefore, all must be to him, says the humble heart.

Now all these conduce directly to uprightness. He is best in walking with God who is most in calling upon God; prayer being like the firm and solid ground which enables the feet to stand best. And God is near to the humble. The weak child is preserved from most falls which is held by the hand of the mother or carried in the bosom of the nurse. Where divine strength is most communicated, there the life is most uniformly ordered. And then humbleness refers all to God's glory; it puts the cause of gifts upon him, and the honor of their use, which is directly opposite to hypocrisy. Therefore, labor to be humble; get to be sensible of yourselves, both for naturals, and also spirituals; in the one, see your vileness; in the other, your emptiness.

4. If you would get and preserve uprightness, then get your hearts to be crucified to the world. Hypocrisy and worldliness are seldom far asunder; it is rare to find a hypocrite, but he is one who is either strongly ambitious of honor, or greedily desirous of riches. Search the Scriptures and you shall find it so, and very clearly in the Pharisees.

Now, when the heart is set upon the world, it is easily drawn aside; it will ever and always be uneven. The bowl which has a bias cannot run long in a straight line. "They that will be rich fall into temptation and a snare, into many foolish and hurtful lusts. For the love of money is the root of all evil," 1 Timothy 6:9-10. A thing of naught turns aside the heart which is worldly. The look of a man, the hope of a nod, a change of garments, a morsel of bread, a meal's meat, a few pieces of silver, all of these are to a worldly heart like the wind is to the ship which turned the sails round about. Therefore, take heed of the world. Most of our uneven carriages arise from lack of faith to exalt God, and from the enthralling of our hearts to the world. We are under either the discouragements of the world (and the fear of them makes us to step awry) or the encouragements of it (and the hope and love of them make us to omit duties or put out our hearts to wickedness). The fear of man, and the too-high account of carnal power, and too much love of ourselves and the world, are sore enemies to uprightness of heart or life. He who will know no Lord but Christ, and no safety like that of God, and no good like that which is heavenly; his spirit is sound and his life will be upright.

Of Exhortation

Now to all that has been said, let me add a few daily meditations which may be of great force to keep us in upright walking. There are four considerations more:

1. One, that God searches my heart, and still looks upon my ways. "Whither shall I go from Thy presence?" said David, Psalm 139. "And all things are naked and open to Him, with whom we have to deal,"

said the Apostle in Hebrews 4. There can be no action hid from an all-seeing eye. Nor can the ground, motives, and ends of our actions be secret to Him who searches the heart and reins, and understands our thought afar off. We may blind the eyes of men, but we cannot delude the eye of God. The Lord sees me in the dark, and my private courses are as obvious to Him as the mountain to the sun at noon-day. What way I take He well observes, and which way my heart runs, what it favors, and what it dislikes; what I do, and what end I have in all my doings, and what principles and rules sway within the chambers of my breast. This daily meditation may be of force to look both to the matter of our doings, and to the manner; and so inclines us to upright walking.

2. Another is that I must one day appear before God, and then all secrets shall be disclosed. The upright man may be shadowed out by a heart in a clear glass, through which any thing may see the pulse and motion of it.

But this is sure, that however in this life our actions and ways may be wrapped up with many devices and hidden conceits of hypocrisy; yet at the day of judgment every man shall be thoroughly opened, anatomized, as it were, and orderly cut up. What his heart loved or hated, what public or private wickedness it acted and would not forsake, what pretenses to cover secret sinnings, what balkings and declinings of known duties, what ingenuous or sordid ends in all, and every performance; all these, and more than these, must be spread open at the day of judgment, before the eyes of men and angels.

Of which did we believingly consider, it is probable

that we would attend to uprightness of heart and life, to present a fair copy of ourselves to the eye of God.

3. A little unevenness will mar the comfort of a great deal of uprightness.

There are two sorts of unevenness in walking.

One is habitual and allowed, which mars the just hopes and expectations of glory; for that is either gross profaneness, or cunning hypocrisy, both which are excluding sins.

Another is actual, which is a trip, a stumble, an outstepping in the course of a pious walking. I confess it may befall the best, yet it will embitter our souls. All the good course which a man has led, and actions which he has sincerely done, cannot so much comfort him as many particular obliquities and unevennesses may sadden and perplex him. As in a wrench of the foot, the present pain shuts out the sense of all former strength; or, as in the sickness of the stomach, the present disease closes up the sense of all health; so the particular miscarriages in a Christian course may fold up, or at least suspend, the taste of all the sensible comfort which uprightness formerly yielded and shot forth. They may break the bones of David, Psalm 51, and melt the soul of Peter, and cast us both to darkness of trouble and sorrow, and the labor of many active endeavors, before we can see God to be our God again, and be persuaded that our estate is really right and sound.

4. God is to be set up above all. It is a hard (yet it is a useful) thing to ascribe unto God the original of excellencies, that He is God, and that power, might, glory, and obedience belongs unto Him; that He made us, and not we ourselves; and that our beings, as they

are depending upon His power, so our ways upon His rule; and He is Lord of Lords, all are under Him and, being the universal efficient, He ought also to be our universal end.

God is set up above all others when His rule and Word sways us against all other, and when His glory is singly or supremely aimed at above all other things, and both these complete uprightness.

Appendix

The Throne of Mercy

and

The Tribunal of Justice

Erected in the remissibleness of all sin,
and in the irremissibleness of the sin
against the Holy Ghost.

In two sermons on Matthew 12:31, preached
before an honorable audience.

By that Reverend and Faithful Minister of the Gospel,

Mr. Obadiah Sedgwick, B.D.

The Throne of Mercy

"Wherefore I say unto you, all manner of sin and blasphemy shall be forgiven unto men; but the blasphemy against the Holy Ghost shall not be forgiven unto men." Matthew 12:31

The best of actions are, oftentimes, subject to misconstructions; and a busy malice will either find or fasten spots upon the purest innocency. This chapter is the map wherein you may read these truths. Christ cannot speak or do, but an envious Pharisee will pry, censure, and slander. Nothing is more offensive to an ill eye than the light; and that which much afflicts an ill heart is the beauty of that good which it sees in, or done by, others.

Let Christ's disciples but pluck some ears of corn, only to make necessary satisfaction to natural hunger, verse 1. The Pharisee will presently pluck at Christ Him Himself, and murmur Him not to be a pattern of obedience, but a pattern of licentiousness, "Behold, Thy disciples do that which is not lawful on the Sabbath day," verse 2.

If Christ steps from the field into the synagogue, verse 9, there also shall He have the catching attendance of the Pharisee. Malicious hatred is like the shadow which will pursue the body of pious actions. Here He no sooner finds a fit object for His mercy, but the Pharisees endeavored to divert the execution by an ensnaring scruple, "Is it lawful to heal on the sabbath days?" verse 10. As though the duties of piety jostled out all offices of charity, and that God, who command-ed sacrifice, had not also preferred mercy. They themselves would reach forth the courtesy of relief to a distressed beast, verse 11, and therefore Christ might justly lend His hand of merciful charity to a diseased person, verse 12.

In the 22nd verse, He heals one possessed of a devil, a miracle that begat amazement among the peo-ple, and some kind of credence concerning His divin-ity; but, in the Pharisees, it vented plain blasphemy. "This fellow casts out devils, by the prince of devils," verse 24. A bitter and high reproach, and such as was for the truth neither probable nor possible; for, first, will Satan cast out Satan? He that seeks the constant support, will he willingly overthrow his own kingdom?

Second, can Satan cast out Satan? He that is cast out must be of lesser power, and he that casts out must be of greater power; but can Satan be greater and lesser than himself? These arguments could not but convince their judgments, yet they did not extinguish their malice. They could not deny these to be truths, yet they will pertinaciously deny their affections to them. What they could not answer, they would resist; and, though they saw sufficient reason and evidence, yet they are resolved not to believe, but to condemn Christ. "Wherefore I say unto you, all manner of sin and blasphemy shall be forgiven unto men, but the blasphemy against the Holy Ghost." These words are like the two mountains of Moses, Mount Ebal and Mount Gerazin, of blessing and of curses. Here is the sweetest mercy, and the purest justice, or the throne of mercy and the tribunal of justice. Or here is set out two glorious attributes of God, mercy and justice.

You have the throne of mercy erected in these words, "All manner of sin and blasphemy shall be forgiven", wherein you have:

First, the universality of the object; every sin, or all manner of sin, which yet must not be taken simply but restrictively; not all manner of sin in comparison of sin to the rule that forbids it (for then the sin against the Holy Ghost should be remitted), but all manner of sin in opposition to the sin against the Holy Ghost; that is, any sin that is pardonable, all manner of sin.

First, whether you respect the several species of sin may be remitted. Noah's drunkenness, Abraham's lying, David's adultery, Manasseh's idolatry, Peter's denial of Christ, all were remissible.

Second, whether you respect the many degrees and intentions of sin, either in the multiplied iterations of sinful acts, or in the accessory aggravations of them from the force of circumstances in time, place, person, object, end, etc.

And that we may not doubt hereof, a special instance is given in a sin of deepest dye and desert, namely, blasphemy; this also may be remitted. The schools tell us it is such a sin as either detracts from God that which belongs unto Him by right, or fastens on God reproachfully and disgracefully that which is not convenient to so pure and sublime an essence and majesty.

And the Scripture tells us that it wounds or strikes through the name of God, Leviticus 24:16. Nothing so dear to us as our name and reputation and, therefore, we are sensible of the least indignities which touch there. God Himself professes how tender and jealous

He is of His name and glory. It goes very near to the quick; yet such is the miracle of His gracious dispositions that He has mercy even for blasphemy. "I was a blasphemer," said Paul, 1 Timothy 1:13, "but I obtained mercy." Only know that blasphemy, here pardonable, is not that which springs from malice and hatred after conviction, but that of ignorance, as Paul's, or of infirmities, as Peter's.

Second, the quality of the act, "shall be forgiven." No such word as that for a sinner; his life and joy lies in it. Some by these words understand:

Certainty of pardon. Thus Theophylact, who holds the event so sure, said that there needs be no repentance to obtain pardon for sins not committed against the Holy Ghost. This erroneous opinion needs the kindness of a large pardon.

Desert of pardon. Thus Origen said, "He who sins against the Son of Man qualifies for pardon, because he seems to have fallen into ignorance." There is some ground of apology in this. This opinion is not very unsound, but not genuine.

Facilty of pardon. Thus Jansenius, in Concord. Evan., "It will be remitted, not as if it will be remitted to everybody, but because it will be remitted easily." There is not so much difficulty to get these, as the other to be pardoned.

Not a certain but a possible outcome shall be forgiven. That is, they are such as are not excluded from hope and offer of pardon; not that they are certainly remitted to all in the event, or that they deserve pardon, or that they are easily pardoned. They do not contract a peremptory incapacity of mercy, but that they may, and if repentance follows shall, certainly be forgiven.

Third, the indefiniteness of the subject (unto men); not a man guilty of any manner of sin, except that against the Holy Ghost; but such is the rich grace of the great court of mercy that he may take out his pardon. Christ does not say not one sin, but all sin; not all sin of one kind, but all manner of sin. All sin of any kind shall be forgiven, not to one man, but to any one; unto men, unto any one of the sons of men. Whence we may conclude this comfortable truth:

DOCTRINE. There is a possibility of pardon for any sinner whatever, and for any sin whatever, to all men for all manner of sin, except the sin against the Holy Ghost.

Hence the infiniteness of divine mercy is, in Micah 7:19, compared to the depths of the sea. The ocean is of that vast capacity that it can swallow up the highest mountains as well as cover the lowest mole-hill. And, in Isaiah 44:22, it is compared to the strength of the sun, which can scatter the darkest clouds as well as consume the thinnest vapors. There is in man a continual fountain of sin; in God a continual fountain of mercy, Zechariah 13:1, still running. Yea, there is in man a multitude of sins which stream from that corrupt fountain; and there is in God multitudes of mercies to heal and stop those various currents, Psalm 51:1, "According to the multitude of Thy tender mercies, blot out mine offences."

In the prosecution of this truth, I shall speak to three things: (1) the explication of the terms; (2) the demonstration of the truth; and (3) the application.

THE EXPLICATION OF THE TERMS

Forgiveness of sin is a gracious act of God in and through Christ, discharging the believing and repenting sinner from the guilt and punishment of sin.

It is an act of God. The Donatists held that man could forgive the sins of men, and St. Austin challenged them for so bold an assertion that in this they were worse than the Pharisees who maintained this truth; "who can forgive sins but God?"

OBJECTION. It is true, Christ committed to his Apostles a ministerial absolution in His name and, by virtue of their office, to bind and loose sins.

SOLUTION. But if we speak of an authoritative right and immediate power, only God forgives. Life and death are only in the absolute power of the Supreme Lord, and, because our sins are directly committed against His justice, therefore it belongs only to His mercy to forgive.

It is a gracious act in no way deserved by the sinner; "*Gratia indebita liberata,*" said St. Austin. Hence, in Scripture, you find forgiveness like a stream issuing out of rich mercy, great love, and the riches of grace; and the prophet, speaking of forgiveness, usually subjoins, "For Thy mercy's sake," or "for Thine own sake;" intimating that forgiveness is a free act, not purchased but given; not merited but granted. There is, I acknowledge, a double graciousness in the discharge of an offender.

One is without any satisfaction at all. I am much mistaken if Socinus and his atheistic accomplices do not run this way.

Another is when the satisfaction of a surety is accepted for the principal debt. In this respect is our forgiveness gracious; not that justice is not at all satisfied, but that the offender himself never satisfied it. He is discharged by the price which a blessed Mediator laid down.

It discharges the sinner of guilt and punishment. There are two things in sin.

One is the stain, pollution, or defiling quality of it; and this is the object of sanctification, which is to it as a medicine to a disease, or as water to spots, or as health to sickness, gradually altering, healing, cleansing.

Another is the guilt which binds over the sinner to punishment, wrath and damnation. This is the object of forgiveness. In it, sin is not healed, but pardoned. The disposition of the sinner is not altered, but his condition is. When the king pardons a thief, his theft now shall not prejudice him; so in God's merciful forgiveness, sinful guilt is so effectually removed that, finally and redundantly, it shall never prejudice the eternal life and salvation of the person. Much more might be said of this subject, but I am unwilling to insist on any more than serves to enlighten the point in hand.

The second is this: of this forgiveness there is a possibility; you must distinguish between the infallibility of forgiveness, which is not to every sin whatsoever or to any sin whatsoever, without some condition. A grant of actual pardon does not issue out of the court of mercy unless persons believe and repent. It is true, there is an infiniteness of divine mercy considered in itself, but in the dispensation and exercise of it, it is pleased to bound and confine itself to some sinners only, namely to such as forsake their sins.

Possibility of forgiveness. Though, perhaps, the sinner never comes actually to partake of mercy, but perhaps refuses his pardon, yet is there a possibility, and that in a twofold respect:

One, in respect of God, who does not, in His Word, shut the door of mercy against him nor exclude him. Nay, so far is He from that that He offers freely the blood of Christ which was shed for the remission of sins.

Another is in respect of the sinner. There is (unless he sins the sin against the Holy Ghost) a receptivity. He is not utterly incapable; he has not such absolute contradictions to the tenor of divine mercy but that God may, without violation of His glory, confirm mercy on him. My meaning is this: his condition is not peremptorily sealed up for wrath, but there is a space and a way for mercy, and some pleas may be made for it.

The third is this: though the sins of a person may be for their nature great, for their kind, gross, vile, abominable, for their circumstances, high and crying, dyed over with many intensive aggravations, not only superstitious, but flagitious enormities as well as infirmities, iterated as well as acted, before conversion and after conversion, all these are capable of pardon.

THE DEMONSTRATION OF THE TRUTH

The extent of mercy, whereupon arises the possible pardon of all manner of sin, is most evident to any considerable apprehension which can or will seriously weigh. The volumes and records of heaven, I mean the sacred Word, reveal and testify to this:

1. *In the commands of the vilest sinners to repent.* They are, in Isaiah 1, for the foulness of their wickedness, called "rulers of Sodom, and people of Gomorrah," verse 10, and their sins are called "scarlet and crimson sins," verse 18. Yet, verse 16, they are called upon to repent, "Wash you, make you clean, put away the evil of your doings from mine eyes; cease to do evil, learn to do well." So it is in Jeremiah 3:1. Though their sin was spiritual adultery (they had forsaken the true God), yet are they called upon to return. Now this is a truth that, though the precepts of repentance do not imply an infallibility of the practice of repentance, yet they do imply a possibility of it, and consequently of mercy.

2. *In the vastness of pardoning promises.* The promise of pardon is equal to repentance, Isaiah 55:7, "Let the wicked forsake his way, and the unrighteous man his thoughts, and let him return unto the Lord, and He will have mercy on him, and to our God, for He will abundantly pardon." Here he speaks to the wicked and to the unrighteous person, and indefinitely to any, and every one of them; and assures them, if they do repent, God will have mercy on them.

OBJECTION. "Yea, but our sins are many and great."

SOLUTION. He replies that God will abundantly pardon. He will multiply pardon. It is as if He had said, "Do but repent, and fear not mercy, whatever your former sins have been." So in Ezekiel 18:21-22, "If the wicked will turn from all his sins that he hath committed, and keep all My statutes, all his transgressions which he hath committed they shall not be mentioned unto him." Mark that phrase, "all the sins which he hath committed."

This takes place in the actual granting of mercy and pardon to the greatest sinners. To instance only a few:

Adam was one of the greatest sinners that ever lived, though not in the respect that he continued long in the practice of sin; yet, in a casual sense, he not only committed a most high sin himself, but was also the cause and occasion of all the horrible sins and dishonors against God that ever were, or all the sons of men have done or will commit. Yet God pardoned him, when He made a covenant with him in Christ in Genesis.

Manasseh seems to be a volume bound up with all kinds of notorious sins, and with every kind of sinful aggravation. View his description in 2 Chronicles 33:3.

He reared up altars for Baalim, and made groves, and worshipped all the host of heaven, and served them. Yea, in the house of God he built altars. For all the host of heaven he built altars in the courts of the house of God. He was a most audacious idolater who dared to provoke God to His very face in bringing of the ark and Dagon together. He caused his children to pass through the fire in the valley of the son of Hinnom. He offered his own children a sacrifice to the devil. Also, he observed times, and used enchantments, and witchcrafts, and dealt with a familiar spirit, and with wizards, and wrought much evil in the sight of the Lord, to provoke to anger. He made Judah and Jerusalem to err, and to do worse than the heathens. And the Lord spake unto Manaseh, but he would not harken.

One would scarcely imagine that the heart of man

could be the womb of such hideous villanies, or that mercy would ever respect such a sinner, yet verses 12-13 say, "He humbled himself greatly before the Lord. And prayed unto Him, and God was entreated of him and heard his supplication."

Who would have risen so high in sin, but a Manasseh? And what mercy would have so exceedingly condescended to forgive but that of God?

Paul's sins, before his conversion, were very high; so high that, as Theophilact and others well observe, they had but one ingredient to stave them off from committing the sin against the Holy Ghost: ignorance, 1 Timothy 1:13. He presents a brief survey of his great transgressions.

He was a blasphemer; that is, one who cast contumely and reproach on God and Christ, whose nature was divine, and therefore every way venerable, but he scoffed and mocked at Christ and His truths.

He was a persecutor too. He not only derided Christ, but endeavored to exile and banish him out of the world, to thrust him away from the society of sinners who, in so great mercy, came to save sinners. St. Austin judged well, "Paul was the quickest persecutor, and therefore the vilest sinner."

Nay, and he was injurious; he not only exercised his thoughts and heart, his tongue and invectives against Christ, but his hand and strength. He consented to the death of persons for Christ. To have a hand in the blood of Christ! To crucify Him afresh in His members, yet said he, "I obtained mercy;" a blasphemer, yet I obtained mercy; a persecutor, yet I obtained mercy; injurious, yet I obtained mercy.

I will give you but one instance more, out of 1

Corinthians 6:9-10, "Neither fornicators, nor idolaters, nor adulterers, nor effeminate, nor abusers of themselves with mankind, nor thieves, nor covetous, nor drunkards, nor revilers, nor extortioners, shall inherit the kingdom of God."

Here are some sins which have destroyed a whole world, and others which have started up hell on earth to devour sinners, and all of them such as meritoriously shut the gate of happiness, yet mercy has stretched out the sceptre to some persons guilty of them. Verse 11, "And such were some of you, but ye are washed, but ye are sanctifed, but ye are justifed, in the name of the Lord Jesus, and by the spirit of our God."

3. *The essential and natural disposition of God.*

Mercy is not a quality extrinsically imposed or acquired, but intrinsical and most natural, and therefore exerciseable with freest facility, and readiest constancy. The eye is not weary with seeing, nor God with pardoning, because that is natural to the eye, and this is natural to God. You know this, the power of any thing is answerable to the nature. The nature of God is infinite, and so is His power: "No incurable disease confronts the omnipotent Physician," said Isodore Pelusiota. And St. Austin said, "What I have is of grace, but I flee to Him who is omnipotent." Therefore is it that his mercies are called "riches of mercies," and "multitude of mercies," and "great mercies," and compared to the depths of the sea, Micah 7, and to the strength of the sun, Isaiah 44, and to the vastness of the heavens in comparison of the earth, Isaiah 55.

As mercifulness is natural in Him, so is it gracious. "The Lord, merciful and gracious," Exodus 34. If mercy were to be bought, there would no hope for any sinner but, being free, now there is a possibililty for any. A sinner may plead for mercy even out of the goodness of mercy.

As it is dispensed graciously without desert on our part, so likewise delightfully without repining on God's part. He delights in mercy, said the Prophet in Micah 7:18. It is a work that God would do. Two things God delights in: our conversion and our remission.

4. *The virtue and sufficiency of the blood of Christ which was shed for the remission of sins, Matthew 26:28.* That was one end to procure our pardon; but for what sins is not expressed, because no sin is excluded. You cannot say that Christ died only for small sins, or only for great sins; nay, the offer of Christ to all sinners confirms it. How can this offer be indefinite? How can it be said, "Whosoever believes shall be saved", unless you grant a possibility of mercy?

5. *The effects of mercy in the creature, which point to an infinite fullness in the Creator.* The virtue in the cause ever exceeds that in the effect; and, according to the generality in the cause, is the intension of the virtue in that cause. If I discern any light in the beams, I apprehend much more in the sun; if I feel any moisture in smaller drops, I know there is much more in the large ocean. All the mercy in the creature is derivative, and so many beams lead us to the infinite fullness of mercy in God, the universal and prime fountain of all compassion. God Himself reasons from the compassion of a mother to his own; and Christ tells us, "If we forgive those that trespass against us, our heavenly Father will also forgive us our trespasses." Surely, if we must forgive seventy times, God much more mulitplies

forgivenesses.

6. *It is all one to the Lord to forgive great sins as well as small, Luke 7:41.* There was a creditor which had two debtors; the one owed him 500 pence and the other 50 pence and, when they had nothing to pay, he frankly forgave them both. There was a difference of the debt; 50 and 500, one of them many hundred times exceeding the other. The debts were different, but the forgiveness was equal, and the manner of forgiveness, the easiness, was alike. Both of them were frankly, that is, freely, readily forgiven.

APPLICATION

Now I proceed to the application of all this. Is there a possibility for the pardon of any sin?

An impenitent sinner is utterly inexcusable, who will continue in sin where so much grace abounds. I confess that many turn the grace of God into wantonness, and, because of the richness and readiness of divine mercy, therefore presume to add drunkenness to thirst, giving the reins to all licentiousness and obduration of spirit. Why? Because God is merciful; but hear what the Apostle says, Romans 2, "Knowest thou not, O man, that the mercies of God should lead thee to repentance; but thou through the hardness and impenitency of thy heart, treasurest unto thyself wrath against the day of wrath." I pray you to remember:

1. *That the end of mercy is not confirmation in sin, but a reformation of sin.* "There is mercy with thee, therefore shalt Thou be feared," said David.

2. *That mercy is the sweetest cord to draw us off from sin.*

When God might justly doom a sinner, yet He graciously presents His mercy to pardon him. Lo, yet there is mercy; I beseech you, by the mercies of God, to leave your sins. This is a melting argument.

3. *That mercy is the strongest argument to draw men off from sin.* The torments of hell cannot work as much as the mercies of heaven. Nothing in the world will prevail upon a sinner, if mercy does not.

4. *If mercy does not prevail, a man's damnation befalls him without all apology.* Ah! What a sad appearing will it be for us when we must die and stand before God, and the Lord shall in that day object to us before men and angels! "This is the person unto whom I freely offered the pardon of all the sins that ever he commited; and offered him in the Word of God that, if he would leave his sins, I would forgive them; but he preferred his sins before My mercy; "for lying vanities he forsook his mercies!"

And your own conscience shall then testify that thus it was, "I had mercy offered again and again, and yet I would continue in my sins." Judge what blackness of darkness and degrees of eternal confusion you shall contract when so great a door of mercy is opened; but, for lust's sake, you will not enter in, you wilt not accept it.

Then no sinner has sufficient cause to despair. I know full well that before God makes us sensible of sin, we are apt to presume; but being once made sensible, we are very apt to despair. It is the great art of the devil either to make us die in a senseless calm, or else to perish in an unquiet storm; either to make us undervalue our sins, and so to slay us with security, or else to undervalue mercy and so to sink us with depair. "Oh!"

says the awakened conscience, "my sins are so many and so great. I have continued long in them, gone on in them after knowledge, after the invitations of mercy, after the strokes of afflictions, after many a secret check, and bitter works from my conscience. Now there remains no hope, no, no! Others, whose sins are fewer in number, lighter in weight, not edged and raised by such circumstances, may hope, but I can have no confidence. Mercy will never look upon such a one as I am."

Nay, but you are not reading the text, and they are the words of a Savior, that all manner of sin may find forgiveness. Though there is cause enough to despair of your own strength, yet there is no cause to despair of God's mercy.

Two things only remember here.

Despair is no remedy to any sinner. It may bind on his sins the faster, but never heals the soul, nor eases the conscience, nor pleases God.

Whatsoever your sins have been, if at length you can find a heart to repent, God can find mercy to pardon. I affirm it, no sinner ever perished because he lacked a heart to make use of his help.

But the main use I would make of this point is to persuade men to make out for this pardon. You see here the extent of mercy, the possibility of pardon. "Why do you look one upon another? (said Jacob to his sons) Behold, I have heard there is corn in Egypt, get you down thither, that we may live, and not die." Why do you stand amazed and backward, you that are so full of spiritual wants? Why do you not come to mercy that you may live and not die? Here is a storehouse of mercy, "Behold," said the servants of Behadad, "we have heard that the king of Israel is a merciful king, let us go to him, peradventure he will save thy life," 1 Kings 20:31. We hear that the King of Heaven is merciful, and yet we do not address ourselves unto Him. We hear that there is balm in Gilead, yet we do not sue to be healed. We hear that the arms of Christ are yet open, and we do not run to be embraced. Ah! It is our folly and madness that, being so greatly diseased, we fly from our medicine; that being in so deep rebellion, we lay not down our weapons, and do not submit upon the tender of the freest pardon. "As I live," said the Lord, "I delight not in the death of a sinner. Why will you die, O house of Israel?" Why do we, by lying vanities, forsake our mercies?

How my soul bleeds at the wretched hardness of our hearts! God is merciful, and we are sinful; yea, we are the more bold in sin because God is the more abundant in mercy. We continue in sin because grace abounds, Romans 6:1. Thus do we abuse the grace of God to wantonness, and bane our souls by the sweet remedy of sin. "There is mercy with thee, that thou mayest be feared," said David, and "he who confesseth and forsaketh his sins, shall have mercy," said Solomon, and "knowest thou not that the mercies of God should lead thee to repentance?" said Paul. Consider:

The presence of mercy does not, but the acceptance of it does. The offer of a pardon does not deliver the malefactor, but the receiving of it does. Only the embracing makes us happy. Mercy does not prove to be mercy except by acceptance; the contempt of it strangely alters it into justice.

The despising of mercy leaves without all excuse. What have you to urge against God, who could not urge and fasten His mercy on your soul? Yes, you would have a license but not a pardon. I know this: you warm your soul with the sound of mercy not to abate, but to encourage your sinful appetite. Why do you not break your arm because there is a skillful surgeon, or fall into the strongest diseases because there is a skillful physician?

Continuance in sin and efficacy of mercy are inconsistent. You, through your impenitent heart, instead of mercy, treasure up unto yourself wrath against the day of wrath, Romans 2:5.

Now that which I would persuade you to is to be wise for your souls, and to get your sins to be forgiven and pardoned. If a company of sick men heard of an able physician that could and would heal them, who would not be carried to him? Or what malefactor is there so outrageously mad, but that would make out to the King, if he were assured that the King would pardon him?

Two things only I propound—motives and means.

Motives to Stir Us Up to Get our Sins Forgiven

1. We are in such a case that we need pardon. Yea, that pardon should be multiplied unto us. Indeed, were we not sinners, then we should need no forgiveness, or could we of ourselves make satisfaction to divine justice, then might we stand off from mercy. But alas! We are sinners by nature and by life; all our days are days of sin. The hairs are not more on our heads than the number of our sins are on our consciences. They are so many that who can tell how often he offends? Therefore, we need mercy to forgive, yea, and

we are without strength. We can find strength to sin, but who can discharge for those sins? The price and ransom could never yet be found in any sinner's hand.

2. How woeful is an unpardoned condition! Men go on in sin and make a work of it, but they speak slightly of it. But the truth is:

1.) Sin makes God our enemy; therefore, it is called enmity, in Ephesians 2, and a provocation, because it stirs up the wrath of God against us, which wrath, if it should seize on your soul, ah, miserable man, then, you can neither suffer it nor decline it. Jesus Christ, standing in our stead, felt some of it, and it made Him sweat drops of blood, and to cry out, "My God, My God, why hast Thou forsaken Me?" How, then, shall a poor, weak, guilty sinner stand under the fierceness of His indignation?

2.) Sin unpardoned makes conscience our enemy. As long as the Lord has a quarrel with us for sin, conscience may not speak any peace unto us. Now the Lord is merciful unto us; if the Lord should awaken your conscience and set your sins in order, who knows what would become of you? Do you know the power of conscience, when it is opened to behold a God angry and sin unpardoned? Read the vigor of it in Cain, and the terror of it in Judas. How it cracked their spirits and brought the one to the utmost desperation, and the other to the grave and hell, in despite of all former advantages!

3.) And who can tell how soon he may die? Go and listen sometimes at a dying bed. The person quakes, the bed trembles, and the heart sighs! What is it that the man speaks so to himself? "Ah, Lord," says he, "I would not die!" And then tears trickle down his cheeks, and his heart is ready to fly in pieces.

But why would you not die? "O no, my sins are many. I now see them, and feel the bitter wrath of God for them. Oh! My sins are not pardonable, and who can dwell with everlasting burnings, or stand before the holy and just God?"

3. What unspeakable comfort is it to have our sins forgiven! "Son," said Christ, Matthew 9:4, "be of good comfort, thy sins are forgiven thee." When the Israelites got through the Red Sea, and looked back, and saw their enemies all drowned, what reviving was this! If the drowning of corporal enemies be such a cause of joy, who could but kill our bodies, what cause of exultation for the drowning of spiritual enemies, of sins in the depths of mercy, which else would have destroyed our souls? How shall I express the comfort of it? David said all in one word, The man is blessed whose iniquities are forgiven. Now blessedness is the center of all joy and comfort. Tell me, brethren, what do you think:

1.) Of freedom from hell, that you shall never see the place of the damned. Is that a matter of comfort? Why, if sin is pardoned, hell is discharged. There is no condemnation if there is remission.

2.) Of God's loving kindness. David said it was life, nay, better than life. Oh, what is this? God is reconciled unto me in Christ. He looks on me not as a Judge, but as a Father with ardent affections and compassions. Why? If sin is pardoned, God is reconciled, enmity slain, all differences between you and God are taken off.

3.) Of the blood of Christ. Is it worth having? Or of interest in Christ, is it worth enjoying? Why, if you are pardoned, then, doubtless, you are united to Christ; and how many and how great are the benefits that result and follow upon union?

4.) Of peace of conscience. It is a mercy that conscience can and may speak peace, cheer us up, assure us, stand for us against men and devil. Why? When sin is pardoned, conscience may not accuse; it has nothing to do but direct us in good ways, and to comfort us with the testimonies of our pardon and reconciliation with God.

5.) Of all outward mercies. Oh! What a life a pardoned sinner lives! If he looks up to heaven, all is peace; if he looks down to earth, all is comfort. He has lands, and sins pardoned too, wife, children, honors, friends, yea, and his sins are pardoned, too.

6.) Last, what do you think of confidence in death? When you are leaving the earth, then you can be assured your next journey is to heaven. After grace to find glory; would you ever be willing to die, be confident in death, live in death, live after death? Oh, then get your sins, whatever they are, to be pardoned!

The Means to Get our Sins Forgiven

If you ask, "What may we do to get our sins forgiven?" I shall answer briefly:

1. Find out your sins and know them, and that is done by the study of the law which gives us the knowledge of sin.

2. Beg God for a contrite heart so as to be sensible of sin, weary of it, and broken for it. The weeping woman was forgiven, Luke 7:44, 47.

3. Ask Him also for a penitential heart. "Repent,"

said Peter, "that your sins may be blotted out," Acts
3:19. See Isaiah 55:7.

4. And ask God for a believing heart in the Lord
Jesus, in whose blood and for whose sake we obtain
remission of our sins. 2 Corinthians 5:20, "God was in
Christ reconciling the world", not imputing our sins.

5. Ask God for a forgiving heart. See Matthew 6:14-
15.

6. Make it a daily and vehement petition for repentance and forgiveness, as David did in Psalm 51, and
sue all out in the name of Christ.

OBJECTION. But these things are hard and labori-
ous.

SOLUTION. But they are for mercy. O mercy, I will
perish without you and, therefore, I will not live without you, sleep without you or die without you! I will
pray for mercy; I will go to Christ for mercy; and shall
it seem so grievous to me to leave a sin which will
damn me, to get mercy which will save me?

The Tribunal of Justice

The tribunal of justice erected in these words, "But the blasphemy against the Holy Ghost shall not be forgiven." Matthew 12:31

These words are the saddest expressions of purest justice that ever were uttered. Oh, what is the height, what the depth of this, for a sinner to rise to such a peculiar degree and form of sinning, as forever to distinguish himself from all hope of mercy, never, never, never to be pardoned!

In this, there are two things into which we inquire:

What this blasphemy against the Holy Ghost is.

The irremissibleness of this blasphemy.

Touching the first of these, there are several opinions, and no marvel; for to find the right nature of this sin is a work not of the least difficulty.

The Novations thought every sin after baptism, especially the denial of Christ in time of persecution, to be the sin against the Holy Ghost. I do not deny but each sin that a Christian commits may, in some sense, be called a sin, but strictly it is not the sin against the Holy Ghost.

This error is abundantly refuted by Cyprian, Hieron, Austin, etc., and is repugnant to all religious reason because, first, thus there should be no opposition between all manner of sin and the sin against the Holy Ghost in the text.

Second, thus no man should ever be saved or have

sin pardoned. And for the denial of Christ in time of persecution, though, indeed, it is a very great sin, yet because it may arise, not out of the strength of hatred against Christ, but out of the strength of fear, and from human weakness, it is, without doubt, an act; though sinful, yet pardonable. Yea, it has been pardoned, as we read in Peter.

Origen thinks that the defection from participation of the Holy Ghost is this blasphemy, and so he places the nature of it in apostasy. This is in part true, for apostasy is a necessary concomitant of this blasphemy; but yet it does not express the full, complete, and certain nature of this sin, because, first, every defection from the truth, or defection alone, is not sin. One may be an apostate, and yet not sin the sin against the Holy Ghost; he may withdraw from the faith and yet not assault the faith; and therefore Jerome, upon this very argument to Marcella, said well, "It is one thing to deny one is a Christian, but a different thing to call Christ a devil"; and to that purpose likewise Cyprian, Epistle 53.

Second, much more is required to the constitution of this sin than a defection; yet we deny not but that an universal apostasy is necessary hereunto.

Third, Austin delivers his opinion by divers phrases in divers places, but most fairly in Epistle 10, where you may apprehend, according to his judgment, three acts in this sin: first, hardness of heart; second, perseverance in this hardness; and third, refusal of remission, which is through malicious obstinacy. This opinion, though it is true in part, yet it is not complete; because one, all this may be without blasphemy and two, all this cannot be till the last gasp, and so may the sin against the Holy Ghost be.

Fourth, the Schoolmen generally run one after another, and place the nature of it in obstinacy or malice; so that to sin against the Holy Ghost is, with them, to sin out of a resolved or determined malice. This, you may see, is more fully delivered by Aquinas and Alexander Ales; which sinning of malice is not barely a vitious and habitual inclination, but further it has the access of contemptuous rejection of those things which might remove this malicious sinning. Hence it is that they break this general into many particulars as, first, of desperation, whereby the malicious offender casts away the anchor of hope, willfully perishing in the gulf of sin; second, of presumption, whereby he rejects all fear of God; third, of impenitence; fourth, of obstinace; fifth, of impugning known truth and sixth, envying and maligning of grace in our brethren.

THE NATURE OF THE SIN AGAINST THE HOLY GHOST

But to omit diversity of opinions in this argument, I shall, as fully as I can, touch the nature of this blasphemy against the Holy Ghost in this brief description.

It is an extraordinary sin wherein the apostatizing blasphemer despitefully rejects and maliciously persecutes the gospel and truth of Christ after a manifest conviction by the Holy Ghost. Let us take this description asunder and consider these parts.

1. *It is an extraordinary sin both for subject and for degree.* For subject, because it is a sin (in comparison with other sins); nothing so frequent, it is not so com-

mon in practice. And also for degree; it is a sin made of the very cream and spirits, as it were, of the vilest and most condemning forms of transgressing; but to let that go as being only general.

2. *The subject of this sin is an apostatizing blasphemer.* He is an apostate, and therefore, in Hebrews 6:6 where this sin is described, the persons guilty of it are said to fall away; not only to fall (for so may the most faithful servant of truth do, he may fall in the way), but to fall away, to turn the heart, and to turn the back upon truth, to renounce our colors. It is a universal apostasy. The Schoolmen well observe two things in an apostasy. One is withdrawal from the faith, the other is adherence to heresy; and I think there was never any branded with the sin against the Holy Ghost but proved guilty of both, as Julian forsook the truth and turned pagan. Hence that conclusion arises among them, "all apostates are heretics."

What a blasphemer is you may collect from the description already given of blasphemy. He is one who is contumelious or scurrilous to God and Christ, either in nature, name, or doctrine. He is such as the Pharisees, who fastened on Christ the most reproachful verbal assaults of a Samaritan, devil, companion and friend to publicans; or as Julian, calling Christ in derision the Galilean and the carpenter's son.

To understand this more clearly, know that blasphemy is sometimes taken, first, most generally, and so it may be terminated in man as the object. Titus 3:2, "Blaspheme no man." Thus, he is a blasphemer who assumes any disgraceful term which may blemish the credit of a man.

Second, it is taken less generally; and so it is applicable to any word uttered in the reproach of God, or Christ, or the gospel of Christ, whether deliberately or unadvisedly, in which respect it may be verified in some cases of the best saints who affix that unto God, in their haste of spiritual trouble, which defames His purity and truth.

Third, it is taken strictly, and so it is a malicious, reproachful word against the known doctrine of Christ so that the blasphemer, who is the true subject of this sin, is not he who speaks evil of other men, nor he, who through inconsideration, violence, vehement distemper or passion, or any extrinsical pressure lets fall some unbefitting speeches of God, Christ, or His gospel; but he that does this out of a resolvedness and willfulness.

A man may blaspheme two ways, either enunciative (so as to affirm that Christ is a devil, or God is unjust, or the Scriptures a lie) or imperative and optative, by wishing any unglorious thing on God, or Christ and His truths; both of which may be in speaking wrong things, which is when the person expresses out in words all this; or in entertaining wrong thoughts. Though he may speak what is true and honorable of God and Christ, yet it is, as Cajeton observes, after a disgracing and despicable manner.

Now, then, the subject of the sin against the Holy Ghost is such a blasphemer, who most unworthily thinks of Christ, and this is inward blasphemy, when a man basely derides and scoffs at Him and His truths, jeering at His holiness, and the excellency and purity of His ways. And this is outward blasphemy, which is not occasioned by co-action of tyranny (as some through torment may speak with their lips that which their heart abhors), nor by the frenzy of the disease, when a person, not mentally competent talks idly he knows not what; but it is a set blasphemy, a deliberate formal blasphemy arising from a direct intention to eclipse, despise, diminish, and disgrace the glory of Christ in Himself, His truths, His ways, or His servants; and, it may be, that even in this sense those that thus sin are said to put Christ to an open shame, Hebrews 6:6.

3. *The object of this is the gospel of Christ.* The common object of blasphemy is God considered in essence and revelation, and man. The object of blasphemy less generally taken, does not go lower than God and His truths; but the special object of blasphemy against the Holy Ghost is the saving part of the word, "It is the gospel of Christ," Hebrews 10:29. The Son of God and the blood of the covenant are the objects of this impiety. Oh, how this raises this reproach-ful sin! It is a high sin to reproach any attribute of God, to reproach any part of the truth of God; but to fasten disgrace on the mercy of God, to pour contempt on the gospel of God, there where His compassions yearn to sinners, there where His freest grace calls upon sinners, there where the Sun of Righteousness and salvation shines to sinners, this is the highest injury; yet, on this most amiable countenance and tenderest affections of heaven, this blasphemer casts his most impure and foulest indignities, which appears in the acts incident to this subject. The acts are two:

1.) A malicious rejecting of the gospel, both in the truth and in the goodness of it. The gospel may be not harkened to where it is represented, and yet the person is not guilty of this sin; it may be refused, though it is harkened to, and yet we are guiltless of the same. All refusal, all disobedience unto it, does not necessarily infer this sin, but there must be a malicious rejecting, which notes two things:

First, a complete and free disposition of the will. He sins not through ignorance, not through violence, but by a spontaneous urging; for there are some actions which arise partly from the will and partly from externally impulsive causes. Second are those which arise immediately and totally from the will. Such is this rejection that it is not caused through the darkness or mistake of the understanding, nor through the powerful impression of persecution, nor through any violent distemper or sudden motion of the affections, nor through the importunity of temptation, nor through any frenetical disease, but through the natural and internal inclination of perverseness in the will; when the person is set in the fairest of circumstances and conditions, not blinded, not agitated, but voluntarily and willfully rejects the gospel of Christ.

2.) Access of deepest malice, and constant hatred in the will; when the person does it of set purpose, and with a secret complacence. He is glad that he can spite and injure Christ and His gospel.

This despiteful rejecting is expressed in Hebrews 10:29 by, first, treading under foot the Son of God, the most base esteem of Christ, respecting Him no more than the impurest dirt in the streets, or the most vile thing, as Ambrose expounds it. It would be fault sufficient not to accept Christ; it is a deeper treason to scorn and reject Christ and mercy. But how infinitely vile is it to do this with disdain, and with a despiteful humour, with a purpose to vex and dishonor Christ

and the gospel? Second, counting the blood of the
covenant an unholy thing. The blood of Christ is the
blood of the New Covenant; it is it wherein promises of
life are made. It is it whereby reconciliation with God is
effectually made; it is it by which we obtain salvation,
and this blood it is called precious in Scripture. But he
who sins against the Holy Ghost abuses this blood. He
accounts it no more than the blood of the most common thief and unhallowed person.

It is a despiteful persecuting of the gospel, second,
as it is evident here in the Pharisees, who hated and
bitterly persecuted the light. And thus was it with
Julian, Lucianus, Porphiruis, and other odious apostates who were so hellishly incensed against the gospel
of Christ that, if it had been possible, they would have
plucked this Sun out of the firmament. They would
have rooted out the very name and naming of Christ,
the reasons whereof I conceive may be these:

First, the strong possession of their hearts by Satan,
who communicates unto them this eternal malevo-
lence and hatred of Christ.

Second, the inward persuasion in their own consciences that they shall never have part in Christ;
whereupon, in the fury of despair, they are maliciously
bent against the possible benefit that any other may
draw from Christ.

The formal aggravation of these acts after manifest
conviction by the Holy Ghost: A man may reject the
gospel, a man may persecute the gospel, and do it with
his very soul and heart, as Paul, who breathed out per-
secutions, and destroyed them that called upon the
name of Jesus, and compelled many to blaspheme, and
waxed mad against the saints, yet not sin against the

Holy Ghost. For all this may be through ignorance, the understanding not knowing, the conscience being not yet convinced, nay, it being persuaded of the contrary as fit and lawful, Acts 26:9. The thing, therefore, that formally contains the nature of this sin is the doing of all this after and against conviction by the Holy Ghost. Hence, this sin borrows its denomination against the Holy Ghost.

Now here I shall briefly open, first, how the Holy Ghost is taken, and, second, what the conviction by the Holy Ghost is.
1. The Holy Ghost is sometimes taken, first, essentially, for that one infinite, indivisible, independent Deity. Second, personally, as the third person in the Trinity proceeding from the Father and the Son. Third, virtually, in respect of energy or operation, and this Origen calls the special quality of grace, and Aquinas calls it a good that belongs to the Spirit; for, though external operations are common to the Trinity, yet the immediate manner of working is more common to one person than another; as the work of creation to the Father, redemption to the Son, illumination and sanctification to the Holy Ghost. Thus is the Holy Ghost here considered in his proper operation, namely, conviction.
2. The conviction of the Holy Ghost is, first, the clear revelation of Jesus Christ in the gospel, both in respect of truth and goodness; of truth, that He is the true and only Son of God; of goodness, that He is the Redeemer of the world and assured Savior to believers.
Second, there is by the Holy Ghost wrought in them an apprehension of all this by a supernatural il-

lumination, as in Hebrews 6:4, "They were once enlightened." He does not speak of natural illumination, for by that light of conscience every one is enlightened, but by that illumination of the Spirit.

Third, it is not a slight apprehension, but a more determinate conviction, so that they cannot deny the truth, the light whereof shines with such clear beams upon the understanding. The testimony of the conscience determinately assents with the testimony of the Spirit, that this revealed gospel is indeed the gospel of Christ and of salvation. "You know who I am, and whence I come," said Christ to the Pharisees. Yea, they professed much, but Christ told them, "because ye say we see, therefore your sins remain," John 9.

Fourth, nay, yet undeniable conviction is not all. There is also some kind of approbation of those truths, which the Apostle calls a tasting of the heavenly gift, and a tasting of the good word of God, and of the powers of the world to come. A man may have a little taste of honey, so that he can say, I know it is sweet; and of wine, that he can say, it is comfortable. In like manner, they who sin this sin against the Holy Ghost may feel His operation, not only in an objective revelation, not only in a subjective apprehension, not only in an undeniable conviction, but also in some degree of approbation. There may drop some effects from the truth imprinted upon the affections so that the conscience may be persuaded, and give testimony assuredly, that these are the very truths of Christ. All of this is very evident in some of the Pharisees, who had Christ revealed to them, who knew, and were convinced in their own hearts who Christ was and what His doctrine was, yet they, with inward malice, broke out against Him and His doctrine, and in words poured the basest assaults and blasphemies upon Him; and in their pertinacious workings constantly persecuted Him, even to the most reproachful death of the cross, and all this against the clearest convictions of the Holy Ghost in their own consciences.

THE IRREMISSIBLENESS OF THE SIN AGAINST THE HOLY GHOST

Thus for the nature of the sin. Now consider the irremissibleness of it: It shall not be forgiven men.

The Arians, Eunomians, Macedonians, and other heretics said the Holy Ghost was a creature, and the Photinians denied to Him a real substance; that is, a personality, as Erasmus interprets it; yet many of these repented (if we believe Austin) and obtained pardon.

The same Father fitly removes this scruple by distinguishing between erroneous opinions concerning the Holy Ghost, and this unpardonable blasphemy against the Holy Ghost. It is one thing to misapprehend the essence or personal subsistence and, hereupon, to pronounce according to the dark misconceits of the Holy Ghost. It is another thing to blaspheme Christ and His gospel after clear conviction by the Holy Ghost. This is the sin which shall not be forgiven.

Hence it is that this sin is called, 1 John 5:16. a sin unto death, and Hebrews 6:4, 6, a sin that casts a man into an impossiblility of renewing, and Hebrews 10:26, "all sacrifice for this sin is taken away." These places strongly refute the errors of Jansenuis, Bellarmine, and

other papists who interpret this of the difficulty and
the rarity only of this remission, not of the impossi-
blilty.

QUESTION. Why is it that this sin shall never be
forgiven?

ANSWER 1. It is not because the Holy Ghost is
greater than the Son, for there is not major and minor
where every one is equal in nature and dignity.

ANSWER 2. Nor is it because this sin is so intensively great that it exceeds the absolute power of God
to forgive it, or the infinite merits of Christ.

But the reasons given are these:

First, because it is repugnant to the immutable
statute and decree of the divine will. It is God's absolute pleasure who, of Himself, sets the extent of His
mercy and the bounds of His justice. Though He will
be pleased to allow a possibility of mercy to other sinners; yet, as a king for some facts will not allow an offender his book, so God is pleased here to deny mercy.
This reason is true, but because it is of common equity
to some other sins, therefore, further satisfaction may
be sought.

Second, it directly resists and repudiates the matter
of pardon and remission, that it, the blood of Christ. If
a patient could be healed only by one medicine, and
he willfully rejected that, it is impossible he should recover; not that the medicine is not of virtue, but that
he willfully rejects this virtual medicine. So here, there
is no other name given under heaven by which we can
be saved, but only the name of Jesus Christ; no plaster
but the blood of Christ, which yet this sinner depite-
fully rejects.

Third, it contemptuously, and with a willful obstinacy, resists that Spirit which should apply this pardon and remission. Pardon cannot be attained unless the Spirit applies it, but here the sinner fights against the Spirit of God, and despites the Spirit of grace, and will not permit any operation, any saving operation of the Spirit to fasten on the soul. All fitness and dispositon for pardon is from the Spirit, who is here rejected.

Fourth, the constant order of operation in the Trinity suggests unto us the reason of the irremissibleness of this sin; which order is always by descent and not be regression. If a man sins against the Father, the Son has an operation for the sinner. If a man sins against the Son, the Spirit has an operation for the sinner in working upon his conscience and offering Christ; but if a man sins against this Spirit, whither should he go? Or who is to present pardon? He cannot go to the Father without the Spirit; he cannot go to the Son without the Spirit, but the Spirit is, by him, rejected and despitefully scorned. He that sins against the Holy Ghost sins against the whole Trinity, the Father's love, the Son's death, and the Spirit's operation. I know that Jerome said that this sin shall not be forgiven, as did Augustine and others, also Hilary, Athanasius, and some of our modern writers.

USES

The uses from the explication of this high sin shall serve us both for, first, information: secondly, caution; and thirdly, direction.

USE 1. OF INFORMATION

First, the greatest illuminations in the understanding, and the most determinate convictions in the conscience, are not able of themselves to save a man. A person may have a deep insight into the mysteries of heaven, an ample apprehension of supernatural truths, a large acquaintance with the rules of graces and life, a yielding in his conscience to the revealed testimonies of the Spirit concerning Christ and His doctrine, yet be so far from the assurance and possession of glory that he may be reprobated to the lowest gulf of misery and damnation. For the damned devils are invested with a most general extent of objective knowledge, and these here who sin against the Holy Ghost participate in divine illumination, even to the measure of approbation in the conscience touching the truth. Yet you see that their condition is utterly incompatible with the just hopes or expectation of happiness; it is not capable of remission and, therefore, eternally desperate of salvation. All of this must be understood by you, not that spiritual illumination is not necessary, but that it is not alone sufficient to save. The strongest abilities of knowledge may only serve to purchase us a more learned and full damnation.

Second, greatest knowledge may be in a subject both deprived of the existence of sanctifying grace, and also filled with bitterest enmity and malice against the truth of grace. I justly question whether any persons incapable of glory are convinced with more supernatural light than those who sin against the Holy Ghost; yet I am sure that none are more enraged lions against the innocence and simplicity of holiness and true grace than these.

A person may put on the external form of godliness, as the Apostle speaks, and yet his heart be void of the inward power of godliness. A dead man may be clothed with beautiful garments, and a heart utterly void of the life and quickenings of holiness may yet be adorned with the fair robes and endowments of knowledge.

Nay, consult the records of the Spirit in the Scripture, and the examples of persons and attempts in all ecclesiastical history. You shall not only find knowledge divided from grace, but often times making strongest oppositions against it. None withstood Christ more than the learned Scribes and Pharisees; none withstood Paul more than the learned Athenians. Whom have we in our age more eager against the doctrine of faith than the subtle Jesuit? Against the independence and immobility of grace more than the Arminian? Dull and blind apprehension are not so serviceable engines for the execution of diabolical malice. The most advantageous servant that ever Satan had was a learned head and a graceless heart. Abstract knowledge will easily blow up pride, and pride will easily fire our malice and contempt, and these will suddenly break out into our tongues with derision and persecution of grace.

Third, our greater knowledge, without sanctifying grace, adds to our greater ruin and judgment. This inference is most conspicuous in the subjects of this sin, whose judgment becomes the more heinous and inevitable because of the greatness of their illumination and conviction.

I know the schools deliver unto us several circumstances whereby a sin, common with another in identity of nature, is yet by the access of them variously altered; but among all the intensive perfections of sinful

guilt, this addition of knowledge is one excessively ag-
gravating. "If ye were blind (said Christ, John 9:41), ye
should have no sin (comparatively for measure), but
now you say, we see, therefore your sin remaineth." An
ignorant offender may have some plea and excuse, but
a willful sinner is without all pretext. None shall find
greater stripes than he who knows and does not, or he
who sees to do, but will not. As the most practical
Christian shall rise to the highest seat and throne of
happiness in heaven, so the most illuminated sinner
shall sink into the deepest dungeon of misery in hell.

USE 2. OF CAUTION

You have heard what this sin is, and you have heard
the sad condition of this sinner, that he may forever
despair to see the face of God! I dare not fasten the
complete guilt of this sin on any who hears me this day.
Only remember that of the Apostle, Hebrews 3:12,
"Take heed, brethren, lest there be in any of you an
evil heart of unbelief in departing from the living
God."

Yet, because this sin is possible unto us, who take
upon us the profession of the gospel, it shall not prove,
I trust, an unseasonable endeavor if I describe unto
you some few steps by which the soul gradually de-
scends unto the bottom of this damned impiety.

First, regardless receiving of the gospel of Christ,
which is done three ways.

1. When the judgment has no reverent estimations
of God in Christ, and of the promises made in the
blood of Christ, or of the necessary conditions of the
covenant of grace to be performed by us.

2. When the heart, either in hearing or reading, is

without life and affections, so that the gospel does not draw our love, joy, and delight, or any adhesion of the mind. Paul tells us, 2 Thessalonians 2:12, of some to be damned. And verse 10, "They were such who received not the truth in the love of it."

3. When there is no conformity to the gospel rules of life. Now what shall I say of ourselves? What accounts do we have of this pearl? What affections have we to this doctrine of grace? Have we any impressions of reverence, any impressions of love unto the ministry of the spirit? Alas! Our stomachs begin to loathe the honeycomb, and we are almost as weary of this gospel as the Israelites were of their manna. Why else do we see those many neglects of this Word of grace? Why else our slight entertainment of it? Why else our very scorn and contempt of it?

Shall I speak the truth? The heavenly strains of the Holy Ghost in the gospel fall too low, and sound too flat in our curious ears. The sharp inventions of some poet, or the brain-raptures of a comedian, shall relish our palates with more pleasure than the sweetest principles and lessons that ever the wisdom of heaven has dictated. The plain tune of Scripture does not strike us unless there are also smart descantings of human wit.

Mistake me not, I do not speak this to banish the convenient use of fitting expressions in our delivery of the gospel of Christ, by condemning our inaffectionate attentions to the simplicity of Christ. I do not hereby apologize for the language of rudeness (no, I would not have the highness of the Word to be made offensive by my barbarisms); only let me tell you that where the Word of life, coming in the strength and beauty of its own elegant plainness, does not find only coldness

of respect and love, but the lashes also of ignorant censure and scorn, we are mounted upon a high step of
profaneness, and are descending to that unpardonable
sin against the Holy Ghost.

Second, private or public scorning of holiness.
Holiness is the glory of God and, in a sort, the rectitude of all His attributes. God delights to reveal
Himself in this holiness, and tells us that, without holiness, none shall see His face. It is the most distinguishing effect of the Spirit of God, and that which is both
an assurance of divine election, and also the seal of our
salvation. Yet may not I confidently affirm to you that
nothing is more fallen into the base derisions of witless
sinners than this glorious image of heaven. Strip a person of the well-spoken complements of dignity, wealth,
conceited projects, and deportments for the itch of the
times, and suppose him only clothed with the endowments of true grace and holiness. Who is there that is
set forth with more disdain, derision, and jeering, than
such a person? This is the only reason of our scornings,
that he is a person of purity, one of the Spirit.

A religious David is the song of drunkards; and the
innocent, objects of mockings, reproaches, scorns and
jestings. Lord, what think we of God, or His Spirit, or
heaven? Is holiness beautiful in God, lovely in the
Word of God, and yet contemptible, effectively considered, in the servants of God? As sure as the Lord lives,
if the bounds of public authority did not awe, and the
secret suspicions of public shame did not check these
enemies of grace, their private sarcasms and blemishes
of grace would break forth into public fury against all
real power and practice of grace.

Who but an Ishmael will scoff at an Isaac? And who

but a Cain will hate his brother because his works are good? And who but an ignorant wretch, agitated by the spirit of darkness and perverseness, will fly out with hellish invectives against holiness in heart and practice, which is the glory of God, the perfection of angels, the sacred work of the Spirit, and the pledge of our immortal inheritance in the heavens?

My brethren, be cautioned to sorrow for this and reform. In offering violence to holiness in man, you fasten indignity upon the very image of God, and despite upon the Holy Ghost, who is the immediate efficient of holiness in the creature.

Third, slighting the checks of conscience. Conscience, especially enlightened, is our Angel-guardian, the private register of our courses, and the faithful monitor within our own breasts. It is the eye of the soul to oversee the whole occasions of heart and life, and it is the tongue that reports to us the rectitude or aberration of our ways. The law testifies *de jure,* and this *de facto.*

There is not, I believe, a sinner partaking of any illumination, general or particular, under the powerful presence of a sound ministry, but his conscience, sometimes in the hearing of threatenings from the pulpit, sometimes in his retired secessions or withdrawings from company, lays unto him the guilt of his sins, and perhaps stings him with unquestionable convictions and horrors. It tells him that his heart is yet desperately foul, and that his ways are not the ways of life and comfort. But now for this person to stop his ears at this faithful voice of conscience, for him to deal with this, as Felix did with Paul, discoursing of "judgment to come, go thy way for this time, when I have convenient season, I will call for thee", or else to quench and drown their private clamors by the untimeliness of other discourses and fouler actions. Oh, what direct injury do we hereby offer to the workings of God's Spirit, and what stronger power do we add hereby to the workings of our heart!

A tender conscience is like a tender eye or stomach; but neglect of motions in the conscience prepares for hardness of heart. It will be with us in sinning, as it is with the iron, which becomes the more hardened after the fire, and the sinner more sinful after the slighting of the checks of conscience, or as with a disease which grows incurable by neglect, yet might have been cured and healed by observance, or as a tree which, after many shakings, takes deeper root and hold in the earth.

It is a fearful judgment to sin against conscience. This will breed custom, delight, and defense and, at length, hatred of that truth which shall present light for reformation. Hereby we grieve the Holy Spirit, and quench Him, and cauterize or sear our consciences with senselessness, whence arises a greediness to sin, Ephesians 4:18.

Fourth, be not peremptory for worldly ends. He who sets up his resolution, that he will be somebody in the world, will have his covetous ends or ambitious projects. No marvel if such a person slights the checks of conscience, derides the beauty of holiness, and looks on the Word of grace without all esteem or affection. Let God say what he will, he will do what he please.

The Pharisees, guilty of this great sin, would not, could not, believe Christ. What was the reason? See John 5:44, "How can ye believe, which receive honour one of another?" Balaam for gain will ride to curse the Israel of God, and Judas betray his Master; and ambitious Haman, rather than his proud humour should be neglected, will endeavor the ruin of all the Jews. What was the reason of Demas's apostasy? The embracing of this present world, 2 Timothy 4:10. Oh, when the heart is resolved for carnal courses it will easily part with, nay, rather than it will be crossed or disappointed, it will fall foul upon the very truths of God! The greatest enemies and opposers of truth have been a covetous Demetrius, Acts 19, or a proud Diotrephes, 3 John 9. Be therefore submissive in your worldly resolutions; and, to bend the mind hereunto, weigh Christ and the whole world in the same balance. See whether Christ is not more advantageous every way; weigh your souls and the world, in the same balance. See whether the saving of the soul is not better than the winning of the world.

USE 3. OF EXHORTATION

The last use shall be to exhort us to use all the means we can to prevent it, and to this end I will commend these advices.

1. Let divine truths reform as well as inform. A naked sword may do much hurt and a bare knowledge may prove dangerous, but where knowledge has heat as well as light, it is useful medicine. He is right whose knowledge does not make him more cunning to sin, but more careful to avoid and forsake it.

2. Strive to love the truth and holiness. Paul's temper was excellent, "We can do nothing against the truth, but for the truth." Why? What was the reason? Surely his great love to Christ and His truth. Love, en-

tire love to Christ, will disarm us of all malice and opposition against Him. Yea, and get love to the gospel,
wherein lies our life, our hope, our stay, our comfort,
our all.

3. Get faith, beg God, the Father of our Lord Jesus
Christ, to give you faith. Faith would not only see a
Christ, but prize Him, too. Two virtues there are in
faith, singular estimations, and inseparable affections.
Faith subjects the heart to Christ, and gives it unto
Him, having none in heaven or earth in comparison of
Him. Should I oppose Him or his truths, who is the
best of all good, and my Savior? He came to save me.

4. Repent in time. Oftentimes, sinning weakens
truth in the mind and raises ill dispositions in the will.
By much sinning, a man becomes a very slave to sin
and a strong adversary to truth. But speedy repentance
draws off the heart and, being often renewed, keeps it
tender and fearful to offend. Divine truths make easy
and ruling impressions upon a heart graciously turned
and mollified.

To close up all, let the Word of God really affect us;
let holiness in the power and beauty of it affect us. Let
the fair and living checks of conscience seasonably affect us; let the blood of Christ and the eternal salvation
of our souls affect us so that we shall not be guilty of
that blasphemy against the Holy Ghost which shall
never be forgiven.

Finis